THE SCHOOL OF INFANCY.

AN ESSAY

ON THE

EDUCATION OF YOUTH,

DURING THEIR FIRST SIX YEARS.

BY

JOHN AMOS COMENIUS.

TO WHICH IS PREFIXED

A SKETCH OF THE LIFE OF THE AUTHOR.

Copyright © 2017 Read Books Ltd.
This book is copyright and may not be
reproduced or copied in any way without
the express permission of the publisher in writing

British Library Cataloguing-in-Publication Data
A catalogue record for this book is available from the
British Library

Loe, here an Exile, who to serue his God,
Hath sharply tasted of proud Pashurs Rod,
Whose learning, Piety; & true worth beeing knowne
To all the world, makes all the world his owne,

TO THE READER.

THE apology for submitting this Essay on Education to the public, is comprised in a powerful impression of the vast importance of the subject, and in the belief that although multitudes of books have been written since it was originally published in 1633, yet that nothing has appeared at all comparable with it, much less as superseding it; and the wonder is, that a treatise of such inestimable value to a faithful Christian mother, should never until now have been presented to the English reader. The same may be said of most of the other educational works of Comenius; a thorough study of which would shew, to the truly Christian teacher of youth, the comparatively small progress really made at the present day in the faithful instruction of the young.

The prefixed Biographical sketch is given with the view of answering the natural inquiry of a reader, "Who was John Amos Comenius?" A question which very few persons, in the absence of such a notice, would be able to answer.

This account of Comenius has been compiled from the following works:—

In Latin:—The author's Letter to Montanus, 10th Dec. 1661. Amsterdam, 1662, 24mo; and such of his other works, including the "Didactica," as could be procured.

History, political and ecclesiastical, of Moravia, by A. Pilarz, and F. Moravitz, Brunn. 1785, 1787, 3 parts, 8vo.

Regenvolscius, Historical and Chronological Conspectus of the Slavonian Churches, Utrecht, 1652, 4to.

In German :—Short Biographies of remarkable Men among the United Brethren, 1846, 8vo.

John Plitt, Contribution to the History of the Unity of the Brethren, MS. 1828, folio.

Dr. Pescheck, Reformation and Anti-reformation in Bohemia, London, 1845, 2 vols. 8vo.

Dr. Anton Gindely, on the life and labours of John Amos Comenius in his exile, 8vo.

The Histories of the Brethren, by Cranz, London, 1780, 8vo. and Holmes, London, 1830, 2 vols. 8vo. and Talvi's Historical view of the language and literature of the Slavonic nations, by Dr. Edward Robinson, New York, 1850, 12mo. have been occasionally referred to, as well as numerous other duly cited works.

Palacky's list of the works of Comenius, as published in a Bohemian periodical of 1829, has also been found useful.

To the Rev. Mr. Clemens, of Baildon, Yorkshire, the Rev. Peter LaTrobe, and the Rev. Mr. Eberlé, of London, and other Christian friends, the compiler acknowledges, with thankful sincerity, his obligation for much of the information contained in the following sketch.

The Portrait is from an engraving by the justly celebrated Wenceslaus Hollar, a Bohemian exile, who most probably took it from the life. It was preferred before that by Glover, which was done ten years earlier. This, with the frontispiece executed by Mr. William Dickes, of Old Fish Street, Doctors Commons, are illustrative of the work, and it is hoped will gratify the taste of the reader. The verses affixed to the portrait were written by Francis Quarles.

In reference to the changes that have taken place in the

names of places during the course of the last two centuries, the reader will observe that

Basil	is now	Basle.
Strassnik	,,	Strasnitz.
Wratislavia	,,	Breslau.
Sednik	,,	Lednitz.
Belse, Belzyce	,,	Belsk.
Boleslavia	,,	Jungbunslau.
Siebenburgen	,,	Transylvania.

DANIEL BENHAM.

18, Regent Square, London.
August, 1858.

ERRATA—"COMENIUS."

Page 3, line 6, *for* 1444 *read* 1434.
    5, line 3, *for* Hugonitorum *read* Hugonotorun.
    29, note, line 1, *for* 1630 *read* 1636.
    37, last line, *for* Sigismund Evinius *read* Sigismund Evenius.
    39, line 9, *for* resarata *read* reserata.
    41, line 13, *for* pietati *read* pietatis.
    43, 2nd line of note, *for* Index Prohibitor *read* Index Bohemicorum librorum prohibitorum.
    56, line 29, *for* it *read* them.
    68, line 25, *for* Charitate *read* Charitativum.
    86, line 26, *for* Lam. i. 10 *read* Jer. iv. 10.
    88, note, line 29, *for* 1640 *read* 1649.
    101, line 19, *for* Cropen at *read* Crossen to.
    111, line 14, *for* Juventate *read* Juventute.
    111, line 15, *for* felicitus *read* felicius.
    128, note, *for* pp. 36, 37 *read* pp. 43, 44.
    131, line 26, *for* democracy *read* democratical.
    157, line 5, *for* 20 *read* 26.
    160, line 27, *for* Bohemian *read* Bohemia.

"EDUCATION."

Page 1, line 15, *for* he *read* be.
    16, line 32, *for* impart safety *read* salute.
    26, line 32, *for* Caligulus *read* Caligula.
    27, line 18, *for* Apolestes *read* Apolephtes.
    32, line 2, *for* to exercised *read* to be exercised.

SOME ACCOUNT

OF

JOHN AMOS COMENIUS.

CONTENTS.

CHAPTER I.

Introduction . . . . PAGE 1

CHAPTER II.

Sketch of the History of the Ancient Bohemian Brethren in Moravia 10

CHAPTER III.

Birth of Comenius—Education—Becomes a Teacher and Pastor—At Prerau—At Fulneck—Driven thence by Persecution—Bereavements—Takes refuge at Slaupna—Consolations in Distress—Mission to Poland—Driven from Slaupna to Poland . . 21

CHAPTER IV.

Leszno—Comenius settles there—Resumes his Scholastic Function and Studies—His Correspondence with Learned Men—Efforts to improve the Schools—Maternal School—Janua Linguarum—Its Celebrity—Comenius ordained a Bishop of the Brethren—Expects to be restored to his Country and prepares for it—His Influence—Lutheran Disturbance—Writes against Socinians—Seeks and partially secures Patronage—His great Designs . 34

CHAPTER V.

Comenius visits England—Civil Commotions there compel his Departure—Accepts an Invitation to Sweden—Interview with the Chancellor Oxenstiern—His Proposals accepted—Settles at Elbing 51

CHAPTER VI.

Elbing—Comenius and his Friends—Removes his Family to Elbing—Limits his Correspondence—An attempt to sever him from his Patron—Reports Progress of his Works—Changes in his Assistants—Called to a General Synod at Orla—Displeasure of his Patron—Attends an Ecclesiastical Conference at Thorn—His Letter to Montanus—Satisfactory Explanation to his Patron 62

CHAPTER VII.

Pecuniary aid from the Netherlands withheld—Distress from Poverty, etc.—Partial relief obtained—Causes of the "Thirty Years' War"—Appointed Senior of the Church of the Brethren—Independents—Treaty of Westphalia, destroys the hopes of the Exiles, who are warned against Declension—Care for the exiled Brethren—Death of Lewis de Geer 75

CHAPTER VIII.

Comenius visits the Princess Rakoczi—Proceeds to Tokay—School at Saros-Patak—Compiles the "Orbis Pictus"—Destruction of Lissa—Escape and Losses of Comenius—He settles in Amsterdam—His Despondency—Obtains help from England for himself and his Brethren—Testamentary Benevolences—Fraternal Sympathy 94

CHAPTER IX.

Comenius at Amsterdam—Publishes his Didactica, etc.—Defends Christian Doctrine against Heterodox Opinions—Adopts means to continue the Episcopacy and Principles of the Unity of the Brethren—Their Church described—Letter to Montanus—Works not completed—Scholastic Plays—Attempts for the Conversion of the Turks 116

CHAPTER X.

Comenius misled by Prophetic Delusions—His connection with Kotter, Poniatovia, and Dabricius—He publishes their Visions—His own Statement regarding them—The One Thing necessary—His last Will—His Family—His Death—Unfinished Work on the Improvement of Human Affairs—His Person and Character—Conclusion 139

INDEX. Names of persons and places . . . . . 163—168

SOME ACCOUNT OF

JOHN AMOS COMENIUS.

CHAPTER I.

INTRODUCTION.

By way of introduction to the following account it may be well to present the reader with a sketch of the history of Christian Bohemia, to the period when that kingdom was dispossessed of its liberties, civil and religious, by imperial Austria and apostate Rome.—In doing this we prefer adopting as a basis the testimony of Comenius himself, who personally shared in the evils he describes, rather than of such writings as have appeared in the defence of his country's oppressors, or such as have so mystified events as to conceal the turpitude of the principal actors in a theatre of blood, perhaps the most terrible of any in which the human family has ever embroiled itself.

The free people of Bohemia possessed, among other distinguished privileges, two of great importance, and of the highest excellence: 1. Liberty, in the exercise of the Christian religion; and, 2. The free election of their king.

1. *Religion and its free exercise in Bohemia.*

Since the liberty of the Christian religion, enlightened all nations as a gift of Divine grace, so did it also to the Bohemians, not under the authority of the Roman Flamen, but out of Sion, and from the Oriental and Greek churches, who assumed no right of dominion over the faith, but ministered to the edification of their converts.

In process of time, through the influence of a certain

princess, an archbishop was obtained from the Roman hierarchy, who found it necessary (even one did it willingly), to preserve and sanction the liberty of the Gospel they had received, the rites of the primitive church, the use of the mother-tongue in the sacred services, and the Lord's supper entire, until and beyond the time of Charles IVth (1378), when, as the most reverend Lord George Prince of Anhalt, and once coadjutor in the archbishopric of Magdeburg, says in his writings, vol. ii. p. 500, " The use of bread alone in the " Lord's supper first began to obtain in Bohemia, a practice " which most of the nobility and the city of Satça could never " be brought to adopt; this city, all along from its first con- " version to the faith of Christ to this day, always preserving " the use of both species,"—proofs of which were declared to be preserved in the citadel of Prague.

And when Antichrist, waxing to maturity, and seditiously opposing Christ, aimed at dominion over the Christian religion, and sacrilegiously changed the institution of its founder in the sacred Supper, the Bohemians adhered not to him, but to the institution of Christ. They, moreover, besides the learned Milicius, the preacher of Prague, who, as early as 1360, began to unmask Antichrist; generously supported other faithful preachers, especially John Huss and Jerome of Prague.

These the Roman Pontiff, violently opposed to their liberty and to religious truth itself, immediately after the year 1400, by means of his Councils of Constance and Basil, endeavoured to suppress. Alleging heresy, he summoned their eminent leaders to councils formed of his own party, and, though not convicted, he, in violation of the plighted safe-conduct, burned them alive: thus unwillingly elevating them to the crown of martyrdom.

When the respectable orders of Bohemia and Moravia expressed indignation at the disgrace of heresy imputed to them, the Pope endeavoured by artifice and arms to destroy them, or subject them to obedience to his chair, and thus excited those cruel commotions, generally, but very improperly, called the Hussite wars.

God, however, imbued the people who fought in defence of his cause with such courage and wisdom, as, about the year 1444, to secure, not only liberty of religion and truth, but the proclamation by authority of the Imperial mandate of the assessors in the Council of Basil, and of the deputies themselves; and in direct contradiction to the sentence of Antichrist, they were proclaimed, *not heretics, but sons of the true Church of Christ.*

The obligation to observe the rites of the church being ambiguously inserted in the proclamation, was understood by the Bohemians to refer to the ancient primitive church, and not to the papal yoke, and hence, through the malice of the Pope, and by the agency of his satellites who construed it otherwise, many preachers and hearers were put to death, fresh disturbances were created, and in opposition to the testimony of the Emperor, the Synod of Florence promulgated a decree, that as Bohemia and its associate Moravia had been proscribed as aliens from the church, they, therefore, ought to be rooted out.

Under these circumstances the Bohemians of all ranks assembled at Prague in 1450, and, condemning the unjust Florentine decree and the papal malice, unanimously appointed a solemn legation to the Greek churches, which would joyously have taken them into their pale, but for the inroads of the Turks about the year 1453, when they were deserted by the occidental churches, who calmly looked on while they were attacked, overpowered, and subjugated by Mohamedans, and thus deprived of Christian sympathy.

The Pope, repeating his fulmination against the proscribed, forthwith sent troops of crusaders, who, aided by such papists as remained in or were but recently drawn from Bohemia, plundered and laid waste with fire and sword the towns and villages throughout the kingdom, and these selected crossbearing administrators of the Roman chair; as if actuated by demons and infernal furies, continued during several years to butcher multitudes of pious and innocent persons, and were so delighted with the murder of children, that they used the little heads of slaughtered infants as balls to play with when engaged in that amusement.—Thus glutting with complacency the Roman conscience by the extirpation of those they called heretics.

The courage and revenge of the Bohemians being excited by the promiscuous slaughter of many thousands of men, women, and children; they seized their arms, and, at a town called Glottovia, conquered and slew three thousand of these crucifixian marauders, and put the rest to flight.

The Pope, having received a blow in this defeat of his bosom friends, and suspecting, as he well might, a general warfare against him, discontinued his open spoliation, but only to try new methods. He sent his legate into Bohemia, and—mark this well—as his minions are now doing in Great Britain, unsettled the minds of certain pastors, and scattered the seeds of divisions, strifes, and hatred among others —thus adopting the method of conquering so often practised by their ancient heathen precursors, and assailing even the regal court itself, instigated it to a violation of compacts and to the infliction of martyrdom on many most eminent Christians for their constancy; as in the example of King Vladislav, in 1483, who, unmindful of his election, and in violation of his oath, passed a most atrocious edict, causing it to be promulgated, by the Senate of Prague and certain nobles, the slaves of Antichrist, "*that on the night of the 25th of September, of that same year, all who took the Lord's Supper entire, should be completely destroyed.*" Had not God, who watches over his own, and the courage of the people, rolled back some portion of that diabolical destruction upon the heads of their enemies, assuredly a more bloody massacre had been perpetrated than that at Paris in the year 1572, which so filled the Roman flamen with delight that he caused a medal to be struck on the occasion with the inscription on it "Hugonitorum Strages, 1572"—*Destruction of the Huguenots*, 1572.*

A few zealous men, detesting the want of firmness in certain ministers on this occasion, obtained letters of credit from the Academy of Prague and proceeded to Armenia, where being examined and approved, they were ordained ministers of the Armenian Church, and returned with testimonials, dated 1499, of the accordance of the two churches in the use of the mother tongue in their services, and in the integrity of the Lord's supper. Joy and gladness now refreshed both teachers and hearers in the Church which had recently been struck with terror by the tyranny of Antichrist.

Meanwhile, certain governors of the Church of Bohemia, who continued steadfast to the ordinances of Christ, even during the hostile reign of King Vladislav, asserted and recommended the doctrine of the gospel, and with the view of composing religious differences, framed this decree: "*Since the multiplication of ecclesiastic rites and ceremonies avails little as regards salvation and Christian piety towards God, they ought therefore the rather to be abandoned than insisted upon, and not to form a subject of controversy.*" This decree was promulgated in 1492, with the consent of the whole of the clergy and masters of the Academy of Prague; and hence superstitions and human tradition falling into disesteem, a purer ministry and primitive doctrine prevailed until the year 1524, when the orders of the kingdom assembled in Synod, (as is evidenced from the synodal decrees,) confessed and sanctioned the form of religion, agreeing with the primitive church, and, excepting some small differences, with the doctrine of Luther and others of the evangelical party in Germany.

* See Medley's History of the Reformed Religion in France, Vol. II. 35-36, for other medals struck on occasion of this massacre.

Such then was the condition of Christianity for more than a century among the Bohemians. Antichrist often condemning and delivering them up to destruction for heresy, and Christ, exalted at the right hand of God, defending and bestowing upon many thousands of them the crown of martyrdom, until other pious men and women, being raised up in other lands, relieved the Bohemians, now much exhausted in their spiritual warfare with the Beast. The breathing time thus afforded to the Bohemians was employed in preparing for future conflict, and the much-wished-for consummation of their desire to emancipate themselves from the thraldom of Antichrist.

As there were no kings or princes at this period in Western Christendom, who were not either tributary or subservient to the Pope, so the kings of Bohemia, freely elected by the Orders of the kingdom, were attached to the popedom, and cherished the snake in its nest; while some, as is usual, turning aside, in order to gain court favour, conformed to the infirmities and errors of the great apostacy, upholding vain ceremonies and impure doctrines, and occasioning perpetual divisions. Yet all attempts to wrest the free, faithful, and open exercise of the Christian religion from the faithful in Bohemia, until the time of King Ferdinand II., notwithstanding every variety of fraud and malice on the part of Antichrist, were ineffectual; and the Prince of Anhalt (at the place already cited), who had travelled through the kingdom and knew it well, declared "the Bohemians are upright and pious men, and *have been unjustly condemned.*"

When, at the time of the Council of Trent, Antichrist attempted everywhere to destroy all persons of piety who opposed the Beast, and dared to condemn and eradicate the whole evangelical religion and its institutes, his slaves laid such accusations of heresy against the Bohemian pastors, as to induce Ferdinand to summon them before the civil tribunals, with the view to their punishment. But they asserted their immunity in a written apology, and appealing to the authority of the Orders and the judgment of the Academy of Prague, exhibited to the King their councils and statutes of 1421 and 1524, which comprised their Christian Confession; and the king, although sufficiently powerful to crush them, yet allowed them to enjoy their Christian liberty, as is evident from the repetition in 1562 of the ancient and constant Confession of Faith of the Bohemian and Moravian Church of Christ, and which was published in that year by authority of the Academy, and again in 1574. Moreover, when the Papists, under the authority of the Council of Trent, attempted to deprive these Christians of their liberty, they composed their differences and unitedly demanded and obtained a Royal letter from the supreme majesty, confirming them in the free exercise of their religion.

2. *Right of the Bohemians to elect their prince or king.*

It is abundantly evident from all well attested history, that the Bohemians, from the period when, conducted by Czech and Lech, they entered into and cultivated the province which was then desert, had always the right of electing their Princes; and observed it so strictly in their laws, that according to the ancient Boleslaviensian Chronicle and other documents, they deprived of their power and deposed no less than eleven of their regularly elected Princes, for daring to violate the conditions of their election, and always elected others who were disposed to govern in conformity with such conditions.

By firmly and successfully defending their territory, during a period of five hundred years against all invaders, they afforded important services to the Christian Emperors, in their wars against the rebellious Italians, and afterwards against the seditious papists, and they thus attained to the dignity of a kingdom, and the Institution of their Orders;

which privileges they asserted, and had confirmed to them, by the golden bulls of Emperors and Pontiffs and at the inauguration of every king. About the year 1086, under the Emperor Henry III. when their last Duke Vratislav became their first king; in 1197, under the Emperor Philip; also under the honoured Frederick II. who offered a determined opposition to the encroachments of the Roman see, confirmed this liberty by successive golden bulls in 1212, 1216, and 1221, and established the right by which in time to come, their kings should obtain the kingdom under the following sacred rescript: "It is our wish that whosoever is chosen to be their king by the Bohemians, should come to us and our successors to receive the Regalia in due form." The same rights were confirmed by golden bulls from the Emperor Charles IV. about and after 1350, which expressly declare: "That the Bohemians have the right of freely electing their king;" and beyond all this when the Emperor at Nuremberg in 1356, in an assembly of the empire, most clearly confirmed this right by the golden bull, then published for the whole empire; under the seventh head decreeing that all secular electorates should devolve to heirs through legitimate succession, expressly excepted Bohemia as an elective electorate in these words: "As to the chief Rulers of the empire, the Emperor will provide; yet always excepting the privileges, rights, and usages of the kingdom of Bohemia, in case of vacation, as to the election of their king by the inhabitants of the kingdom, who possess the right of electing and creating the King of Bohemia, that the same privileges and long observed usages may be continued, and these we decree to remain in unquestioned security, both during the present and for all future time, in their entire bearing and form." And this public Constitution in the Imperial assembly was decreed, although in 1348 the Emperor had, by declaration, restricted the said election to "the case of a vacation, when none of the regal race survived." Moreover, their king, George Podiebrad, was confirmed by Pope Pius II., and all their kings afterwards, to whatever family they belonged, solemnly professed in a reversal letter, "that they attained the royal dignity by the decree and free election of the Orders,—a more glorious and honourable ascension than by inheritance."

And when the will of the Popes directed everything, and Sigismund, the Emperor, even carried on wars against religion, the Bohemians used their right, and maintained it openly; and so matters continued down to the year 1617, when Ferdinand II., in an assembly held at Prague, being recommended by Matthias, the Emperor and King, to the chiefs of the kingdom, and being elected and crowned King of Bohemia, fully acknowledged the voluntary election in the reversal letters customarily given, and by the prescribed oath.

It is unnecessary to repeat here what has already been presented before the English public in Dr. Peschech's admirable work on the Reformation and Anti-reformation of Bohemia; how the Papists assailed, and eventually suppressed their liberties, both in religion and election, with every artifice, every fallacy, and every deception; by false interpretations of the Word of God and of ecclesiastical writers, by corruptions, by concealments, by apocryphal documents, by feigned objections, by clandestine counsels, by open councils, and by illegal force. So also their free election of a king was sought to be destroyed by the Austrians, by wonderful contrivances, by political artifice, by false interpretation of laws, by corruptions, by concealment, by novel arrangements, by declarations, by extra-legal writings, by clandestine compacts, and, finally, by open force; until the iniquitous purpose of the mystery of iniquity was at length cruelly obtained, through the manifold machinations of the great apostacy, which, in the inscrutable hand of the Divine government, became instrumental in effecting that which the purpose of God had predetermined to be done.

CHAPTER II.

SKETCH OF THE HISTORY OF THE ANCIENT BOHEMIAN BRETHREN IN MORAVIA.

WE shall now lay before the reader a sketch of the history of the ancient Unity of the Bohemian Brethren in Moravia, down to the period when the kingdom of Bohemia, which included the Marquisate of Moravia, was dispossessed of its liberties, religious and civil, by Imperial Austria and apostate Rome.

As early as the year 1498, the most vigilant Stanislaus Thurzo, Bishop of Olmütz, spared no labour in his earnestness to eradicate the tenets, which, having been propagated from Bohemia, had in the course of years struck deep root in the hearts of the Waldensian Brethren or Picards, names by which they were distinguished by the enemies whom they opposed, and sometimes also by themselves.

These Brethren had found a permanent settlement, and acquired so firm a footing in Moravia, that they could by no means be dislodged, although under the kings George Podiebrad and Matthias, they had been obliged to hold their assemblies in caves, and underground hiding places. At first they taught that there were to be found in the Roman church three kinds of things: *good*, which they followed; *good intermixed with evil*, which intermixture they had purified; and *evil things*, which they carefully eschewed. But, in addition to these, they in process of time discovered innumerable other evils, the correction of which, (from closer examination of the Holy Scriptures, the apostacy of Rome becoming more apparent to them) they endeavoured to defend by various apologies, and especially by one entitled " Vindication of the so-called Waldensian Brethren, against two letters addressed to the King, by Dr.

Augustin, Councillor at Law, of Olmütz," who was his majesty's epistolary Secretary, a most deadly enemy of evangelical truth, and whose two letters were declared to be signally false and calumnious, and intended to bring odium upon the objects of his attack. His was a melancholy end; being seized with apoplexy while at dinner in his house at Olmütz, he suddenly expired.*

These Brethren abominated the Roman priesthood, and affirmed their own to be without interruption apostolic, alleging that from Christ it passed to the apostles; from thence to the Greek church, and from it to Michael and Stephen, formerly priests of the Roman church, but now superintendents of the Brethren; that, finally, by them others had also been initiated, and by this succession five superintendents were ordained in Moravia, in the year 1499.

These ministers of the Brethren had an attached auxiliary to their cause, in the illustrious Martha de Boskovitz, a lady of very superior education, who had become a member of their Unity, and made it her principal care to introduce them among her kindred, mostly of equestrian rank.

She even applied in the behalf of the Brethren to the King, who replied, that it should be left to each of the lords of the states to act as he chose towards heretics: and thus the Brethren were tolerated; but these things coming under the notice of Pope Alexander the VIth, "apostolic letters" were transmitted from Rome to Austria, with instructions for the suppression of this Picardic heresy, under the counsel of the Bishop of Olmütz.

In 1500 another Papal brief was issued, commanding all the writings of the Brethren to be sought for, seized, and publicly burnt; especially a book written by Peter Chelzicius, which being compiled in forty chapters, he named Kopita. He was a pious man, and, although by trade a shoemaker,

* Regenvolscius, p. 182.

very learned, and wrote this book against the abominations which had crept into the church.*

In 1501, at the instigation of the above Dr. Augustin, King Vladislav proscribed the Brethren by a public edict; and, annoyed by the importunities of their enemy, who now brought the Imperial power to bear upon him, he issued a second edict; in both which he commanded them to be driven from the royal domains, removed from the magistracy and prohibited from preaching; and moreover that they should be regarded as ensnared by the devil, and that the faithful should abstain from commercial intercourse with so vile a community. Little however was effected by these edicts, extorted by the clergy from the king, inasmuch as the Brethren were legally protected by the nobles on their estates.

The Brethren, nevertheless, desirous of conciliating the favour of the king, at that time in Hungary, forwarded to him their Confession of faith, and made the greatest possible efforts, by preaching and teaching among the people, to strengthen the cause of God. It was entitled "An apologetic Oration of the Waldensian Brethren."

Yet in 1505 Bishop Thurzo succeeded, at a diet of the Marquisate held at Brunn, in procuring a general statute, condemning the Brethren, by which the churches they had erected were interdicted and their doctrine was prohibited. It was also decreed, in accordance with the papal mandate, that none of their writings should be published, and that every one that could be found should be burned; and, finally, directed that Austin Kosenbrot, Provost of the church of Olmütz should write them down. But since their doctrine could not be eradicated, the Bishop was compelled to allow it to prevail; King Vladislav being unwilling to persecute their protectors, although prompted to it by priestly interference.

* Regenvolscius, p. 27.

Since nothing has been handed down to us of the history of the Brethren between the years 1510 and 1516, their congregations probably edified themselves, in what may be considered as a breathing time from the efforts of their persecutors, which however do not appear to have relaxed, although not exhibited by open aggression.

In the year 1523, under the counsel of the same Bishop Thurzo, Lewis, the successor of Vladislav in the kingdom of Bohemia and Marquisate of Moravia, proscribed the doctrines of the Brethren and of Luther, and promulgated the edicts, which gave exclusive toleration to the papists and high church party only, and commanded the expulsion of the Brethren and the Lutherans. Other edicts were issued by the papal legate; and under these, some were imprisoned, some were branded, and many thousands of the Brethren were driven into exile.*

On the 25th of May, 1525, King Lewis, at the instigation of the Bishop, again sanctioned an edict, now under penalty of death, repressing these courageous men, whose doctrines were both in private and public making progress increasingly.—But death relieved the King from adding to the miseries already inflicted upon the Brethren.

John Dubravius, Bishop of Olmütz, in the year 1543, so excited King Ferdinand against the Brethren, that he proscribed them from his dominions; yet, in 1547, we find them protected in various domains of the Moravian nobility, and continuing to hold meetings and ordain ministers—at which period their numbers so increased daily, as greatly to trouble Kuenus, who became Bishop of Olmütz in 1553. They now held public conventions, at which their superintendent John Czerny, a physician presided; the same who, in 1555, in a general Evangelical Synod held at Kozmin, zealously with others promoted and ratified the consent and union of the Churches of Bohemia, Moravia, and Great and Little

---

* Pelzel. Hist. of Bohemia, 3rd edition, p. 519, &c.

Poland. This venerable and eloquent man died at Boleslavia, 5th February, 1565.*

In 1557, the clergy of the Brethren in Moravia numbered more than two hundred.—Upon these the Bishop made war, and called in the aid of the so-called "Society of Jesus," as auxiliary forces from Prague and Vienna; upon whom, in 1570, it was enjoined that they should spare no efforts to restore the Brethren to the papal church. But these efforts only stimulated them to greater exertion; and in 1571 they printed the New Testament at Kralitz in the Bohemian language, as a corrective of a papal German translation, which, in the previous year, had been prepared and printed at the expense of Jerome Emser, a Romish priest.

In 1575, when the Emperor Rudolph permitted the Brethren to live according to the prescript of their Confession, such was the low condition of Romanism through the zealous labours of evangelical men in Moravia, that it was said of Bishop Albinus, who held the episcopate of Olmütz little more than a year, that the greatest privilege, next to not ruling at all, was to govern for the shortest period of time.

In 1602 the Emperor Rudolph, however, at the instigation of Cardinal Dietrichstein, then Bishop of Olmütz,† made provision by edicts sufficiently severe that the Picards or Brethren, and all non-romanists, should be debarred from the use of their places of worship and religious services; prohibited their assembling together under penalty of exile; removed the wealthy from the magistracy and

---

* Regenvolscius, p. 318.

† He who among other things provided for the perpetual worship of the so-called *mother of God*, under which name the Romanists of our day have virtually restored the idolatry of Pagan Rome in the worship of their "Mater Deorum," whose great festival was held on the 25th of March, *Lady-day*, and to whom the ancient Romans annually sacrificed a *Sow!*—See Tressan Mythology, by North, p. 62-63, Dr. Rees' Cyclopædia, article Cybele.

places of trust; and finally decreed that none but Romanists should be admitted to the rights of citizenship—yet still the evangelical doctrine prevailed, and with it the desire of establishing by law that freedom, which would emancipate men from the tyranny and selfishness of a vicious priesthood.

Hence when Matthias, the brother of Rudolph, succeeded to the kingdom, men's minds had become so enlightened, that many privileges were explicitly demanded from him; and one, which was regarded as the most important, had respect to religious toleration: *That all should be at liberty to worship God in such manner, as should, according to the doctrine of Christ set forth in the New Testament, be deemed right:*" and hence that in the formula of the public oath the words "to the mother of God and all the saints" should be omitted. Matthias at length acceded to this, reserving, however, that the ancient oath in its original form should be previously read.

Notwithstanding this, the Romanists, in 1609, priestly and laic, headed by Cardinal Dietrichstein, prevented the Brethren and Lutherans from exercising their sacred rites within the regal and episcopal cities; and the Cardinal, having bought the township of Cropin, and added it to the episcopal domain of Kremsier, in 1615, completely demolished the high school of the Brethren there; and in other respects, by the assistance of the Jesuits, and the military which they managed to quarter upon the non-romanists, so exceedingly worried them, as eventually to goad them in self-defence to the infraction of law; which, being made the pretext of denouncing them as traitors to the government, induced further persecutions, until at length the States of Bohemia and Moravia were induced to repudiate the Emperor altogether. And in 1618 they elected in his stead another king, the Elector Palatine Frederick, who was afterwards driven from the country by the issue of the battle of the Whitehill at Prague in 1620, when the imperial papal party prevailed.

In 1621, the Emperor Ferdinand II., as a mark of his approval of the conduct of Cardinal Dietrichstein in this most iniquitous affair, appointed him Governor of the Marquisate of Moravia, with instructions to seek out the promoters of the rebellion, which, of course, at once sealed destruction to all non-papists.

On a certain day the leading men of the Protestant nobility, who were charged as having been concerned in the affair, were arrested, and their domains were committed to the administration of the papistry. Dietrichstein substituted a magistracy of his own party in place of that of the subdued; everywhere appointing a Romanist under the title of Imperial Judge, as President of all the Councils of the States. Such citizens as had been active in the revolt, he adjudged to public prisons, and confiscated their property; and, finally, he compelled the mayors of cities, governors of citadels, and guardians of the public peace, to take an oath of obedience to the Emperor in the ancient form, invoking "*as present witnesses* the blessed Virgin Mary and all the saints."

Dietrichstein, having thus succeeded in chaining the Moravians to the imperial footstool, now adopted means to bind them to the papal yoke. In the first place he ejected and restrained by military force the Protestants of Nikolburg, Austerlitz, Hradisch, and Fulnec. Such of the military of Moravia in general, as had acted against the Emperor, were pardoned by him, the leaders and the Protestant preachers being excepted. Hence Dietrichstein's great difficulty, from a sense of personal insecurity, was with the military, which he removed by directing that such as were not papists should quit either their faith or the camp.

He and his council now proceeded with the trials of the accused, whom he divided into three classes, Barons, Knights, and Citizens; their punishments were also classified under death, amputation and mutilation; imprisonment, exile, confiscation, fines, and property placed under the administration of others; the memories of such of the accused as had died were condemned to infamy, and their property was confiscated. In this way the spirit of the oppressed was suppressed, and by this means the Imperial and Papal coffers were enriched.

The Emperor Ferdinand, no doubt prompted by ghostly incitement, alleging that the source of the revolt must be attributable to the diversity of religious sects, resolved to bind the Moravians by a *new* obligation, the so-called UNITY *of the Papal belief,* perhaps the most specious and, at the same time, the most really monstrous of all its monstrosities. He consequently issued mandates empowering the Cardinal to prosecute with all zeal the work he had *so meritoriously* commenced.

Dietrichstein, as before, began with the Anabaptists, who had become so from the absurd and abominable abuses adopted in this respect by the Church. They were at this time very numerous, including many of the Brethren, and chiefly from the lower classes of the people. These he commanded, within a short space of time, and under the penalty of death, to depart from Moravia and all the Austrian provinces, unless they agreed to attach themselves to the ritual of Rome; assigning as causes of this exile, that it was a principle of the Anabaptists not to obey the civil magistrate, and that they were guilty of seducing simple people, and, therefore, they were proscribed from the whole empire. This measure was shortly followed by the departure of seventy thousand of Anabaptists from the provinces of Austria—so mightily had the word of God prevailed over the minds of these noble and faithful confessors of Christ. Others, about ten thousand, not so firm in their principles, unwilling to part from their patrimonial possessions, submitted to a profession of the pretended religion of Rome.*

To the so-called "fathers of the Society of Jesus" must

* A faithful account of this most cruelly misrepresented people is still necessary to the English readers of Christian Church History.

be attributed this scourge to the country, by whose means the Protestant nobles were now deprived of their right of patronage to parochial churches, and compelled to give the Emperor "letters of reversal," as they were called, promising, under loss of the imperial favour and confiscation of their property, not to allow any other than the dogmas and rites of Rome to be exercised within their respective possessions. Thus Moravia was rendered a dead mute and a desert, and the so-called Society of Jesus being encouraged by the imperial munificence, and aided by the equestrian order of the "*Christian Militia,*" which was instituted in 1617, first at Olmütz, and then at Vienna; they arrogated to themselves the education of the people, and thus formed, according to their own principles, numerous youths for the administration of political and ecclesiastical polity, as well of Moravia as of the other portions of the kingdom of Bohemia, and as a finishing stroke to the whole, the Emperor, in a letter to Dietrichstein, dated the 12th of August, 1624, decreed that none but Romanists were competent to be the inhabitants of Moravia.

Yet for all this many Protestant Preachers still remained concealed in the cities, who, under the protection of certain baronial lords, that no doubt well knew the vast difference of principle, in respect of faithful service, between true Christianity and the mockery of it under a vicious priesthood, emerging into the rural districts, confirmed numbers of the inhabitants in the Protestant faith. With the view to the complete extirpation of these, the Emperor, by an exceedingly severe decree sent forth on the 27th of December, in the same year, 1624, commanded that, without any exception, all non-papal preachers should be driven by military force out of the country, debarring the denounced while they continued in the kingdom from employment, from compacts, from commerce, and from marriage, and consigning all again to exile.

In the next year the Emperor's mandates were promptly and diligently carried into effect by a most rigorous search instituted by the Jesuits, and the indiscriminate expulsion of Protestants from every part of Moravia. The people, accompanied by their ministers, went into exile in masses to Lower Saxony and to Denmark, King Charles IV., son-in-law of Frederick, Elector of Brandenburg, then reigning. This extreme severity of the Emperor was undoubtedly instigated by a fiendish apostacy, which in pursuing its diabolic ends, by exciting the evil passions of men, always exults in the destruction of those who by their conduct exhibit any real approach towards that Christianity in doctrine and life, which necessarily must condemn its infidelity, idolatry, superstition, and craft.

In 1628, on the 9th of March, the Emperor, in addition to what had been done before, sent an edict for promulgation in Moravia, enforcing the departure within six months of all Protestants, both nobles and commoners, from the Marquisate, unless they should conform to the so-called Roman faith. The nobles were also bound to sell their possessions to Romanists, whether of their own friends or others of the inhabitants. This edict being enforced by the increased avidity of the Roman clergy, non-papists of every kind throughout the country were ferreted out with implacable enmity, and very many of the nobility, maintained the dignity of their Christian profession by withdrawing to Hungary, Transylvania, or Saxony.

To complete the annihilation of every thing sacred in the annals of a free people driven into exile, the officialties of the Marquisate of Moravia, were transferred to the Emperor; the right of the orders of the states to create barons and knights, was wrested from them, and declared to appertain to the *regalia* of the supreme prince ; the whole of the distinctions of nobility must henceforth be obtained from the Royal chancery ; and the municipal cities were left in the hands of Dietrichstein to be deprived of their privileges, as his cardinalship should determine.

To close this sickening sketch of what has been really effected in a Protestant country, by the admission of a political agency in the shape of an apostate foreign priesthood, always either secretly or openly intriguing destruction to everything sacred to the cause of humanity, and which is now insidiously working its way in our beloved country, it will be only necessary to add that the war in defence of religious toleration, excited by the Roman Flamen and his satellites, and which began in 1617, continued with unabating severity until the year 1648, when four successive campaigns being decisively unfavourable to the Emperor Ferdinand III., he was at length compelled to think seriously of ending the contest, and this was finally brought about by a peace made at Munster, in Westphalia, which terminated the so-called "Thirty years War." By the conditions of which peace, the Bohemian and Moravian crown being secured to the Austrian family, that once free and Christian country, has ever since continued under its despotic sway, and the tender mercies of the Inquisitors of papal Rome, which from rejecting the means of improvement presented to her in the course of Divine Providence, stubbornly persisted in her own defection and faults; and being in this condition it would be vain that even God himself should speak to her from heaven. All means of improvement divinely presented, have been recklessly disregarded, and from age to age Babylon remains Babel still.

As to the exiles, they were entirely disregarded in the treaty; and thus abandoned, they did their best in the countries to which they were driven, where, from the benignity of God, they mostly found asylums and means of subsistence through the sympathy every where expressed towards them by their brethren and sisters in Christ.

CHAPTER III.

BIRTH—EDUCATION—BECOMES A TEACHER AND PASTOR—AT PRERAU—AT FULNECK—DRIVEN THENCE BY PERSECUTION—BEREAVEMENTS—TAKES REFUGE AT SLAUPNA—CONSOLATIONS IN DISTRESS—MISSION TO POLAND—DRIVEN FROM SLAUPNA TO POLAND.

ALTHOUGH the Unity of the Brethren, as an ecclesiastical association without the pale of the Papal but afterwards within that of the Evangelic church, was dissolved by the one of its branches (in Bohemia and Moravia) being destroyed, and the other becoming attached to a more extensive establishment, the Reformed church in Great and Little Poland, yet various remnants survived; and among these preserved ones was a man, who, possessing excellent genius and talent, while he became pre-eminent in every department of learning, attained the most desirable of all fame, the greatest reputation for virtue and goodness. This man was John Amos Comenius, the last Bishop of the ancient church of the Bohemian Brethren, and who by means of his writings preserved their cause, and rendered possible its renewal after it had, by the exertions of the emissaries employed by the Arch-flamen of Rome, become almost hopelessly extinguished.

Jan Amos Komensky, *i.e.* from the village Comna (Komna) near Brumovium (Brumow) in the vicinity of Ungrish-Brod, in Moravia, was born on the 28th of March, 1592.* His family name, the concealment of which became necessary for the safety of his person when driven into exile, was, in German, Töpfer,† (English, Potter.) Of the

* Regenvolscius, p. 322.—Plitt's MS.—Holmes I. 127.
† Dr. Pescheck, Vol. II. p. 419, note.

circumstances of his family and the history of his early life very little is known; his father, a corn miller, belonged to the Unity of the Brethren, whose congregations were very numerous in the locality of his birth.* His modesty was such that he seldom spake of himself, even where he might, and ought to have done so in his history of the body to which he belonged. The one thing needful to the souls of men; his devastated country; and his expatriated Brethren, were the subjects which completely engrossed his whole soul.

We learn, however, that he received early education after the death of his parents in 1604, for a year and a half at the public school of Strassnik, where he lived with an aunt,† and that in his sixteenth year he was at a grammar school in his native land; but the wretched condition of the schools there,‡ through the persecuting spirit of the times, induced his friends who belonged to the Brethren to send him in the year 1612 to the high school at Herborn, in the duchy of Nassau, where having become desirous of devoting himself to the service of the Lord, he might be subjected to the necessary theological training; and where, under the superintendance of John Henry Alstedius, a learned man, skilled in the interpretation of the prophets,§ and afterwards at the reformed University at Heidelberg, in which he continued until 1614, he made great improvement in liberal learning, in the Latin and Greek languages, and in philosophy and theology. Afterward, making a tour in the Netherlands, he returned to Heidelberg and was there seized with a very severe illness. Recovering from this attack he left Heidelberg, and partly from the hope of gaining strength by bodily exercise, and partly from lack of pecuniary means, he

* Dr. Anton Gindely, p. 6.
† Hist. Revel. Kotteri, &c. p. 138.
‡ Knight of Born, Vol. i. p. 79.
§ Subsequently professor of Theology in the Academy of Weissenberg. He died in 1638, aged 50. Regenvolscius, p. 379, 461.

travelled alone and on foot to Prague, which city he reached at the end of the same year.

In early life a desire seized him to compose certain books in his vernacular language for the benefit of his own nation only. This desire never left him, and in order to make himself master of his mother tongue he began in the year 1612, while living at Herborn, to compose "a Lexicon, &c.," the rudiments of which was a collocation of all the roots of the Bohemian language, with a large collection of derivatives and compounds.*

Returning home in 1614, and being too young to enter into the ministry, at the invitation of Baron Charles de Zerotin,† he undertook the superintendence of the school of the Brethren at Prerau, where he began his endeavours to improve the method of juvenile studies by writing some "Grammaticæ facilioris præcepta," *simple grammatical rules,* which in 1616 were published at Prague.‡ To such labours he declares himself to have been originally stimulated by the celebrity of Wolfgang Ratich's plan of a reformed method of studies,§ which in a public written document obtained the approval and praise of the Universities of Jena and Giessen, and being published in 1612 immediately reached Comenius at Herborn, where he was then pursuing his studies.

On his appointment to the pastorate of Fulneck in 1616,‖ being compelled to treat of matters and cases of conscience, he composed Liſtowe do Nebe, &c., "Pauperum oppressorum

---

* Balbini Boh. Docta, p. 318.

† Of whom some most interesting particulars are already before the British public. See Dr. Pescheck, Vol. ii. p. 50, 53.

‡ Palscky's list, No. 1.

§ In which as the Swedish Chancellor Oxenstiern expressed it, he well enough laid bare the evils of the prevailing system of education, but the remedies he proposed were inadequate to cure them. He was a native of Holstein, and born in 1571. See Chambers' Journal, No. 263, p. 23, 24.

‖ On the 26th of April, at Zerawitz, with five and twenty others. Hist. Rev. Kotteri, &c. p. 138.

clamores in cœlum"—" *The cries of the oppressed poor to heaven, &c.*" which little book was printed at Olmütz in the next following year,* and probably referred to the oppression of his countrymen which led to the revolt of 1618.

His "Theatrum Divinum," *Divine Theatre*, the subject of which is the six days' work of creation, was written in the Bohemian language and is declared to be replete with various learning.†

In the year 1618 he was called to be superintendent of the school recently erected at Fulneck, where at the same time he was also appointed to administer the sacred duties of congregation pastor.

Whether the school at Fulneck was a mere town-school or one of a higher grade, which is the more probable, since the classics were taught in it, is not known. It was situated above the market place, half way up the hill, upon whose summit stands the castle which commands an extensive prospect over the lowland district called "Kuhländel," and of the range of mountains, Lissahora, &c., bearing the name of the Moravian Carpathians. The parish of Fulneck includes several villages of the fruitful vale whose inhabitants, partly Bohemian, partly German, at the present day shew to the curious traveller the meeting house (Zbor) of the congregation of the ancient Brethren and the dwelling of Comenius, now divided into two portions, the one used as a school the other as an hospital for females.‡

Here the enlightened mind of Comenius, occupied in the instruction of youth in the Latin and Greek languages, which he did with great ability and in a peculiar manner discovered by himself, brought first into practice in the sombre precincts of the school, the simple true idea that

* Letter to Montanus, p. 75.
† It was printed at Prague in 1616. Balbini Boh. Docta, p. 316.
‡ Fulneck was a seat of those Waldenses who joined the first Brethren in 1480.

"*children acquire a knowledge of words by objects*," and that "while learning *words* they should also be taught *things*," a practice which he afterwards elaborated in his writings, and which has subsequently proved to be so universally beneficial in the education of the young.

Comenius observing that clouds of persecution were gathering, as lightning indicates the coming thunder, wrote, Retuňk, &c., " Præmonitiones adversus Anti-christianas Seductiones," *Premonitions against anti-christian seductions.** The censures of superiors, deliberations, delays, and final ruin itself prevented this work of pious purpose from being published. It was, however, variously transcribed by several hands, and thus being privately circulated, is most likely yet extant in manuscript.

Driven from his church almost among the first by the course of the war in 1621, when the little town of Fulneck, together with the house-family, library, and manuscripts of Comenius were plundered by Spanish troops, this calamity greatly afflicted him; and he composed a small treatise, "De Christiana perfectione," *on Christian perfection;* the object of which was to elucidate to himself and others that the whole perfection of Christianity consists in doing and suffering everything in accordance with the will of God; that when we are languid and fail to obey with alacrity and become uninfluenced by the sweetness of the Divine promises, to be driven onward then by a cross is a work of Divine goodness, &c. This little work was printed at Prague in the year 1622.†

Shortly afterward, when ordered to confine himself in a hiding place on account of persecution directed against his own person, he wrote for the consolation of himself and others a little book entitled, "Hlubina Bezpecnosti," *The Centre of Security.* In this work he demonstrated that all human things are undergoing continual changes, that those

---

* Letter to Montanus, p. 75.   † Letter to Montanus, p. 76.

who resign themselves to these revolutions are secure from the distress of being forcibly driven hither and thither and drawn in different directions; and cannot ultimately fall and perish. He also clearly shewed and illustrated by examples that security from ruin and everlasting repose are in God alone, the eternal centre of all things.*

Some time after this, for the sake of a friend who was to him in the place of father, Comenius wrote another small tract on the same subject: Nebobyteblnj hrad gmeno hospodinowo, "Arx inexpugnabilis Nomen Domini," *The Name of the Lord is an impregnable stronghold.*†

In the same year 1622, the companion of his life, of whom nothing further is known, was taken from him by death, and shortly after this his little first born son perished by plague.‡ By these heart-rending afflictions his thoughts were turned to the subject of bereavements. Hence for the consolation of himself and many others similarly visited; of the orphan churches deprived of their pastors, he composed a tract entitled, "De Orbitate," on *Bereavement*. It was published in Bohemia in the Bohemian language, and in the Polish language in Poland.§

Plitt in his manuscript, quoting a writer named Knoll, p. 137, mentions two works written by Comenius entitled, "*Moravian Antiquities from the more ancient sources,*" particularly notes by the senior of the Brethren Matthias Czerwenka of Celakowitz, dedicated to Baron Charles Zerotin, senior;‖ and a treatise "*Concerning the origin of the family

---

* Published at Lissa, 1633, at Amsterdam, 1663. Letter to Montanus, p. 76. Palacky's list, No. 5.

† Letter to Montanus, p. 76, 77.

‡ Probably the common epidemic, a continual contagious malignant fever, called the Hungarian disease, which broke out in 1622. See History of the Air, &c. London, 1749, Vol. i. p. 302.

§ Letter to Montanus, p. 77.

‖ Balbini, Bohem. Docta, p. 315, says, they remain concealed in manuscript, p. 316, 317. These were compiled from a MS. of Matthias

of Zerotin," both which are quoted from then extant manuscripts by Pessina the historian of Moravia.

Although Comenius was compelled to secrete himself from his merciless pursuers, it does not appear that he became altogether separated from his people at Fulneck, until the year 1624, when driven from the place of his activity by the Imperial mandate banishing the Evangelical clergy from the country, he removed to Slaupna, among the Bohemian mountains, near the sources of the Elbe, the citadel of George Sadowsky a Bohemian Baron, and, in as far as it was allowable, a great patron and Mæcenas of the proscribed, where they remained concealed. From Slaupna he visited his orphan congregation as often as circumstances permitted.*

It was in the middle of a night which, like many others that had preceded it, was sleepless on account of the darkness of calamities increasing in the year 1623, and there was no hope of counsel or aid from man, being harassed with inextricable difficulties and severe trials; appealing with great fervour to God, that Comenius sprung from his couch and seizing his Bible, he earnestly prayed that as human consolation availed nothing, God in his own secret place would not desert him and his persecuted brethren. Opening the Holy Book at Isaiah, and continuing to read for sometime with unutterable distress, he perceived that his sadness was beginning to be dispelled. He then seized a pen to record his previous anguish, and the Divine remedies applied to it, believing that such instances of Divine sunshine arising and dispelling the gloom might be serviceable to himself and other pious men in case such dark horrors should return. Writing to Montanus he says: " Proceeding to the other prophets and the rest of the

Erythræus or Czervenka who from 1553 was Senior of the Brethren at Prerau in Moravia. Pilarz, Hist. Morav.

* Crantz, p. 69.

Divine code, for no food was ever sweeter to me than this collecting of Divine consolations, I discovered that there was abundance of materials calculated to tranquillize the mind in God, and began to digest them in the form of a dialogue. First, an afflicted mind, by the aid of its own reasoning powers, endeavours by various consolations to raise itself up.* Then faith applies her emollients from Scripture to the distress of the mind so labouring: but ever and anon she fails to effect much. At length Christ comes, explaining the mysteries of His sufferings and shewing how beneficial it is to man to be humbled by afflictions in the sight of God, to be broken and bruised and reduced to nothing; and in this way at length restores to the troubled soul complete tranquillity, consolation, and joy." Towards the end of the year 1624, afflictions becoming still more severe, the anxiety of his mind returned, which gave rise to the second part of the above book, wherein new sorrows accompanied by despair, and victories over them by the intervention of Christ, who "smiled to peace the demon of despair," are described. These books were transcribed by some of the Brethren who had experienced similar sufferings, and being afterwards brought to Prague were there printed. The title of the Bohemian original was "Truchliwy," *On Sorrows*. A Dutch translation of this work was published under the title "Trauren über trauren und Trost über trost." A third part was added in 1651, and the fourth and last part in 1660.†

In 1623 he also wrote "Labyrint Sweta a rág Srdce," *The Labyrinth of the World and the Palace of the Heart*, which he dedicated to Baron Charles Zerotin, senior, the great patron of learned men with whom Comenius held

---

* "This portion is," as he says, "chiefly from the two books of Lipsius 'On Constancy,' a work much read, but to little purpose in those days of execrable persecution.

† Letter to Montanus, p. 78, 79.

frequent literary intercourse.* This was a work of great and universal application, in which are described the wanderings, bewilderments, errors, vanities, and miseries of all of every age and sex, in all circumstances and conditions and of all orders and dignities. Then is shewn in vivid colours under various emblems the impossibility of attaining true repose otherwise than by a complete union with Christ through faith, secured by an indissoluble bond of reciprocal attachment and love.†

After the publication of the edicts in 1624, against all ministers of the gospel who refused to abjure their principles, when it was feared the nobility would soon be also proscribed, the seniors of the Brethren met as secretly as they could in the Bohemian mountains, at the village Daubrawitz, near the sources of the Elbe in 1625, when it was resolved that some of the younger ministers should proceed to Poland and Hungary, with letters of recommendation, to solicit places of refuge for their countrymen. Among these, Comenius, and with him John Chrysostom and Matthias

---

* He died at Prerau in 1630, many of his letters were in the Hortzowitz Library of the illustrious Lord Count Eugenius de Wüerben when Balbini wrote his Bohemia Docta, which see at p. 314. Balbini, only knowing the edition of this work printed in 1631, supposed that Charles Zerotin of the order of Malta, a General in the Imperial Army, repeatedly victorious over the Turks, and who died in 1660, was the patron to whom it was dedicated.

† Some years after, in 1631, "this work which in itself, says Dr. Gindely, was sufficient to prevent the name of Comenius from being consigned to oblivion," was printed at Pirna in Misnia. It was also translated into the Belgian language by John Gay, rector of the school of Campen in the Netherlands; but the death of the translator prevented its publication. Talvi says, "this work reminds us strongly of John Bunyan's celebrated Pilgrim's Progress," and that it was first published at *Prague*, which appears to be a mistake for Pirna. After undergoing several editions in other places it was printed at Prague in 12mo. in 1809. —Talvi, p. 199, note. Palacky, No. 4, says it was published in 1633 at Lissa, and at Amsterdam in 1663.

Probus, were deputed to Poland on this hazardous and difficult errand. They proceeded to Baron Zerotin the younger, at Görlitz, thence to Sprottau, and thence to Poland. On this occasion he unexpectedly made a visit to Berlin, and having fulfilled his mission returned to his retreat by way of Silesia.

At this period of his seclusion, by no means agreeable to him, during the leisure resulting out of his removal from the functions of his calling, the following circumstance occasioned him to turn his attention to poetical composition. Lawrence Benedit Nudozierin, a professor in the University of Prague, having successfully cultivated Bohemian poetry, had composed a rendering of the Psalms of David in various kinds of measure similar to Buchanan's translation. In 1614, when this work had scarcely received its final correction, the author died and by his will bequeathed it to a certain person, who, neglecting to forward its publication, deferred it until the year 1620, when in the plundering of Prague it was lost. This coming to the knowledge of Comenius, he was grieved that his country should be deprived of so great a treasure, and stimulated by a desire of supplying the loss he began to compose " A metrical version of the Psalms of David," and about twenty-six of them were finished. He was afterwards, however, called off to other duties which prevented the completion of this work, as it did also of another, in which he so reduced his poetical version to the Gallican melodies of the Psalms as to assign to every long note a long syllable, and to every short note a short syllable, so as to produce an admirable sweetness. The completion of this work he left to others.

Cato's moral Distichs, though, as Comenius says, of questionable Latinity, he translated into heroic verse, and composed some verses in imitation of Virgil and Ovid, as specimens for those who might be disposed to translate these authors into the Bohemian language, which is better adapted to measure than to rhyme, and possesses all the requisites that render Greek and Latin poetry so admirably pleasing. Excusing himself to Montanus for having entered into the region of poetry, he says, "In case any one should blame the theologian for wandering into poetry, I may here make my apology, which is, 'that I am a man, and think nothing foreign to me which appertains to man.'" Man has been so constructed by his Maker as to be sensible of harmony; if, therefore, on any occasion he be delighted with harmony, who can blame him?

A circumstance took place in the year 1627 which occasioned a return to the same scholastic studies which had occupied his attention at Prerau and Fulneck. It happened that Baron Sadowsky committed his three sons, 1. Wenceslaus Ferdinand, 2. John George, and 3. Peter, to John Stadius one of the proscribed, for their education; and Comenius, at the request of Stadius, wrote "*some canons of a better method*" for their use.

Having, during the dog days in the heat of summer, made an excursion to the neighbouring citadel of Wilcitz, to see the celebrated library of the most noble Lord Silver, he unexpectedly came upon the "Didactica" of Elias Bodius, recently brought thither from Germany. The reading of this book stirred up Comenius to compose and publish in due time a similar work in the Bohemian language. The rest of the Brethren, when informed of this purpose, highly approved of it, and expressed an earnest desire for its completion. In the meantime, however, a new imperial edict was directed against the evangelic nobility, enjoining expatriation upon every one who refused to change his religion, and they consequently were preparing to emigrate.

Such vast ruin of churches and schools in their native land, and the grief occasioned thereby, and the hope—"Why," asks Comenius, "should I conceal it?"—of being at some time, through the mercy of God, enabled to return, compelled them to much solicitous meditation on the means to be adopted for repairing the ruins. And, upon mature deliberation, no other plan seemed to be more eligible than, if God should at any time deign to look upon them with an eye of compassion, to, above all things, give succour to the young by the erection of schools with all convenient speed, and those to be supplied with good books and directed by a lucid method, so as to carry forward in the best possible manner the various studies of letters, morals, and piety. They, therefore, entered with fervour on the duty, Comenius discharging the office of a whetstone to another, and accomplished what could be effected while still remaining concealed at Slaupna, within the innermost recesses of their country. But in the next following year, when the same storm of persecution began to rage with still greater and greater malignity, they were all compelled to fly their native land and be dispersed.

For as the edicts of the Emperor began to be carried into effect with increasing severity, Comenius became painfully sensible that Sadowsky's citadel was no longer a place of security to him. He therefore went into exile to Poland, with others of his brethren. The companions of his flight, among whom was Lord George Sadowsky himself, according to the Fulneck record, departed by way of Upper Silesia. On the frontier mountains near Troppau, from whence is an extensive view in the direction of Fulneck and Moravia, or on the Giant mountains in the direction from Bohemia to Poland, Comenius and his brethren kneeled down, and, their eyes streaming with tears, prayed to God, imploring Him that he would not entirely and for ever withdraw His word from Bohemia, but that He would preserve a seed there to serve Him.* And God heard their cry.

* Tradition reports this to have been done by Comenius in 1624, on the brow of the castle hill at Fulneck, when he removed thence into Bohemia.—*Plitt's MS.*

This was the last sad lingering look of Comenius on his devoted country! From this time he never beheld the land of his fathers, but lived an exile in foreign regions; yet unceasingly labouring for the cause of his brethren, and the welfare of mankind at large; and, as we shall see, presenting himself to our view most truly as a Christian practical philosopher in all respects.

CHAPTER IV.

LESZNA—COMENIUS SETTLES THERE—RESUMES HIS SCHOLASTIC FUNCTION AND STUDIES—HIS CORRESPONDENCE WITH LEARNED MEN—EFFORTS TO IMPROVE THE SCHOOLS—MATERNAL SCHOOL—JANUA LINGUARUM—ITS CELEBRITY—COMENIUS ORDAINED A BISHOP OF THE BRETHREN—EXPECTS TO BE RESTORED TO HIS COUNTRY AND PREPARES FOR IT—HIS INFLUENCE—LUTHERAN DISTURBANCE—WRITES AGAINST SOCINIANS — SEEKS AND PARTIALLY SECURES PATRONAGE—HIS GREAT DESIGNS.

ABOUT nine hundred years ago, when Miczislaus, Duke of Poland, united himself in marriage to the daughter of Boleslaus, Duke of Bohemia, and with her received the Christian faith, there happened among the nobility who accompanied him to be one Peter de Bernstein, whom Miczislaus, desirous on account of his virtues of detaining in Poland, induced to remain, by bestowing upon him rich possessions, the chief of which was a locality called Lezsyna—*i.e.* Hazelgrove.

From this place Bernstein and his family assumed the patronymic Leszezynski, now Lescynsky, and were afterwards admitted to all kinds of rank and dignity, among which they enjoyed the title of Earl of the Empire. But the name of the place, in course of time, became contracted to Leszna, and the Germans call it Lissa.

This village, which is situated on the confines of Silesia, twelve German miles from Wratislavia, five from Glogaw, and ten from Posen, was raised by Sigismund, about two centuries ago, to the dignity of a market town, and tradesmen, with whom the German tongue was introduced, were invited to it from Silesia.

Through the influential exertions of the Lescynski family, the Reformation prospered here extensively, and the tide of immigration setting in from Bohemia and Moravia and Silesia, on account of the atrocities inflicted on their inhabitants after the battle of Whitehill (Weissenberg) by a brutal soldiery at the instigation of a merciless priesthood, between the years 1620 and 1629, the town so grew in size and importance that it is said to have contained three market-places, four churches, a large school, more than sixteen hundred houses, and a fixed population of two thousand citizens, with their families, households, and others. There was, moreover, a handsome edifice erected for the service of God, according to the rites of the Confession of Augsburg, which is that of the Lutherans.

This town, like every other where the inhabitants being Christian, and left to the free exercise of their religious views, are relieved from the tyranny of priestly domination, at once rose in strength as well as importance; for the citizens by a wise economy raised sufficient means to surround it with fortifications. They also erected a beautiful town-hall in which to transact their public affairs. In a word, with the Reformation, civilization, trade, and commerce—for it became a mart for all the country around—and religion so flourished as to render the town second in the kingdom to Posen, for its attractions as a place of resort, not only to exiles for conscience-sake but to strangers who visited it from all parts far and near.

At this place a congregation of the Unity of the Brethren had existed from an early period, which afterwards was greatly increased by the influx of Brethren driven from Bohemia and elsewhere. Here Comenius fixed the seat of his future fortunes; he had probably selected it on his visit to Poland in 1626. Raphael, Count Lescynsky, was its Lord, and on the estates of that nobleman and his family, the Brethren found another Pella. Here, formed into one church under the superintendence of their own Bishops Gertichius and Erastus, with two of the former members of the Consistory at Prague, John Cyril and Paul Fabricius, the cause of the Brethren began to flourish so much that it almost appeared as though their Unity were to be renewed at Lissa. They had three places of worship for the accommodation of those of them to whom the languages of Germany, Bohemia, and Poland, were vernacular.

The school of the Brethren here, which had been in existence from 1555, was formed into a Grammar school, in which Comenius found a very pleasant sphere of activity. As he had been in his own country, so he became at Lissa, an instructor of youth; but on a more enlarged scale. He thoroughly understood the defects of the existing systems of teaching, and their disadvantages in regard to the Unity of the Brethren. Thus, for instance, he observes in his concluding discourse to the 8th book of Lasitius, "When our people visited schools for the sake of the learned languages, what did they bring with them on returning home? What beyond that which they obtained there, the tinkling of human eloquence, love of disputation, and knowledge that puffeth up instead of the charity which buildeth up. Some, moreover, acquire corrupt morals, a desire to make themselves agreeable by a show of external civility, and in several instances the habits of intemperance, and finally a hatred of strict discipline, or at least a distaste and indifference for it. And yet these very men were to be the lights of our church and the pillars of our constitution! O that instead of such an education we had retained the simplicity of children! O that some one could have brought back the ancient custom of the Spartans, who more than all the other Greeks, intent upon the education of their youth, prohibited them from visiting other towns! We on the contrary sent ours to places where, in accordance with the prevailing character of the schools, it was too easy for them to forget their Christian simplicity, the one thing so needful to them. Hence the former blooming condition of our church, which was pleasing both to God and man, has gradually faded away."

Comenius was under the necessity, in order to sustain himself in exile, to enter upon the scholastic function, and being anxious to perform the duty with efficiency, a new incitement was added to induce him to return also to the study of didactics which he had commenced before. There were, moreover, many such writings published at this time; and above all the ray of a certain new hope "shone forth to the outcasts, of returning from exile, although alas evanescent."

These various circumstances induced Comenius to revise his educational works from the very foundation, and to endeavour to render the whole more full and efficient than all former works on the subject, either prepared by himself or by others. This renewed effort he designated " Didactica Magna, universale omnes omnia docendi artificium exhibens," or, *the art of teaching all things to every body.* The hope, however, of returning to his native land was not realized, and he consigned his work to silence; only permitting his other books written with the same view, in consequence of the solicitation of friends, to go forth to the public.

Comenius soon after his settlement at Lissa re-entered the marriage state, by uniting with Elizabeth, daughter of the above mentioned John Cyrill, who had arrived from Prague on the 3rd of August, 1627.

With the renewal of his scholastic usefulness, Comenius also commenced a correspondence with many learned men, among whom are named Sigismund Evenius, Abraham

Mencel,* Paul Paliurus,† Johnstone,‡ Dr. John Mochinger,§ Justus Docem, George Winkler, Martin Moser, Albert Niclassius,|| and Samuel Hartlib.¶ To these he communicated his ideas concerning the necessity of a reformation in the system of teaching, and the compilation of books most suitable for the promotion of this object. It does not, however, appear that many of the learned with whom Comenius entered into negociations did anything more in furtherance of his views, than simply corresponding with him, excepting Hartlib, who embraced the ideas of Comenius with ardent zeal, and during a long succession of years rendered him valuable aid with the most disinterested activity.

Earnestly desirous of emancipating the world from the thraldom into which the papal system had involved it, the thought was ever uppermost in the mind of Comenius to prepare, as an essential groundwork for the rising generation of those and future times, a simple system of training and instruction suited to the capacity of early childhood, and of so awakening every faculty, as to qualify youth for the discharge of the important duties of life, and fit them for their highest, their eternal calling. He strove to discover

---

* A much esteemed Prussian Divine of the Reformed persuasion.

† A senior of the Churches of the Brethren in Great Poland, to whom was committed the charge and publication of the Polish Bible. He died at Ostrorog in 1632, aged 63. See more in Regenvolscius, p. 391.

‡ John Johnstone, a Pole of Scotch descent, of whom Krasinsky, Hist. of the Reformation in Poland, ii. 330, gives an interesting notice. See also his " Lectures on the Religious History of the Slavonic Nations," p. 254.

§ Pastor of Catherine's Church and professor of elocution in the Gymnasium of Dantzic. Regenvolscius, p. 361. He was present at the Charitative Conference at Thorn, and was one of the twelve disputants of the Lutherans there in 1645. MS. collection relating to that Conference, p. 33, 52.

|| Incumbent of the parish of St. Peter and Paul in Dantzic. Regenvolscius, p. 113, 118, 403.

¶ Of whom Chalmers gives a biography in his Gen. Biogr. Dict. Vol. xvii. p. 200.

the readiest way to the attainment of these most noble ends:
"Children," says he, "should learn not *words* merely, but *objects*, together with words; it not being the memory alone which requires culture, but also the *reasoning* faculties, the *will* and the *affections* of men; and this should be done from early infancy, by a clear and well arranged mode of thinking and friendly intercourse with them."

As Comenius wrote so he acted; for in the year 1631 he published his "Janua linguarum resarata," *Gate of Languages unlocked*, which was subsequently republished as the "Orbis pictus," *Pictured world*. His object in this was to impart to youth in the schools at one and the same time a knowledge of the things around us, and of the Latin and other languages most commonly in use.*

By way of preparing for the attainment of this, he published in 1633 his "Schola materni gremii," *School of the maternal bosom;* that is, how in the most rational manner, to the honour of God, the comfort of parents, and the salvation of children, godly parents, either by themselves, or with the aid of nurses, may educate and exercise their offspring during the first six years of their lives, before they can be entrusted to other preceptors. In the latter of these books the parents instruct their child in those things which are common to either sex; in the former, the preceptor prepares the boy for the duties of the man.

The "Janua" was printed in the office of the Brethren at Lissa, and had a very extensive circulation, by which means the name and reputation of its author became known throughout many countries, but especially in the Protestant states of the north of Europe,† and it brought Comenius

---

* This book is used at the present day, by the students of the Latin language, in the Gymnasia or Schools, throughout the Austrian dominion. Pilarz, Moraviæ Historia.

† We learn, from the introduction to the earlier editions of the Janua, that some years before it was written, a certain Jesuit, of the Hibernian College, at Salamanca, in Spain, observing the advantage likely to arise

into such repute that his writings were afterwards eagerly
sought for in various countries, with the view of effecting
from a compendium of the Latin language, compiled the whole into one collection, and published it under the title of "A Gate of the Latin and Spanish Languages," in which are comprehended about twelve centuries of sentences, wherein all the words of common use in the Latin, are so disposed that none of them, excepting the particles *sum, ex, in,* &c., recur a second time. J. F. Noltenius in his Lexicon antibarbarum, vol. ii. 68, suppt. gives this as the work of William Batty, published at Salamanca, in 1611, but that he had never been able to procure or even to see a copy of it.

This invention was first approved and commended by the English, and enlarged and published with the English language, by William Welde, in 1615 and 1616, who translated it from a copy communicated to him, by Edmonds, clerk of the privy council. Two years afterwards Isaac Habrecht, a German, of Strasbourg, added the French, and published the work in the four languages. On Habrecht returning to Germany he annexed a German version, recommending at the same time this method of teaching and learning, and describing this system as the most compendious, certain, and useful, and inestimably valuable. In which opinion he found many supporters, and the work was published in many parts of Germany, where it was so eagerly circulated, and introduced to the most celebrated schools, that in 1632 it came out in no less than eight languages.

Comenius, after carefully reading this work a third time, found that it did not reach up to its title, and considering it a worthy labour, he resolved to perfect what had already been imperfectly done, stimulated thereto by an overwhelming desire of being serviceable to youth, upon the principle first discovered by himself, "that the understanding and the tongue should always move together in the instruction of the young." The preface of Comenius, is dated March the 4th, 1631.

This work appeared very soon in England, under the title "The Gate of Tongues unlocked and opened;" and in a second edition, much enlarged by the labour and industry of John Anchoran, licentiate in divinity, it was published at London, in 1633. "In Latine first, and now, as a token of thankfulnesse, brought to light in Latin, English, and French, in the behalfe of the most illustrious Prince Charles, and of British, French, and Irish youth." The preface to this edition is subscribed by Anchoran and Comenius. Regenvolscius (p. 322) states the work to have been "translated into the English and French, by John Ancoran und Samuel Hartlib."

Comenius says of this book, "It was received with almost universal applause throughout the learned world;" and he had the grati-

by them a reform in every stage of the education of the young. Moreover, it now appeared to many to be their duty to support the author of such a work, lest being hindered by care for his outward subsistence he should be prevented from pursuing such studies. Hartlib endeavoured to procure a rich patron for him in England, and wrote to inform him he hoped to secure him an annuity of two hundred pounds. This hope was not realized, although Comenius urged the procurement of half the amount, to enable him to compensate with salaries two of his assistants, Mr. Wechner, a Bohemian exile, and Dr. David.*

We learn from Palacky's list, No. 12, that in 1630, a work entitled " Praxis pietati," *Practice of Piety*, by Comenius, was published at Lissa and at Amsterdam, in 1661; it was similar to that of the bishop of Bangor, Lewis Bayly, which has the same title, and was most extensively read.

About this time Comenius wrote " Astronomia ad lumen Physicum reformanda," *Astronomy reformed according to Physical light;* not established at will on strange fictions, but founded on true and real hypotheses derived from the nature of the heavens. This was not published, indeed never completely finished, inasmuch as Philip Lansbergius, to whom he had proposed to dedicate this work, died in the meantime, and then other avocations occupied his attention. Lansbergius died 8th Nov., 1632, aged 67, at Goez in Zeeland.†

The care of Comenius for the welfare of mankind did not supplant his sympathies for the body of which he was a

fication to receive the congratulations of many distinguished men of various nations, upon the valuable discovery,—to learn that translations were promptly made into all the vernacular languages of Europe, and that it had been published in Latin, Greek, Bohemian, Polish, German, Swedish, Dutch, English, Spanish, Italian, French and Hungarian; also in the Asiatic languages of Arabia, Turkey, Persia, and even of Mongolia.

* Dr. Gindely, p. 8.
† Letter to Montanus, p. 91. Bibliotheca Belgica, II. 1036.

distinguished member; and his Brethren well understood his value to them. Of this the Synod of Lissa, in 1632, amply testifies, at a time when the victorious career of Gustavus Adolphus, king of Sweden, animated the exiles with the prospect of returning to their homes, and awakened new hopes for the church of Christ. Among the three bishops consecrated at this Synod for the Bohemian branch of the Unity, in the expectation that it would be restored, Comenius was appointed the one to succeed his father-in-law, Cyrill, whose death happened this year, on the 30th of May. It was chiefly owing to the influence of Comenius that the Synod resolved to publish the "Ratio Disciplinæ," *Rule of Discipline*, or account of the Constitution of the Church of the Brethren, which had been written in 1616; as a memorial of the past and a model for the Church which should be renewed. This writing seems to have been prepared for the press by Comenius, who, as appears from its style, translated it into Latin, in which language he published it; and thus, in all probability, became the originator, or, at least the promoter of the synodal resolution which, contrary to the ancient rule of the Brethren, gave such publicity to their synodical transactions.* There was now no necessity for secrecy.

The hopes of the banished returning from exile, though vain, led Comenius to write "Haggeus redivivus," *Haggai renewed;* or, a counsel not to give heed primarily to houses, mansions, farms, vineyards, &c., but in the first place to apply with earnest mind to the restoration of the worship of God. And he embraced this occasion to remind all, both young and old, in every condition, of their sins; to urge them to repentance, and to counsel them as to the way in which they ought to improve the present severe chastisement of their past transgressions, &c. It was a pious work,

---

* Plitt's MS.

and would have been suitable at any period, yet, although its publication was recommended by the Synod, it never appeared in print.

It is probable that Comenius promoted the publication, if he did not himself compile the work, entitled " Historia persecutionum Ecclesiæ Bohemiæ." *History of the Persecutions of the Bohemian Church,* from the year 894 to 1632, treating principally of the Unity of the Brethren, a work which originated in an application from England to some Bohemian exiles in Holland, for additions to be made in a contemplated new edition of Foxe's " Acts and Monuments of the Christian Church."*

While in Lissa, where at this time more than thirty ministers of God's word were driven by persecution, Comenius suggested that they should apply themselves to compose complete " S. Bibliorum Indices," *Indexes to the Sacred Scriptures,* or Concordances, as they were called. His counsel being adopted, the several parts were assigned to each, and the work was finished in two years, but could not be committed to the press for want of pecuniary means, and eventually it was destroyed by fire, as was also another work of greater diligence, " Evangelistarum Harmonia," *Harmony of the Evangelists,* accompanied by a continuous context, and illustrated by commentaries divided into one hundred and thirty chapters.

" Manualnyť Gabro cele Biblí fwate." Enchyridion Biblicum, *Biblical Manual,* or nucleus of the whole of sacred Scripture,† was likewise composed by Comenius, in order that the exiles for the faith of Christ might bear with them the shield of their faith for their defence, and the wanderers through the world, the staff of their hope for their support. In this work all the scripture histories are given in a concise form,

* It was published in English, at London, in 1650.

† Index Prohibitor, p. 124. It was published by Gabriel a Roi, at Amsterdam, in 1658. Balbini, Bohemia Docta, p. 316.

but yet in the words of the Holy Spirit; sententious sayings, however, being stated at length. The same compendium of sacred Scripture, but in a less compendious form, and in a larger type than the intention of the book required, was afterwards published for the use of schools, with the title "Janua seu Introductorium in Biblia Sacra," &c., *Gate or Introduction to the Sacred Scriptures, being an epitome of the books given by God to man, as the rule of his belief, of his conduct, and of his hope.*

His essay entitled "Physicæ ad lumen divinum reformandæ," *Physics reformed according to divine light,* was written at Lissa, the date of the preface being the last day of September, 1632.* In this glance at the natural sciences in the light of divine revelation, he endeavoured, at great length, to shew that the peripatetic philosophy is not only defective in many respects, but likewise intricate, and occasionally doubtful and perplexing; in some parts erroneous, and not only unprofitable, but also hurtful to Christians. Then in his own new system he separates the true science of natural history from the alchemystic and astrological dreams, by which writers of that age pretended to unravel the mysteries of nature and revelation; and carefully distinguishes the three sources of knowledge given to man by God himself: the *senses,* to observe outward objects; *reason,* to judge concerning truth; and *the Scriptures* (Revelation),

---

* It was printed at Leipsic, in 8vo. in 1634, and at Amsterdam, in 12mo. in 1645 and 1663, by the Janssons, and shortly after at Paris, from whence Comenius received a letter, in 1647, from D. J. D., advocate of the Paris Parliament, (perhaps Mons. Jacques Danet, who became advocate in 1619. Armorial des Officiers de Paris, fo. 97.) saying: "We reprint all your works here. You will not be offended that one sentence in your preface has been altered. It has been corrected with candour, &c." Letter to Montanus, p. 91. It was translated into English in 1650, and published at London in 1651.

to prevent the conception of false notions and practical errors in things divine.

In 1636 Comenius's sphere of activity was more definitely prescribed at the Synod of November 25th, which assigned to him the ministry of the congregation at Lissa, the oversight and maintenance of church discipline, but more especially the superintendence of the schools, all other spiritual labours being committed to the care of the co-senior, Martin Gertichius. His labours becoming increasingly productive of benefit to the Brethren, their attention was naturally and proportionately directed towards him; and many of the Polish magnates were induced from his influence and reputation among them to send their children for education at Lissa. It was hoped that by the aid of his very extensive connections, the exiles might be restored to their homes; and, indeed, there appears to have been no other channel more likely than this of affording to the oppressed such desired aid, which, however, never reached them.

Since even the exile of the Brethren was disquieted by reason of certain restless men, Lutherans, for whom, chiefly through his personal influence, Comenius had obtained in November, 1633, the privileges of a church community at Lissa,* he wrote, by command of the superiors, *A defence of the innocence of his church*, entitled, "Obrana, &c." and shortly afterwards, with the view of tranquillizing the minds of both parties, *The way of peace*, entitled, "Cesta pokoge, &c."†

In relation to these works, both which were published, we learn that M. Samuel Martinius of Drazovin, formerly assessor of the Bohemian Evangelical Consistory at Prague, and pastor of the Bohemo-Lutheran church at Pirna, who was an exile in Misnia; from a desire to bring over the Brethren to his party, injudiciously published against them a work in the Bohemian language in 1635, another in 1636,

* Plitt's MS. † Letter to Montanus, p. 84.

another in 1638; but when threatening more he was interrupted by death in 1639. To the above two refutations of his writings the Brethren added a tract in the same language, also written by Comenius, on the method exhibited in Scripture of attaining ecclesiastical peace. Martinius finding his polemical writings unavailing, made a journey to Dresden, where, by the aid of the Court-chaplain, he procured a mandate from the Elector, commanding the Brethren either to embrace the Lutheran liturgy or quit the country. Some accepted the alternative and repaired to Lissa, among whom Paul Fabricius, a senior of the Brethren, was one. With such calamitous assaults were the Brethren harassed both in their native land and in their exile.*

Comenius fostered in his mind most magnificent designs, and aimed at the composition of works which should be useful in every age. His principal concern was not so much to superintend a model school, and practically to labour for its success, as to exercise an abiding influence upon mankind at large by the power of his pen. This was his principal reason for declining a call which he received from Sweden in 1638, with the view that he should effect an entire reformation in the schools of that country. Although he thought it not prudent to undertake a work of such difficult attainment, or to submit his shoulders to an office obnoxious to so much envy; yet he recommended that some one of their own nation, competent for the duty, should rather be selected, and expressed his willingness to assist with advice such as should be commissioned for that purpose.†

It was in this year that Comenius, full of the fervour of zeal for every subject of real interest to mankind, wrote two books against the shallow Scripture illustrations of Socinians.

* Regenvolscius, p. 203. Crantz, p. 83. Knight of Born, ii. p. 67.
† Introd. to his Didactic Works.

1. On the one God of Christians, Father, Son, and Holy Spirit, addressed to Jonas Schlichting.*

2. On the question, whether our Lord Jesus Christ rose from the dead by his own power, against the German Melchior Schäfer. This part, by order of the superiors, was written in German, and printed at Leszna, at the time of its production, in 1638, at Amsterdam in Latin, 1657 and 1659.

His straitened circumstances and an indomitable desire to accomplish the means of disenthralling the world from the meshes of false principles in the affairs of religion and state, made it necessary that he should seek out a Mæcenas, whose pecuniary assistance might enable him to devote all his energies for a few years, with the help of assistants, to the accomplishment of his views, and the compilation of suitable educational works.

Such assistance was partially secured to Comenius in the patronage of a Polish magnate, whose name is not now known, but whom in one of his letters he styles "the chief in the kingdom of Poland," and therefore in all probability was Count Bohuslaw de Lissa, between whom and Comenius a conversation took place in 1640, in which the latter expounded his ideas and plans; and at his patron's request, under date September the 12th, committed to paper the course he himself pursued in his studies, and had endeavoured to expound at the above interview.

This document, still preserved and in Comenius' own hand-writing, is well calculated to exhibit the lucid and systematic characteristics which pervaded the man in the midst of his diversified employments. The following are its leading topics. He writes:—

* Jonas Schlichting à Bukowiec, a Polish Knight and a leading man among the Socinians, was pastor of Racovia. He died in exile at Zelichovia, in the marquisate of Brandenburg, Nov. 1, 1661, aged 59. Bibliotheca Antitrinit. p. 126, 127.

"The vastness of the labours I contemplate demands that I should have a wealthy patron, whether we look at their extent, or at the necessity of securing assistants, or at the expenses generally. As to their *extent*, I purpose to render the study of the sciences, of philosophy, and theology, more accessible to all parties and of greater usefulness in the regulation of human affairs, than has hitherto been the case. In order to this, two kinds of books are necessary, *a.* for philological researches, and *b.* for elementary training.

a. Books of the first class would primarily and chiefly have reference to the Latin language; and of this class I would adopt eight.

1. Vestibulum Latinitatis. *The Vestibule (introduction) to the Latin language.*
2. Janua Latinitatis. *The Gate to the Latin language.*
3. Palatium Latinitatis. *The Palace (essentials) of the Latin language.*
4. A Dictionary, giving the etymological meaning of the *Latin* words in the vernacular language.
5. A Dictionary, giving the meaning of all the words of the native language in the Latin, and more especially supplying phrases of the former language with corresponding phrases in the latter.
6. A Latin Dictionary, giving an explanation of all the peculiar idioms of the language.
7. A short Grammar, containing all the declensions and conjugations, and to be used in connection with the Vestibulum or *Introduction* (1).
8. A large Grammar, in connection with the Janua or *Gate* (2).

b. Books to be used for elementary training, are three:

1. Pansophia, *Universal Wisdom*. This book should comprise the sum-total of all human wisdom, and be so expressed as to meet the requirements of both the present and future ages. The method to be followed in such a book, would be, to

reduce every thing to and deduce it from certain fundamental principles, beyond the compass of which no part of human knowledge can reach. Such first principles are, *God—the World—Common sense.* Such a book would prove a real blessing to mankind.

2. Panhistoria, *Universal History.* This work must comprehend the most remarkable facts of all ages. Universal history is a most valuable handmaid of the imagination; searching into the causes of all things, and inquiring into the laws of cause and effect, surveying, as at a glance, the whole universe. Instruction in history must be imparted in gradations, beginning as early as possible, at the lowest point. It might be best arranged in six classes, as follows:

1st, Bible History. 2nd, Natural history. 3rd, History of Inventions. 4th, History of the most celebrated examples of virtue and morality. 5th, Historia ritualis, or history of the various religious rites of the various tribes of the earth. 6th, Political history of the world.

3. General dogmatics. These have to treat of the different views which human ingenuity has taken in dogmatical science, both false and true, and would thereby prevent a relapse into vain speculations and dangerous errors.

" One man is not able to accomplish an undertaking of such magnitude. Fellow labourers are requisite. There ought to be some clever linguists, perhaps three, imbued with philosophy; one able historian; and lastly a man of comprehensive knowledge, thoroughly acquainted with biblical literature. As regards the philological labours, I have already met with an excellent assistant in Mr. Wechner. Nor are clever coadjutors wanting for the Pansophia, who have not only offered with freedom the treasures of their libraries, but have given themselves and their cooperation to this work. Among these my friend Hartlib far excels. I don't know his equal in the extent of his knowledge; his daily increasing acuteness of reasoning, his zeal to become useful for the welfare of mankind, his fervent love for a philosophy unmixed with error and fanciful speculations, which I designate Pansophia, and his self-denial in order to further the objects in view.

"Am I not justified then, with such a task before me, in appealing to you, who are the chiefest in the kingdom, and in soliciting your support? We give you spiritual blessings; may I not be permitted to ask for temporal aid? All required is to maintain for a few years, say, three or four men at an annual stipend of from 200 to 300 thalers,* according to the extent of their attainments, and proficiency, and the number of their family."

This, however, could not be obtained for him at Lissa.

* German Dollars, £30 to £45.

CHAPTER V.

COMENIUS VISITS ENGLAND—CIVIL COMMOTIONS THERE COMPEL HIS DEPARTURE—ACCEPTS AN INVITATION TO SWEDEN—INTERVIEW WITH THE CHANCELLOR OXENSTIERN —HIS PROPOSALS ACCEPTED—SETTLES AT ELBING.

It appears by letters of Comenius to his patron, of the early part of the year 1641, that sufficient assistance was not received from this quarter to meet the claims of his own people; for in the autumn of the year he had already accepted an invitation to England, which Samuel Hartlib had procured for him from the Parliament, whose attention to Comenius had been attracted by his writings. Accordingly he arrived in London in September. His own account of his visit will best explain the circumstances of it. Speaking of "new occasions for the continuance of Didactic studies," he says, "The truth of the words of the prophet Jeremiah, *I know, O Lord! that the way of man is not in himself, that it appertaineth not to a man to direct his own steps*, must be forcibly felt by every one that attends to his own contemplations, desires, and purposes, and observes what things eventuate or fail to eventuate in conformity with them. For, according to the common proverb, which moreover agrees well with the mind of Solomon (Prov. xvi. 9. xix. 21), *man proposes, God disposes*. An instance of this has occurred to me; for when seriously purposing to abandon the thorny studies of Didactics and pass on to the pleasing studies of philosophical truths, I find myself again among the same thorns. I shall now state how this occurred, so that if any thing have been done otherwise than was proper, they may sustain a portion of the blame who drove me against those rocks.

"After the Pansophiæ Prodrŏmus* had been published and dispersed through various kingdoms of Europe, many of the learned approved of the object and plan of the work; but despaired of its ever being accomplished by one man alone, and, therefore, advised that a college of learned men should be instituted to carry it forth into effect. Mr. S[amuel] H[artlib], who had forwarded the publication of the "Pansophiæ Prodrŏmus," *Harbinger of all wisdom*,† in England, laboured earnestly in this matter, and endeavoured by every possible means to bring together for this purpose a number of men of intellectual activity. And at length having found one or two he invited me also with many very strong entreaties. As my friends consented to my departure, I proceeded to London, and arrived there on the day of the autumnal equinox in the year 1641, and then learned that I had been called thither by an order (jussu) of Parliament. But in consequence of the king having gone to Scotland the Parliament had been dismissed for three months, and consequently I had to winter in London, my friends in the meantime examining the *Apparatus Pansophicus*, small though it was at that time.

"On this occasion a tract was produced by me, entitled, "Via lucis," *The way of Light*, that is, a national disquisition as to the manner in which wisdom, the intellectual law of minds, may now at length towards the evening of the

* Probably this was the work which was translated into English, and published by Samuel Hartlib under the title, " A Reformation of the Schools, &c." London, 1642, in two parts, 4to.

† Published at London in 1639, the work—" Porta Sapientiæ resarata seu nova et compendiosa methodus omnes artes ac scientias addiscendi," *The Gate of Wisdom opened, or a new and compendious method of acquiring the knowledge of all arts and sciences*—having been printed at Oxford in 1637.

world be felicitously diffused through all minds in all nations; supplying, moreover, a better elucidation of the oracular words of Zechariah, " *and it shall come to pass that in the evening it shall be light.*"

"By this time the Parliament having assembled, and my presence being known, I was commanded to wait until after some important business having been transacted, a commission should be issued to certain wise and learned men from among themselves to hear me and be informed of my plan. As an earnest, moreover, of their intentions, they communicated to me their purpose to assign to us a college with revenues, whence some men of learning and industry selected from any nation might be honourably sustained, either for a certain number of years or in perpetuity. The Savoy (*Sabaudeum*) in London, and beyond London, Winchester (*Winthoniense*), and again near the city Chelsea (*Chelseum*) were severally mentioned, and inventories of the latter, and of its revenues were communicated to me; so that nothing seemed more certain than that the design of the great Verulam (Lord Bacon) to open a Universal College of all nations devoted solely to the advancement of the sciences was now in the way of being carried into effect.

"But a rumour that Ireland was in a state of commotion, and that more than two hundred thousand of the English there had been slaughtered in one night, the sudden departure of the king from London, and the clear indications of a most cruel war being on the point of breaking out, threw all these plans into confusion, and compelled me and my friends to hasten our return."*

It happened, however, that a letter sent to Comenius from Sweden to Poland and thence to England, reached him almost immediately after his arrival in London, in which that magnanimous and vigorous man, Mr. Ludwig De Geer, a wealthy Dutch merchant, and a warm admirer of his

* Didactica, tom II. Introd.

writings, invited him to his own residence, there to pursue his studies without interruption. Desirable as this proposal may have appeared to Comenius, he felt obliged to decline it for the present, and therefore replied, "I am not certain when I may be released from my engagements in England. My own people particularly wish my continuance here, inasmuch as I can secure them pecuniary help in this country, if no where else. Beside which I here enjoy the assistance of some brethren in London which is invaluable. My congregation would never consent to my removal to Holland, unless Mr. De Geer could pledge himself to support my co-adjutors. As regards the chief object of my visit to England it is in great measure frustrated by internal commotions throughout the country. I would be thankful for a quiet resting place."

Mr. De Geer, so far as related to Comenius personally, repeated his proposals through a Mr. Hotton, his agent, upon which Comenius in a letter dated in February, 1642, expressed his readiness to accept them, on condition that his expenses for the support of one assistant, a man of learning who should aid in compiling the Pansophia, should be paid; for if this work was to become what he contemplated, it would be necessary that a man of intelligence should travel in France and Italy to inquire into and report what had been and was being effected there. "Such a journey would employ two or three years. Among all mortal men I know none so suitable as Fundanius for collecting the materials of all those things not yet known, and which would escape the notice of every other person, not excepting myself. He possesses uncommonly keen powers of observation, even to the smallest minutiæ, and is gifted with a very sound judgment. His good taste and rare abilities qualify him for intercourse with the most learned, whose confidence he well knows how to gain. Through his literary correspondence with some of the principal men of science in

France, for example Mersennus, whose acquaintance he has formed, he has discovered some of their secrets in physics, mathematics and mechanical knowledge. Rest assured, dear Hotton, that nothing will further this work on universal wisdom so effectually, as my patron undertaking to defray the requisite cost of a pansophic journey of two or three years duration. I do not call it a *philosophic* journey because that word does not convey my full meaning. Of what consequence is it, whether or not my patron be acquainted with the peculiar religious views of Fundanius? If Fundanius retains them, the loss will be his alone; if he abandons them, as I hope he will, it will be to his personal benefit. His views will neither injure ourselves nor our work."*

In the end it appears that Lewis De Geer proffered his readiness to support Comenius in his studies, and also one or two learned men, whom he should select to be associated with him. And Comenius having consequently communicated this to his friends, he determined to leave England; they, however, urgently beseeching him to permit himself to be employed in nothing except the Pansophica.†

The fear of meeting with misunderstandings in religious matters, induced Comenius to decline Sweden as a place of residence during the pursuit of his studies. He therefore in a letter to Hotton mentioned Poland or Prussia, as quiet places of retreat; but considered Holland, where his personal safety would be secured, preferable to either of those countries.

Meanwhile, he communicated the state of affairs in England, and the proposals made by Mr. De Geer to the congregation Elders at Lissa, who on his undertaking to visit Lissa, and confer with them on the subject, gave their preliminary consent to his acceptance of Mr. De Geer's offer. Upon which Comenius applied for the means of

* Dr. Gindely, p. 13. † Didactica, II. Introd.

enabling him to make the voyage, and received from him a hundred thalers. (£15.) His departure from England was delayed till the end of July, as many of his friends, particularly Hartlib and Duræus,* were very desirous to detain him among them.

In the estimation of Comenius, this Duræus (John Dury) was a man of great learning, and of indefectible zeal. From the period of the publication of the "Janua," if not earlier, an intimacy had sprung up between these two men, which was greatly fostered by the similarity of their pursuits. Dury's absorbing object, was to combine all Protestants into one common bond of union; for the attainment of which he laboured personally, from the year 1628, and succeeded in securing the auspices of many learned men, and reigning princes, whom he made familiar with his plans; which, through the cooperation of Comenius, met with a favourable reception at Lissa, where the subject was discussed in a synodal assembly, held in 1636, which resolved to recommend general fastings and prayer, and to republish a work of Bartholomew Bythner, written in 1618, and bearing the title "Book advising Unity," which was very well suited for the purpose; further, to obtain the approbation of all influential noblemen. And, in the event of a general conference being held, in furtherance of this object, it was also agreed to send deputies to it with proper instructions.†

These efforts of Dury made a deep impression on the minds of many, particularly that of Comenius, who also conceived and often expressed his sentiments concerning it, that every wall of partition between different confessions of faith ought to be abolished, and it must be ascribed to the impulse given by these efforts that so many conferences on religion were held in Poland and Prussia, between

---

* Respecting whom, Chalmers, in his General Biographical Dictionary, vol. 12, p. 520, and 17, p. 200, gives some interesting particulars.

† Dr. Gindely, p. 14.

the Protestants and the Brethren on the one side, and on the other the Romanists, without however the slightest real approach on the part of the latter to concede an iota of those principles which constitute their apostacy from the Christian church.

Comenius, before he left England, received an invitation to visit France; but it is not known by whom this overture was made, neither the nature of the prospects presented to his view. Perhaps it came through the medium of the already mentioned Mersennus, (Mersenne) a man of universal learning, of whom it is said that the philosopher Des Cartes scarcely ever did a thing without taking his opinion, and with whom Comenius had held a correspondence for several years.*

At length Comenius departed from England, toward the end of July or the beginning of August, 1642; and, arriving at Sweden, he found his new patron in his house at Nort-

---

* An extant letter of this man, shews what extravagant notions he entertained, when he tells Comenius, that a certain Le Maire had discovered a method of teaching, by which boys six years old might acquire in nine months a perfect knowledge of three languages, say Hebrew, Greek, and Latin, so that the translation of any book written in either of these, should be an easy task. That after twenty years close study he had invented an alphabet, by the aid of which people might write without the need of an interpreter to men of every nation, even to the Chinese and Japanese, yea even to the inhabitants of the mountains of the moon, if there were any, and receive answers of every kind connected with human affairs. That he taught boys and girls, with the assistance of a young man named Gouy, and by means of notes of a peculiar kind, to understand in the course of only three lessons any musical composition. That he himself was engaged upon the construction of a new and universal language, exceedingly simple in its form, having but one conjugation, the first principles of which he had laid down in a work that had already become rare, entitled "Libri Harmonici," the study of which he commended to the attention of Comenius, who probably struck with the thought of possibly uniting the world together by means of such an invention, regrets, in a note to this letter, that he never received a specimen of so remarkable a production. In Chalmers' Biog. Dict. Vol. 22, p. 31—33, is a notice of this M. Marin Mersenne.

coping, where he was benignantly received by him. After several successive days deliberations, he was sent to Stockholm, to the illustrious Lord Axel Oxenstiern, Grand Chancellor of the kingdom, and also to John Skyte, Doctor of Canon and Civil Law, and Chancellor of Upsal University. These distinguished men exercised him in conferences during four successive days; but especially the former, that "Eagle of the North," whose inquiries pierced to the foundations of both subjects—the didactic and the pansophic—with an acuteness of discernment such as had not been hitherto displayed by any of the learned. During the first two days he examined the Didactica, and, addressing Comenius, at length concluded thus: "From my early youth I have observed something forced and incoherent in the method of instruction commonly used, but could not discover where the impediment lay. At length, being sent by my king, of glorious memory, as a legate to Germany, I held conferences there on the subject with various learned men; and when I learned that Wolfgang Ratich* had attempted an amendment of the method, I could not rest until I had a personal interview with him; when, instead of favouring me with a conference, he presented me with a large quarto volume. With avidity I executed the task thus imposed upon me; and having perused the whole book, I discovered that he had succeeded in detecting the diseases of the schools, but the remedies he suggested seemed to be deficient. Your remedies rest on surer foundations: proceed, &c." Comenius replied that he had already done what he could in these matters, and must now pass on to others. "I know," answered Oxenstiern, "that you are attempting greater things; for I have read your Prodromus Pansophiæ. To-morrow we will consider that; at present I am called away by public business."

On the next day the Grand Chancellor, purposing to examine the pansophic attempts of Comenius with still

* Born in Holstein in 1571.

greater severity, premised this question, "Can you bear contradiction?" Comenius replied that he could, and that the Prodromus was sent forth, not indeed by himself, but by his friends, in order that it might elicit the sagacity and censures of others, and when thus admitting strictures from all quarters, why not admit those of men of mature wisdom and elevated judgment? Upon this Oxenstiern began to reason against the idea of hoping for a better state of affairs from any rightly instituted study of pansophiæ; alleging, first, political reasons of profound importance, and then adducing Scripture testimonies which seemed rather to predict darkness and worse things towards the end of the world than light and an improved state of affairs. To all these objections such answers were returned by Comenius, that Oxenstiern concluded with these words: "I think that such things as these have hitherto entered into the mind of no one. Stand firmly on those fundamentals, and we shall both eventually arrive at the same result, or but little difference between us will remain. My counsel, however," he added, "is, that you first satisfy the wants of the schools by rendering a knowledge of the Latin language of easier acquisition, and thereby preparing the path of a readier approach towards those more sublime studies."

The Chancellor of the University likewise importuned Comenius to accede to this counsel of Oxenstiern, requesting, moreover, that in case he objected to remove with his family to Sweden, he would at least come nearer, by making Elbing, in Prussia, his place of abode.

As Mr. De Geer, to whose house at Nortcoping Comenius returned, judged that he should agree to both proposals, and earnestly pleaded that he should implicitly acquiesce both in respect of the place and of the task to be executed first, Comenius yielded to his advice, in the hope that within a year or two, there would be an end of these impediments to his applying himself to higher studies.

The facility with which Comenius thus yielded to the wishes of the Swedes greatly displeased his English friends, who attempted to recall him in a prolix letter abounding with reasons : " that the specimen already given in Didactis was sufficient ; that a way to rectify all these things more fully was already sufficiently opened up ; that it was otherwise in regard to philosophical studies ; that others could prosecute the former ; that educationists were now everywhere springing up and challenging each other to industry with mutual emulation ; whereas the foundations of Pansophia, to say nothing of its superstructure, were not yet visible. That infinitely greater service would accrue to the world from the ways to true wisdom being made plain, than from labouring on Latin letters." To these and other arguments in the letter Samuel Hartlib added this poetic solecism : " Why rush upon death, and dare things *less* than your strength ?" thus imputing inconsiderateness to Comenius ; who, delighted at this recal to the "royal way," communicated the import of the letter to his Swedish friends ; and not doubting but that they would yield to these reasons, he resumed and devoted himself entirely to pansophic studies, purposing, if not to pursue them permanently, at least, in case he should be detained in scholastic labours, or in the event of his death, so to search out and place in a clear light the foundations of pansophics, respecting which their not being sufficiently disclosed was complained of, that they could not possibly continue any longer unknown.

A reply, however, came from Sweden, in which Comenius was directed to prosecute the proposed arrangement by completing the Didactica first ; it being observed, " that no doubt it was proper that the *better* things should be performed, but that the things that took priority should be completed *first;* that it would be improper to proceed through greater things to the lesser, but contrariwise, &c." And thus Comenius, compelled to obey much against his will, was held fast fully eight years in what he called "the miry entanglements of logomachy."

Two things afforded Comenius consolation when thus forced back to didactics. First, that even during the time thus spent some valuable philosophical observations might be collected, and that he would be allowed a longer period for digesting with maturer judgment the contemplated greater work, and thus benefit would result from the delay. Secondly, that together with the study of languages, the germs of a more internal wisdom might be everywhere spread abroad; thus dexterously turning to beneficial account, among the young, the want of reflection in the human mind, which, as things generally still are, constantly prefers the *shell* to the *kernel*.

At the close of the interviews with the two Chancellors, and under their sanction, and with the approval of Mr. De Geer his patron, Comenius, having selected as his future dwelling place the town of Elbing, in Prussia, proceeded by sea, and after a very tedious voyage, rendered dangerous by contrary winds, arrived there towards the end of the month of October.*

* Letter to Ludw. de Geer, dated Barsand, 3/13, Oct. 1642.

CHAPTER VI.

ELBING — COMENIUS AND HIS FRIENDS — REMOVES HIS FAMILY TO ELBING—LIMITS HIS CORRESPONDENCE—AN ATTEMPT TO SEVER HIM FROM HIS PATRON—REPORTS PROGRESS OF HIS WORKS—CHANGES IN HIS ASSISTANTS —CALLED TO A GENERAL SYNOD AT ORLA—DISPLEASURE OF HIS PATRON—ATTENDS AN ECCLESIASTICAL CONFERENCE AT THORN—HIS LETTER TO MONTANUS—SATISFACTORY EXPLANATION TO HIS PATRON.

THE town of Elbing, situate in the palatinate of Marienberg, and distant thirty-six miles south-east from Dantzick, in West Prussia, is interesting as having been connected with the Hanseatic league entered into in the twelfth and thirteenth centuries, to protect the commerce of a number of German ports against the piracies of the Swedes and Danes, but more particularly as having included in its population from 1577 to 1660 an English trading company.*
Here were an eminent grammar school, places of worship for German and Polish Protestants, and a congregation of the Bohemian Brethren.†

Comenius found this a very suitable place for the pursuit of his studies. Here the town council granting him liberty to take up his permanent residence, he hired a house for his exclusive use.

His first care on arriving at Elbing was for his friends in England, Hartlib and Fundanius, on whose account he wrote to Hotton on the 11/21 of October: "It is true that I have somewhat neglected the latter, but thinking I should ere this have received two hundred pounds, which the London booksellers, to enable me the more readily to complete my

---

* Rees' Cyclopædia, art. Elbing.   † Regenvolscius, p. 52, 112, 402.

Pansophia, had agreed to advance me, I had designed this sum for Fundanius and Hartlib. As the payment of this is uncertain, and I am quite sure that both are suffering from want, I would most earnestly entreat my patron to allow them two hundred thalers each, at least, for the present year, and so long as Fundanius is not otherwise provided for." In this letter he states further, that M. Rossigniolo wished him to dedicate his work to the most excellent Cardinal (perhaps Mazarine),* but he was quite satisfied with the liberality of his present patron, whom God had raised up for him. He would, however, commend in his stead M. Fundanius, and his work on Universal History, to the attention of the Cardinal; and in this way his friend might, as he hoped, be provided for.

Comenius lost no time in visiting Lissa, for the double purpose of conferring with his elders there, and for the removal of his family, from which he had been separated during his journey to England. Returning with them to Elbing, he entered at once upon his task, assisted by his fellow-labourers, Paul Cyrillus, Peter Figulus, Daniel Petreus, and Daniel Nigrinus, whom, although of inferior literary attainments, he employed, because of his unwillingness to tax too severely the liberality of Mr. De Geer, who had actually undertaken to maintain Hartlib and Fundanius at his sole expense, beside giving five hundred thalers for the Bohemian exiles in Poland, and a like sum to those in Hungary.†

In order that he might work out the results of his studies

---

* Dr. Gindely, in Note 1 of his pamphlet, at p. 9, declares himself unable, after a most diligent search, to discover either the name of this Cardinal, or anything respecting this Rossigniolo, or in what way Comenius was connected with either. An equally unsuccessful search had been made respecting Fundanius.

† In April, 1643, he remitted five hundred Austrian thalers to Comenius for his personal use, and, two months later, one thousand Prussian thalers for distribution among the poor.—*Dr. Gindely*, p. 17.

without interruption, Comenius resolved to break off for a whole year all correspondence with his numerous friends. This of course did not include his patron, whose undoubted claim to be informed of the progress of his exertions, he most fully recognized in a letter to Mr. Wolzog, a well educated man, then residing with Mr. De Geer. Comenius hoped by the help of God to be enabled within the year to complete a new edition of his "Janua Linguarum," together with an entire newly arranged Dictionary and Grammar; and, should time permit, a rough draft of his Pansophia.

His retirement at Elbing was not altogether free from vexatious annoyance. An attempt to sever the connection between Comenius and his patron was made in the beginning of 1643, by a certain Nigrinus, formerly chief president of the Reformed Congregations at Dantzick, who under the notion of uniting Protestants and Romanists, and being liberally supported by the King of Poland, settled at Elbing for the purpose of preparing the necessary materials to carry out his plan. Comenius successfully resisted this attempt. What the overtures were which Nigrinus made to him are unknown, but it is quite certain they were rejected. In the spring of the same year, however, Nigrinus went openly over to the Papal Church, and thus Comenius was relieved at once from the conversation and seducements of an unprincipled man.

In the summer of 1643 Comenius sent Figulus to Sweden, with instructions to furnish Mr. De Geer, the State Chancellor, and John Matthias* with an account of his progress, urgently commending him to the favourable consideration of Mr. De Geer, with the view of the young man being trained at his expense in some university. His "Hypomnemata," *Suggestions,* relating to a settlement of the points in dispute between the churches he sent to John Matthias in particular; accompanying the manuscript with a letter in

* Perhaps successor to Dr. Skyte.

which he said, "A careful study of this subject is useful at the present time, when representatives of the various states are on the eve of assembling at Osnaburg on account of a projected treaty of peace. At any rate it might tend towards extinguishing the never to be sufficiently deplored differences between the evangelic parties."

The circumstance of Comenius not receiving a stipulated salary from his patron, exercised a considerable influence upon the relative position of these two men towards each other. When the former had been scarcely eight months at Elbing, the latter began to complain of the slow progress in the work, of which nothing had yet been committed to press. This, to a certain extent, disturbed the good feeling between the two; and although Mr. De Geer and his children held Comenius in high esteem, yet a sentiment of lamentation is said to be perceived as running throughout the letters of the befriended one, until towards the close of the year 1650; partly because of insufficient support, and partly from an impression of his services having been unfavourably estimated. Whether Mr. De Geer or his friends were the cause of these differences is not quite clear. After the destruction of Lissa in 1656, when Comenius, at the invitation of Lawrence De Geer, settled at Amsterdam, a better understanding ensued, which was never afterwards disturbed.

In relation to these complaints, Comenius, writing to Wollsog, in September, 1643, says: "We compose books and do not copy those of others. I can assure you our proposed work is not merely a book, but a real treasure, for the aiding of whose production my patron will assuredly have no cause of regret. It had been my intention to follow the opinion of friends by completing and publishing the 'Methodus Linguarum,' which I intend to dedicate to my patron: But first one and then another disapproved of this plan, and advised me to devote my greatest attention to the more philosophical works, suggesting that all other subjects of minor import might be added afterwards. Every one is looking out for something very weighty, and there is reason to apprehend, that while engaged in these matters of less moment, I may die. My own view of the case is this; that if permitted to consider and pursue every subject in a systematic and not irregular manner, things will move forward much better."

In addition to the departure of Figulus, other changes took place among the assistants of Comenius, who was obliged to dismiss Daniel Nigrinus, as he turned out to be a very worthless character. Comenius engaged the services of Melchior Zamorski, a Pole, who with his family had made Elbing their abode. There was a Dr. Kozac of Bremen, to whom Comenius, expecting great assistance, on account of his depth of knowledge in physical science, sent a gratuity with the view of inducing him to unite in his great undertaking. Indeed, he even wished the Doctor to reside at Elbing. "Should my patron," he writes, "allow me in the next year, as much as he has in the present, I may secure Dr. Kozac a sufficient maintenance, inasmuch as his family is fewer in number than my own." Another assistant, named Olyrius, to whom Comenius sent money in 1643, lived in England, and as the sum allowed Mr. Hartlib by Mr. De Geer was insufficient, he sent him a present of forty pounds, which he himself had received from England, and which he at once transmitted to his friend.

The fame of Comenius attracted many scholars to the public Grammar School at Elbing; the parents of the wealthier pupils desiring him to impart private weekly instruction to them, a request to which, it being seconded by the Town Council, he was declared to have consented. Besides this, Comenius was called to a General Synod held in August, at Orla in Lithuania, for the purpose of effecting a union among the Evangelical bodies, at which he was detained during some weeks. These impediments to the progress of his works excited the displeasure of Mr. De Geer, who considered the acceptance of other engagements as necessarily interfering with the one made with himself.

Hearing of this displeasure, on account of these alleged causes of delay, Comenius, in a letter to Ludwig De Geer, of September, 1644, begged him to have patience, explaining that in the past two years it had been altogether impracticable, on account of the extreme difficulty of the subject, to publish any part of his Didatic labours. In a letter to Hotton of the same date he gives expression to his injured feelings: "Admitting that my labours progressed but slowly," he asks, "what were the distracting engagements by which the completion of my works have been thought to be so much impeded?" The journey to Orla he had as a theologian been necessitated to undertake, and the attacks of the faithless Nigrinus had compelled him in justice to reply by a little book, which had only taken him several weeks to compile and publish. Nothing less than the earnest solicitations of the Town Council of Elbing would have induced him to give private instruction, which extended only to one individual, the son of a highly respectable layman. By doing all these, he never imagined that he had entered upon new engagements, having all along considered himself pledged to the service of his patron; for which very reason he had declined a most magnificent proposal made by Prince Racoczy of the one-fourth of his whole revenue for his services. He certainly should hold by his present patron as long as his patron stood by him; and knowing that his charity had been required in other quarters, he had not applied to him for assistance during the whole year. As to his patron declining to maintain the ingenious Dr. Kozac, *that* he attributed to a dislike of the Doctor's eccentric opinions; which, however, neither prevented him (Comenius) from rendering to him the respect that was his due; nor from aiding him with means until he had finished the work entitled, "Spagyria," which had been intrusted to his hand.

Towards the close of this year, 1644, Comenius engaged the services of two new assistants, Ravius and Ritschelius,* and informed Mr. De Geer of his having done so; they did not, however, arrive. He mentioned also, that the Elbing Town Council had decreed that he should live in his present house rent free. At the same time he begged of his patron to state without reserve whether or no it was his intention to afford him future support. This had the effect of renewing and confirming their former friendly relations, and Mr. De Geer at once remitted him four hundred thalers; in his acknowledgment of which Comenius, with an overflowing heart, assured his patron, that by thus sowing he would be instrumental in providing a harvest abundant beyond all expectation; for the benefit of his labours would extend to future ages.

Meanwhile it was contemplated to hold, in the spring of 1645, another Conference at Thorn, with the view of uniting Romanists and Protestants, a project in which the King of Poland took a personal and lively interest; inviting the different churches to delegate qualified theologians or representatives to this assemblage, since known as the "Colloquium Charitativum." Comenius, knowing what had been before attempted in this direction, anticipated no good as at all likely to result from such a Conference; well aware as he was of the intolerant bigotry and arrogant dogmatism of the papal system, and fearing a great impediment in the rigid orthodoxy of Lutheranism.

---

* George Ritschel, a Bohemian, born in 1616, educated at Strasburgh, driven into exile by Ferdinand II. settled at Oxford in 1641. Afterwards head-master of the free school, Newcastle on Tyne. Then vicar of Hexham, where he died in 1683. See a particular account of him and his writings in Bliss, Athenæ Oxon. Vol. IV. col. 124-126.

Upon learning that the town of Dantzick had elected Botzak* and Colovius,† as its representatives, two zealous Lutherans, who severely attacked the Reformed and the Brethren with all their adherents, Comenius wrote to Zbignxus De Goraj,‡ the castellan of Chelm :§ "Would that all party differences, with their abettors and defenders, were annihilated and destroyed! Christ, to whom I have dedicated myself, and whom the Father has given as a Light to all nations, that He should be the salvation of God to the whole world, knows no sects but hates them. He gave peace and mutual love for an inheritance to his people."

The progress of the revolution at that time in England confirmed Comenius in his hatred of all extreme party views,‖ and created in him an ardent desire to take no active share in the proposed Colloquium; yet as it was expected that his own congregation would send representatives to it, he undertook a journey to Lissa in April, 1644, in order to confer with his Brethren on the course it might be proper to pursue. At his own particular desire his fellow-labourers gave up their original intention to depute him as their representative; but the "politici,"¶ *lay-deputies*, most strenuously urged his being sent. Comenius, therefore, wrote to Mr. Ludwig De Geer, his patron, in May, 1645, requesting his recall to Sweden, in order that he might

---

* John Bothsac, Doctor in Theology, and parochial pastor of St. Mary's Church, Dantzick.

† Abraham Colovius, Doctor in Theology, and rector of the Gymnasium at Dantzick. Regenvolscius, p. 360.

‡ He acted at this Conference as president of the Reformed. MS. of the Conference.

§ Culm, a town on the Vistula, nearly 30 miles from Thorn.

‖ In a letter to Goraj, 3 March, 1645, he says, respecting the English, "they do nothing temperately—by opposing extremes to extremes they cover blood with blood." Dr. Gindely, p. 22.

¶ The Brethren called their lay-deputies *Politici*, and these as representing the lay-brethren, accompanied the clerical deputies.

fortify himself with a sufficient ground of excuse, beyond his own personal desires to be relieved from a duty which he foresaw must be useless, for, beginning in remediless disagreement, how could it lead to union? The Papists contemptuously abhorred all those whom they were called to meet, and the Lutherans of Dantzick refused to be placed upon a par with the Brethren. It could not be otherwise; for, as it has been well said, "The unity of the church is spiritual, and not formal or geographical, or political, or dependent upon human laws; but a unity which has its seat in the minds and hearts of men. Its centre is CHRIST, the head of the church. Its producing agent is the SPIRIT of God. It reigns through the medium of the TRUTH, received by faith. Its conservative principle is devotion [not devoteeism.] Its bond is the common sympathy of regenerate natures—the attraction of minds kindred in moral tastes, purposes, and interests. Its spontaneous and proper manifestation, is LOVE!" *

Mr. De Geer, deeming nothing more desirable than the removal of every hindrance to Comenius in the completion of his labours, recalled him to Sweden. In the interim, however, Comenius, perceiving that many voices would be raised against his return to Sweden, and that he must yield to circumstances over which his position in the church left him no control (for the claims of his church necessarily took precedence of his engagement with Mr. De Geer), he yielded to the desire of a person of high rank, no doubt instigated at the suit of his Brethren, and consented to remain at Lissa and take a part in the Conference at Thorn. He communicated this determination in a letter to Wollzog of the 16th of June, stating that he should labour at his works in the meantime; that he willingly consented to his patron's wish for him to dedicate his work to the Swedish monarch, inasfar as that could be done in the name of his patron, adding that

* Schism, p. 185, 186.

at present he had not determined to whom his great work, the Pansophia, should be dedicated; whether to mankind at large, or to Europe, or to the three great Northern Empires. Such vast importance did he attach to this work. He concludes his letter by saying he had found a valuable assistant in Dr. Kinner,* to whom for the year he had promised four hundred thalers.

The Conference at Thorn was opened on the 25th of August, and Comenius attended its sessions from the first down to that of the 18th of September. Respecting this Conference, his letter to Montanus states: "I was present in the way of my official duty at the Charitative Conference held at Thorn, assembled by authority of Vladislaus, king of Poland; and was interrogated by various persons on various subjects. Various things were also there recorded. But as the whole object of this Conference, was frustrated through the intractability of certain persons; and the king was therefore said to contemplate the assembling of another Conference, by the advice of certain of the leading men, a small treatise was written, with this title: " Christianismus reconciliabilis reconciliatore Christo," *Christian people a reconcileable community, Christ being the Reconciler.* Or that Christians, provided they would truly and seriously *be* Christians, can easily live in concord, is a fact evident as the sun at mid-day; addressed to the most illustrious King Vladislaus IV. Since the Royal purpose was not carried into effect, this treatise did not appear in public. It consisted of eight chapters: 1. A statement of the true cause of such cruel dissensions among Christians. 2. Remarks on their abominable turpitude, and injurious consequences. 3. Reconciliation among Christians most desirable. 4. Reconciliation, if desirable, ought to be sought. The reconciliation to be desired and sought ought to be universal and

---

* Dr. Cyprian Kinner, a Silesian, whose "Thoughts concerning Education" were published by Hartlib about 1648 or 1649.

complete; so that the very roots of dissensions should be cut out. 5. Whether and upon what grounds a reconciliation so complete can be hoped for? 6. The means necessary for such a reconciliation. 7. On the legitimate use of the means, so that they may not fail of the desired success. 8. The triumph of Christ, the Prince of Peace, if Christians could be brought to live under the influence of the laws of peace."*

The letter of the 15th of June does not appear to have satisfied Mr. De Geer, who addressed Comenius in an outburst of high displeasure, reproaching him on his conduct as the sole cause of the very slow progress of his undertakings. The mind of Comenius was evidently much aggrieved at the reception of this letter, to which the deputies of the Brethren at Thorn, on the day it was received,† wrote an apologetic reply in the behalf of Comenius; urging that he had been compelled by a moral necessity to attend the Conference, and that he was on the very point of leaving Thorn when the above letter reached him.

On the 12th of October, the day of his return to Elbing, Comenius wrote to Mr. De Geer, and also to Hotton, who had likewise written to Comenius on the subject. To the latter he expressed feelings of deep-felt sorrow at the displeasure of his patron; that he had been thinking of relinquishing his former connections, and entering into an entirely new sphere of life; that his letter had come just in time to pacify his troubled mind; and thanking him and Laurentius De Geer, for their kind mediation with Mr. Ludwig De Geer, to whom for their sakes alone he had endeavoured to write with all the calmness he could possibly control.

In his letter to Mr. De Geer, he says: "It appears to be quite the settled opinion of your mind that Comenius has

---

* Comenius to Montanus, p. 94, 95.
† 12th of Oct. 1645. Gindely, p. 23.

a great fondness for subjects diverting his attention, because he has not published anything in the last three years. It is certainly true that these years have passed and that nothing is yet published; but it ought to be remembered that Comenius is engaged in a very arduous undertaking, the component parts of which are so closely interwoven with each other, as to make it impossible to separate and publish the different portions until the whole shall be completed. It is doing me great injustice to say, that I have secured the services of Dr. Kinner at an extravagant rate, inasmuch as I have received the means of meeting this outlay from *another source*, in the same way as I paid my former assistants *out of my own purse;* you having given nothing towards their support. Although you should now forsake me, be assured that on my part, I shall never cease to remember your many past favours, and will endeavour to repay your generosity by dedicating to you my didactic works, which I hope to publish this winter at Dantzic. I still trust to find a friend for myself personally, but however the case may be my entire dependence is upon God."

The differences between Mr. De Geer and Comenius, if indeed there were really any, which however may very properly be doubted, are easily understood to arise out of the anxiety of the former to keep the latter to the task he had entered upon, and for which his talents were so peculiarly adapted. Admitting that Mr. De Geer, really did feel himself neglected, it must have been from a very oblique view of the matter, since as Comenius had given the highest evidence of a disinterested reliance upon the generosity of his patron, by not stipulating for a fixed income, his patron was certainly not entitled to press an exclusive employment of his whole time on his account. And Mr. De Geer must certainly have known the position of Comenius, who, as a leading member of his church, and as a general lover of mankind, was profoundly interested in the welfare of the

Christian world; which, as his whole life shews, he intensely desired to extricate from the vortex of puerility, superstition, idolatry, bigotry, and selfishness, in which it had been engulfed by an increasingly avaricious, tyrannical and impious priestly domination, which in the long succession of ages had permeated Christendom with all its impurities.

Mr. De Geer, who with every Christian man was equally interested in redeeming the world from its thraldom, saw, by the reply of Comenius, that he had borne too severely upon him, and at once laying aside all irritation, sent him, at the commencement of 1646, five hundred thalers for his own private purposes, and an equal sum for distribution among the Bohemian exiles. Aided by this remittance, and in dependence on some other hard-earned means of support, Comenius laboured on without repining throughout the whole year 1646, at the close of which he went to Sweden, and presented his patron with a report of his several years' employments. A Committee was appointed for their review, which approved them, and Comenius, receiving instructions to give them a finishing revise previous to publication, returned to Elbing in December, where, amidst much personal privation, he completed his task.

CHAPTER VII.

PECUNIARY AID FROM THE NETHERLANDS WITHHELD—DISTRESS FROM POVERTY, ETC.—PARTIAL RELIEF OBTAINED—CAUSES OF THE "THIRTY YEARS' WAR"—APPOINTED SENIOR OF THE CHURCH OF THE BRETHREN—INDEPENDENTS—TREATY OF WESTPHALIA DESTROYS THE HOPES OF THE EXILES, WHO ARE WARNED AGAINST DECLENSION—CARE FOR THE EXILED BRETHREN—DEATH OF LEWIS DE GEER.

COMENIUS, on his return to Elbing, found that the deacons of the Reformed Congregations in the Netherlands, which had afforded him some pecuniary assistance, now, through their pastors Caladrinus and Optebekius, declined sending him further remittances, on the plea of what appeared to them very great tardiness in the completion of his works. He assured them in a supplicatory letter, dated December 28, 1646, that he was no beggar on his own account; but, that he pleaded in the behalf of his assistant Ritschel, who was in great distress, and whom it would be highly unjust to forsake in his present adversity; especially as Mr. De Geer had convinced himself of the impossibility of publishing any thing just now, and when at this very time the works required him to employ no less than five assistants. In closing his letter he breaks forth in a pang of anguish: "O ye friends of God, if you could see me as naked as He who sees all things sees me, you would find no place there of a sinister motive to excite your groundless suspicions!"

In January 1647, writing to his friend Hartlib, he grievously complained of his manifold privations, which shew him to have been bordering on a state of wretchedness, more on account of the obstructions to the completion of his works than of his pecuniary wants, which, however, appear to have been very great. As this letter throws much light upon the condition in which Comenius, and his fellow-labourers in his literary pursuits were then placed, it will be proper to give it in a note below.*

* "I replied to your last two letters on the 5th, but lest my letter be lost I now forward a copy of it. I had promised further particulars by a certain Englishman, who, as our merchant, John Slavke, gave us to understand, would soon leave this for your country. He has already sailed. His name is Ambrose Grigges, and by him you will receive 50 imperials for Ritschel; the rest will probably be supplied by the Belgian clergy, to whom I have recently written, and I forward a duplicate list in order that you may have a correct account. I am unable to do more, and have scraped together these 50 imperials with great difficulty. They who are constantly around me witness my overwhelming cares, and how I have found an almost intolerable burden, from a quarter whence I had looked for relief. Ritschel comforts himself with the hopes of better times; he has repeatedly written to me that splendid offers have been made him for the future."

Concerning the "sluggish" progress of his labours, Comenius writes, "I have already stated and repeat it again, that had I been alone, I should, by the help of God, long since have completed what had from the first been marked out for me. My thoughts were arranged and expressed in preface full fourteen years ago, when my mind was alive to the work, and the Lord's blessing was very perceptible, while we laboured in secret relying upon His help alone. But since we began to come before the public, to expect help from man, and to attempt a display, I don't know how it happened, but the vigour of our mind appeared to be shaken and moved from its centre, to waver and be unsteady, whilst we were confused with the multitude of different counsels, and hence our progress was evidently retarded. I know, my beloved Hartlib, that it was with the best intention, when you drew me into public notice, and secured me my patron's favour, and obtained me the help of fellow labourers; but you witness now how contrary to our wishes these things have proved. You have pitched me into a quagmire, out of which, if I myself cannot discover the way, you cannot help me. My conscience witnesses that it was from no sinister motive I accepted the proffered assistance, such as for riches, or fame, or ease through the help of assistants; but chiefly because, habitually thinking better of others than of myself, I expected greater things from others than from myself; and finally, because when considering our dying state here, it seemed far better, instead of imposing so great a task upon one mortal, to let the work begun by myself, be accomplished by many, so

Comenius spent the whole of 1647, in revising his works, which he completely prepared for publication; and receiving a remittance from Mr. De Geer, of five hundred Austrian thalers, he was relieved from great distress.

It was in this year that Comenius published the work ascribed to him by Balbini:* "*On the causes of the war that arose in* 1618." From this spirited work the first part of our introduction, in as far as Bohemia is concerned, is an abstract. The work being extremely rare, a notice of it may be ac-

that whatever might happen to the individual, it should by the many be uninterruptedly carried forward. No blame seems to attach to such an arrangement, which appears to have been carefully considered, yet why was not the issue more favourable? I think the multitude of counsels threw no increased light upon our subjects, inasmuch as the primary ideas still prevail, and we proceed rather slower with assistants than without them. At least we are led into difficulties, and thus into endless obstructions. I cannot see how things can progress in this way, for if I should die before the work has reached any thing like completion, I do not think any one of those around me capable of preserving it from destruction. It would be better to close our labours and give their results to the public now, so that the sparks being scattered abroad, might probably ignite more talented minds than our own.

"Moreover, by having to seek a provision for those whose assistance we have invited, an amount of trouble has been imposed proportioned to the impediments, thereby accruing to our labours. Added to which we are compelled to pursue the disagreeableness of mendicancy, unmindful of the saying, "It is better to die than to beg." I am thoroughly ashamed at having to write such begging letters, and do hope that the one to the Belgian clergy will be the last. So also I feel shame at being compelled to remind my patron, who has promised to help me this year, that I am in want. Under these circumstances I contemplate how, when the most elaborate didactic studies are completed, I may possibly return to my old sphere, so as to quietly enjoy my own bread, without having to seek for that of others........Farewell, salute the Rev. Dr. Dureus from me; to whose as well as to your prayers I commend myself, and pray that Christ may not cease to guide you with His Holy Spirit.

Dated 11th January, 1647.   COMENIUS.

* Bohemia docta, p. 317.

ceptable. Its title and a synopsis of its contents are given below.*

* "Consideratio Causarum hujus Belli, &c." *A Dissertation on the causes of the war, which like a terrible conflagration, broke out in Bohemia in the year 1618, and still raging throughout Christendom, would but for the hand of God, and the virtuous courage of good men, consume the City of God itself.* It was written at the request of one of illustrious rank, and published for the information of those who had not yet thoroughly investigated the causes, and who, erring in this respect, were thus led to form wrong judgments.

"Happy the man who has been enabled to discover the *causes* of events."

"The *causes* of events are always more important than the events themselves." *Cicero to Atticus.*

Not who? But what?

Printed at Liberty (In Libertate) anno 1627.

Synopsis of Contents.

This Dissertation embraces and examines the genuine causes of this most cruel war.

In the First Part, the subject is treated historically and summarily.

In the Second Part, the causes are classified under the following seventeen heads.

1. Sin in general, that of Satan and of men, which is the source of every evil.

2. The defection or apostacy of the Bishop of Rome and his followers, from the true faith; from the simplicity which is in Christ; and from the usages of the primitive Church. Their transition to customs and errors at once Pharisaical, Idolatrous, and Heretical; and consequently a real Transubstantiation into the very form or type of Antichrist.

3. The pestiferous "polypragmosyne" *interference in many matters* of the Roman Flamen and his accomplices, by which, not content with ecclesiastical or episcopal duty, he mingled himself up with political, warlike, and juridical affairs.

4. The ambition of the Roman Pontiff, by which he would be Lord over all men and all things.

5. The impudence or harlot-like effrontry of the Pope, by which he is rendered incapable of feeling shame.

6. The malice and lust of vengeance of the Roman Flamen when enraged

Comenius, whilst working at his desk, for his industry never ceased, received intelligence that the principal senior of the exiled Brethren, Laurentius Justinus, had departed this life at Lissa. He was a Hungarian born, and superintended the Brethren in Scalica.* In 1632 he had been

against Christians, who detect or convict him. Under this head are related the histories of the Holy War, of Frederick Barbarossa, and others who have been harassed by Popes.

7. The introduction of the sect or heresy of the Jesuits into Christianity, and the incautious admission of their false principles and most turbulent counsels into courts and kingdoms. Here some account is given of some of their peculiar tenets and conduct.

8. The fraudulent, wicked, and violent conduct of the Council of Trent, and of their secret clandestine decrees. The Council encouraged to act at the instigation of the Popes.

9. The haughty disposition of the Spaniards and Austrians, who claimed for themselves the government of the world. An account of their League.

10. The indifference of the Saxons, and their disgraceful seduction by the Austrians and Spaniards, through the aid of Moguntinus† and others, subservient to the Popish faction.

11. The execrable and frequent violation of faith and treaties on the part of Magisterials.

12. The most iniquitous oppression of the Bohemians, and the inhabitants of the Palatinate.

13. The hypocrisy, confidence, and neglect of discipline by many of the Evangelical party.

14. The indecorous dissension, discord, and virulent writings of some theologians.

15. The negligence and tergiversation of certain statesmen.

16. The ill feeling, malice, tyranny, and perverted zeal of the Papists generally.

17. The frequent apostacy of many from known evangelical truths; doubting respecting the providence of God; and the omission of primitive or true charity.

Who can suppress the VOICE OF BLOOD crying from the ground?

---

* Skalitz, where the exiled under an Imperial grant had obtained a parish and erected a church and a school. Laurentius had a son John, who became a pastor among the Brethren in Poland. Regenvolscius, p. 322, 324, 404.

† Atto, Bishop of Mentz.

appointed senior at Lissa, and now (1648) finished his course there in his seventy-eighth year. Comenius being chosen his successor removed to Lissa, and was thus relieved from embarrassment as to a means of subsistence, and enabled to publish his carefully prepared Didactic works, of which we shall have to speak hereafter.

For the purpose of advocating the laws of peace, Comenius, in the course of this year, 1648, wrote a tract, entitled, "Independentia Confusionum origo," *Independence the origin of Confusions;* (religious strifes on the question of Church Government, then prevailing among the Brethren in England). This work earnestly recommended moderation to both parties.*

Comenius had written to his friend Hartlib on the 27th of Dec. 1646, respecting the "Independents." "In the erroneous dogma and almost irresistible struggle of the Independents, I can discern that most precious gem of excellence in the human mind, and of the liberty restored to our souls by Christ himself, in which is reposed the balmy power of expelling the poison mixed up with our nature. If we can find nothing to satisfy their desires, and allow their consciences to enjoy good in the church, without however breaking all the bonds of order, whatever else we may try, will only be an act of compulsion, the wounds will not be healed, but rather deepened without end. This, however, I say to you as a friend, not to those who cannot understand us; and, perhaps, if they were to hear our judgment, would only put a wrong construction on it. I have from this cause conceived a problem of profound wisdom and great use : *To extract from every error its own antidote."*

With the exception of his Pansophiæ Prodromus, no preparatory works had been compiled for the Philosophical Sciences, the usefulness of which Comenius strongly re-

---

* It was printed at Leszno in 1650, and reprinted at Amsterdam in 8vo. in 1661. Letter to Montanus, p. 95.

commended. His expectations of great things for the Pansophia, from the pen of the metaphysician Ritschel, were disappointed on account of the absence of perspicuity in style of the essays he had prepared. Comenius therefore himself pursued the study of philosophy with all his energy, and prepared and published, in 1649, "A Fragment on Metaphysics."*

The termination of the treaty of Westphalia in 1648, gave a death blow to the hopes of the Brethren, inasmuch as nothing was provided in that treaty for a return of the exiled Bohemians to their country. The Brethren, from the generally victorious career of the Swedes, had constantly been enlivened with hope for the future; and the intimate connection between the Swedish Court-Chancellor, Oxenstiern, and Comenius, who was known and respected far and wide, had led to the expectation that from motives of honour and in remembrance of the very first origin and cause of this "thirty years war," Sweden would not forget the men in whose behalf it had been undertaken. But they were treacherously doomed to remediless disappointment.

When a rumour that the stipulations in the treaty were adverse to the Bohemians began to spread, Comenius wrote a powerful letter, which, although the address is not preserved, was in all probability to Oxenstiern himself, and in which he says: "My people have aided your arms with their weapons, the unceasing offerings of tears and supplications to God, and now when they see your success and may rejoice in the hope for a more favourable issue of affairs, they are at the same time troubled with dread apprehension lest they should be forsaken. They have, therefore, requested me to

* So small a number of this pamphlet of five sheets was printed, that it became very scarce in 1678, and was rarely to be met with, even among his own friends and relations. Palacky does not name it in his list; but it is mentioned in a letter of Nigrinus to Hessenthaler and others, of the year 1678. Dr. Gindely, p. 26.

make known to you their cause of lament in the possibility of discovering a channel for my grievance to the heads of the Council, or even to the person of her most gracious Majesty the Queen. What other way could I find than through you, whom God has raised up to be the executor of His own holy will? I, therefore, lay all before you, leaving it to the decision of your righteous judgment, whether you will immure it in the recesses of your own bosom or make it known to those whose prosperity you are called upon by the Almighty to vigilantly watch. The oppressed of my people and of our neighbours fostered the hope that you would prove yourselves to be the instruments raised up by the Lord for putting an extinguisher upon our spiritual murderers. On which subject numberless promises were made by those holding high positions among you, that either by the power of the sword, or by the force of peaceable negociation, our cause should be well remembered, and that we and all other exiles should be replaced in our former positions. But now, seeing themselves forsaken by you, how can the distressed look for anything at your hands? What has become of your many solemn asseverations? How comports it with your declarations, that the liberation of the oppressed is the every object of your aim? Are a few casks of gold a worthy reward of such efforts, while many thousands, even myriads of souls are suffered to be surrendered to the fangs of Anti-Christ? Where among you is the zeal of Moses, who, when Pharaoh would have allowed *a portion* of the people to depart, determinately answered him—' Our *cattle* shall go with us; not a *hoof* shall be left behind?' "

On the 11th of October of the same year, three, or thirteen days before the treaty was signed, Comenius wrote to Lord Chancellor Oxenstiern—" Pleasant as it was wont to be to my countrymen, who are persecuted for the sake of the Gospel, to listen to what your Excellency communicated to them through myself and others, by which they were assured of your constant remembrance; just so agonizing is it now to be informed that we are deserted and entirely disregarded in the Treaty of Osnaburg. Of what use is it to us, who are now deprived of every hope of peace, to have assisted you with our tears in obtaining victory; when, although it lay within your power to release us from our prison-house, you surrender us anew into the hands of our oppressors? Of what avail now all those holy, evangelical alliances, formed by our ancestors, and consecrated with their sacred martyr-blood? Why, when you have no anxiety for the restoration of the Gospel to our kingdom, why have you called upon us for assistance? . . . . . I write in the name of many, and, impelled by their lamentations, fall prostrate before you and your Queen, and your Directorial Board, adjuring you all by the wounds of Christ, not to utterly desert us, who are persecuted for His sake."

This language was of no avail, for although an elevated principle may have formed an important ingredient in the origin of the "thirty years' war," that principle had entirely evaporated towards its end, in a mere conflict of the commonest interests; and the Swedes, in particular, cherished inclinations quite the opposite from those of restitution to the despised portion of a nation devastated by its oppressors. The position of Comenius more than justified his plain dealing, which was by far too mild and lenient for the occasion; and Oxenstiern, being galled by it, was of course prompt in exhibiting his displeasure. Comenius, however, did not at once abandon all hope of service from the Chancellor, to whom he wrote again on the 1st of November, 1649, availing himself of the death of his Lordship's wife as an occasion of addressing him. In this letter Comenius excuses the strong language he had employed, on the ground of the grief with which he was overwhelmed, and which he could not conceal, and of his acting not on his own individual account, but in the name of thousands of his fellow men, who were groaning under their helpless and hopeless condition.*

"Most illustrious Count and most gracious Lord,—

"Whatever your godly mind can wish for your own welfare, and that of your friends, I place all upon the altar of my heart, and offer it up to God, with the fire of my most ardent desires. My son-in-law, who has lately returned from you, has filled my mind with the two-fold grief by the tidings that you, most illustrious lord, have become a widower, and that we have given you cause of offence. As regards the first, I pray, and shall not cease to pray to God that he will sustain you with His consolations, and with the wise reflection that the lot of our present mortal state is never otherwise than vacillating and changeable; and that even those who make life dear to us must be taken from us, and we must either send before us our dearest friends, or go hence before them, where at last true life will begin, a life undisturbed by any fear of death. Abraham sent Sarah before him; David left his Bathsheba behind; the one, however, follows the other, and both, and we all, are separated from each other, that we may be gathered again in the bosom of Abraham. A little while and we shall meet again. Husbands and wives, as they are rarely born on the same day, so also they rarely depart at the same time, though they may have long been joined together in the same road. When I was still a boy in Moravia, John Ferdörfer, toparch of Banovia, died in the 106th year of his age, and very shortly after his wife followed him, at the age of 104, having, if my memory be correct, lived 85 years together in their married state. Such examples are very rare in our days. O! that it had pleased the Lord, the disposer of life and death, that you and your now happy partner could have left this world at the same time! But since He has commanded her to go before you long before the age above alluded to, I implore the adorable Disposer of all ages that He may command you not to follow her until you have attained that period, and that the number of years wanting in her case may be added to yours, in order that now, when peace has at length been restored to Christendom, you may enjoy the fruits of those things accomplished by your counsels.

"But as regards the offence you have taken at my plaintive letter, I must crave forgiveness for my guilt if any imprudent word or imprudent expression has been mingled with it; and I must say that very recent grief was its cause, and that it was not deliberately intended. May ingratitude, a crime deserving the abhorrence of all men, ever be far from me and mine. We have heard that you wished to advocate my cause, but

Whilst at this treaty equal privileges were granted throughout Germany to the Lutherans, the Reformed, and the Romanists, in Bohemia and Moravia, the ritual of the

that *our neighbours* were unwilling to plead their neighbour's cause alike with their own. Let God alone be judge. My grief, to which I gave utterance in my letter, was not, neither is it now, my own merely, but a public sorrow, not merely because I myself, or a part of those who are of my faith, had been forsaken, but because my whole nation had been forgotten. The great grief and zeal of the Apostle Paul from this very cause is evident from Romans ix. 1—3. He wishes that he might be accursed from Christ for his brethren. So Moses also, in Exodus xxxii. 32. This is an excess of grief which God himself does not disapprove, for it springs from an exuberance of charity which God, who is love, cannot disapprove. If God does not suppress such complaints in anger, but tolerates, yea, even commiserates them, as our Lord clearly teaches us by the example of the unjust judge, I cannot see why our cry for help should be an occasion of exciting displeasure. But God is still powerful, and will show to our neighbours that by deserting us they have deserted their own cause; and if we can find no comfort in man we can find it in God, whose help generally begins when human help is no more, as Philo the Jewish author observes—' Finally, if there be no consolation for us in this life, we shall obtain it in that hereafter, to which the Prince of Life leads his people by the same path on which he has trodden before them.

"Meanwhile, it will be our duty, in order to gain some profit, even now to turn our present calamities into the occasion of improvement. Epictetus very wisely observes—' To upbraid others in adversity is the practice of ignorant men; to upbraid oneself, of him who begins to learn; and to upbraid neither others nor oneself, of the wise and learned.' It would, therefore, be folly on our part to accuse others, and complain of them in our calamities; but the beginning of wisdom to accuse ourselves. It would betray real impenitence towards God, who is now chastising us, and confessedly sluggishness on our part, to sleep and neglect our own interests, while we desire others to undertake our cause. This matter has given rise to the publication of a little pamphlet, which I now send to your Excellency, the tendency of which is, if possible, to awaken our people, who are almost stupified by the blow, to repentance. I have selected such arguments as I could hope would influence our countrymen, and at the same time to produce some fruit among our friends in the evangelical churches. Should you not think it too much trouble, and your public duties permit you to read it; and I may say also that it treats of

latter alone was established, and that reformation was finally extinguished which had been begun long before the time of Huss. Comenius thus expresses his feelings on this deathstroke to the hopes of his countrymen:—" The Bohemians deservedly suffer the chastisement of the Almighty which is poured forth on our nation. But how will those men justify their actions before God, who, forgetful of the common cause of evangelical Christians, and of ancient treaties between the nations, not only did not help the oppressed, but actually stirred up our enemies against the Brethren and their neighbours, by saying like those of old (Ps. cxxxvii. 7), 'Rase it, rase it, even to the foundation thereof.' (He alludes here to Saxony, which in 1635 had sacrificed the cause of the Bohemian Brethren in a separate treaty with the Emperor.) And others, in concluding peace for their separate benefit (such as France and Protestant Germany) have quite forgotten that the Bohemians, who were the first and the most manly in resisting Anti-christ for centuries past, were all deserving of assistance, at any rate in so far as not to permit the light of the Gospel to be extinguished in the very locality where it was first of all put upon a candlestick."

His lamentation addressed to his scattered brethren is truly affecting: "This last general treaty of peace, what comfort did it bring to us and many others besides? As we are called to exclaim with Jeremiah (Lam. i. 19) 'Woe unto us, they deceived us. Very often they promised us,

public affairs, the welfare of the Church, and the various means for promoting it, I feel confident you will not regret the having perused it.

"Farewell, most prudent lord, and may you carry forward with the greatest zeal the work of wisdom, justice, and Christian sympathy. May it be the crown of your old age to have accomplished such deeds as to which the crown of life is promised. May Christ fill you more and more with His spirit, the Spirit of wisdom and of a sound mind. Amen! Amen! Amen!

"So prays again and for ever, your humble client,

"COMENIUS."

Ye shall have peace, but behold, the sword has pierced our inmost souls!' So we must now seek for peace within, the peace of a pure conscience, according to the word of the Lord, 'That in me ye might have peace. In the world ye shall have tribulation: but be of good cheer, I have overcome the world.' Nevertheless, the Lord liveth! He can raise again the dead bones; He can give renewed and larger increase to his congregation!"

At the same time the deep interest of Comenius in the welfare of his brethren was greatly excited by the prevailing spirit among the remnants of the scattered flock, both at Lissa and in other localities. He thus addressed them: "Beware, lest you dishonour your martyr's crown by an unworthy course of life. Cease to pollute your Christian profession, as some began to do when in our native land, and continue to do while in exile, by your indifference to godliness, by your warmth of desire for earthly things, by intemperateness, by vanity, and bitterness towards one another! Others, observing you, say we have left the footsteps of our forefathers, and are no longer those to whom Luther united in fellowship. Alas, it is true! but not in the sense to which they refer; but by declining in *godliness*, we have lost our charity too, and cannot bear that our brethren should differ from us in non-essential points, while we *can* bear with intemperance, covetousness, pride, anger, malice, as though those sins were less flagitious than diversity in religious sentiment."

The dishonourable and unmanly conduct towards the kingdom of Bohemia and its exiles, of the Protestant parties who negociated the conditions of peace, although necessarily striking a wound which could not easily be closed, did not entirely interrupt the intercourse between Comenius and the Swedes, who with others equally or even more to be blamed than themselves, must have felt conscious of their guilt, and were, of course, proportionately less willing to listen to deserved reproaches.

Henceforth an uniform strain of mournful lamentation

pervades all the correspondence of Comenius, who thought this, 1649, a proper time to publish " Historia ecclesiæ Fratrum Bohemicorum, Johannis Lasitii epitomata: cum exhortationibus ad ejusdem ecclesiæ reliquias:" *History of the Church of the Bohemian Brethren, by John Lasitius, epitomized: with exhortation to the remnants of that Church.** Of this book he sent a few copies to Sweden to Wollzog, Tobias Andreæ, and Oxenstiern, being anxious thereby to excite their sympathies for his suffering people. But the effect of it was merely a small grant of money, the Queen sending him two hundred thalers and to his son-in-law fifty. At the same time he received from M. De Geer, for himself, four hundred, two hundred for his son-in-law, and for the poor one hundred and fifty-eight.

* In relation to this book, Comenius, intent upon transmitting to posterity the jewel once possessed by the Church of the Brethren, dedicated it to the scattered Bohemian Brethren. In the preface he remarks that he accidentally found this work of Lasitius in the library of Charles de Zerotin at Breslau. Grieved at the conduct of their forefathers in neglecting the publication of their Church history, and at the indifference of the people and want of attachment to their own Church, he resolved upon the publication of an abstract of the first seven chapters relating to this history, and of the entire eighth volume, which describes the ecclesiastical and social Regulations of the Unity of the Ancient Brethren. According to the preface, he felt impelled by the strongest motives to publish this work, such as the following:—to translate *himself* in spirit into those better times of the past, to instruct and encourage his *Brethren*, and to preserve to *posterity* a memorial of one of the most beautiful phenomena in the Church of Christ. At the conclusion he expresses his thoughts and admonitions, which is an excellent essay rendering the work intrinsically valuable on account of its merit, while, at the same time, the descriptions of Lasitius are important by way of comparison with the " Ratio disciplinæ," which treats on the same subject. The ideas expressed in this Latin publication were republished at Lissa in 1640, in an altered form, in a Bohemian book for the use of the Brethren, entitled, " Kssaft umjragjcj matky, Gednoty bratrske," *The testament of the expiring mother of the United Brethren*, who, speaking collectively and through her separate members, divides all the treasures entrusted to her by God among all her sons and daughters.

From the date of his appointment as Senior of the Brethren at Lissa, Comenius found little time to devote to his great work the Pansophia, whose completion would have added considerably to his reputation and fame. He was now obliged to engage in matters of a very different kind, amongst which the care for his dispersed brethren being increasingly requisite, he felt himself called upon to provide for many of the exiled nobility who had no means of supporting themselves. His anxiety was also extended to young men of education and learning, for whom respectable situations, in which they might be able to settle for life, could not be met with at Lissa. And such was the influence of Comenius, that there was no country in Protestant Europe where Bohemians might not be met with, as instructors, teachers, clergymen, or artists. Several Bohemians successively became pastors of Reformed Congregations in Switzerland; and in Poland there were very few families in which a Bohemian or a Pole, proposed by Comenius as the instructors of their children, might not be found; and thus the ever blessed God used those very men who were supposed to be entirely crushed, as His instruments in disseminating His truth very much more efficiently and extensively than if they had been allowed to return to their native land. (Acts viii. 4.) In England certain stipends were provided in connection with the University of Oxford, for the education of Bohemian youths,* who were thereby enabled to acquire the requisite training for an honourable maintenance throughout life. This state of things continued down to the year 1680, or even later, and, generally speaking, a very friendly feeling was long cherished at Oxford for the Bohemians, many of whose descendants in England are said to have adopted English names.†

The Bohemians being held in reputation as excellent

---

* From a letter of Hartlib to Dr. Worthington, 5 May, 1659, it appears the University of Cambridge was then unable to maintain any exiled Bohemian students.—Dr. Worthington's Diary, p. 132.

† Dr. Gindely, p. 29.

teachers, their services were eagerly sought after for Grammar schools. Thus even after the death of Comenius the Council of Education at Dantzic applied to Nigrinus, when engaged in publishing his own literary works, to recommend teachers for their public schools. Distinguished by great talents for languages, many a Bohemian was conversant in the Bohemian, Polish, German and Latin, and most of them in the English; and, as far as can be gathered from the correspondence, many were acquainted with the French. It was by no means an easy task for Comenius to satisfy the demands of applicants for teachers, and great ingratitude was often the reward of his exertions in this direction.

Another duty bearing upon Comenius was the care of the scattered congregations throughout Hungary. It is difficult to form an adequate conception of the frequent intercourse, according to the circumstances of that age, between the Slavonians of Upper Hungary and Lissa, the central station of the Brethren, by whose means the charitable beneficences sent for the relief of the exiles were distributed in due proportions between those at Lissa, and such as had migrated into Hungary;* in which kingdom and Poland

---

* The following letter shews that these distributions were not always satisfactory to the recipients:—

" To the faithful servant of Christ, Peter Securius of Scalic, my greeting and love.

"Brother beloved in the Lord,

"On the day of my receiving your papers, the 27th of January, I also received those of your brother-in-law, D. Joseph, dated the same as your own, of the 23rd of November last year, both having been sent by Br. Adam Hartmann, from Thorn. I replied at once to him by the ordinary day-courier, and waited a suitable opportunity to answer yours, to which an instant reply was not necessary.

" I congratulate you on your good health, and on the labours you piously contemplate for the church meetings. But as to your complaints about the multitude of your engagements, and the smallness of your income, and therefore that you intend to abandon your present post and go into Switzerland, I hardly know how to commend you; for we must approach

some candidates for the ministry in the one country found promotion in the other. When the Con-senior Paul

this sacred office only with an apostolic spirit—the office of a bishop is described as "a good work," not as "ease or gain or honour." And you know that the Apostles worked with their own hands that they might not be chargeable to the churches. And here too we do not all live upon a ready and prepared sufficiency, but are content to obtain assistance such as may arise out of the compassion of strangers, and the surplus of the church collections, and are often very scantily supplied. As for myself individually, I do indeed eat my bread in the sweat of my brow, lest I should be burdensome to the church.

"In respect of labour and toil, we are born and destined for them, and if you have the heart to adopt this language, we may say with Homer's Achilles: 'O that my portion of work were greater!' If at times you have to undertake the duties of those fainting old men, undertake them with alacrity; for it often happens to every good man to have much laid upon him, and if God finds you a faithful workman He will increase your strength.

"Meanwhile, I can but ill bear to be again reproached by you, for not promoting *you* rather than Figulus, Olyrius, and I know not who beside, whom you say I have favoured to the neglect of yourself; nor do I like to be told that you have to continue your studies without the aid of myself or any one else. I desire to see a little more prudence, my brother, and more gratitude. Have not I promoted you wherever an opportunity offered? Did I not call you from a very uncertain mode of life to the study of theology? and in order that you might study it did I not at my own expense take you from Switzerland to Bremen? Did not my particular and effectual recommendation procure you an excellent situation with the Councillor? Did I not more than once assist you with money? as Dr. Kozak can attest, through whose hands my remittances were sent you. What is there else that I have not done for you to the extent of my power? I have moreover suffered the haughtiness of your mind long enough, who are continually putting forward your literary labours as deserving commendation.

"To what purpose is it that you again promise me a sight of the testimonials you received at Basle for your proficiency at the examinations? I pray you to imitate the example of Christ, who said, *I receive not honour from men*. Who compels you, like Paul, to become a fool in glorying? Why do you sign your letter with "Peter Securius, candidate for the sacred office of the ministry at Basle, and, God willing,

Fabricius died in 1649 at Lissa, Comenius called three Slavonian brethren to care for the spiritual offices there.

minister of the same; and German and Bohemian preacher of the Helvetian confession among the Sakolcenses (*i.e.* people of Skalec), &c., &c.?" Alas! how many words full of vanity! Have the people of Basle some particular kind of ministry by which they must be distinguished from all others? and how can you call yourself a candidate for the ministry when in reality you are already a minister? Is not this making broad your phylacteries like the Pharisees? and enlarging the borders of your garments? I pass over the remainder. But I ask why do you send me this long notation of all your titles? Was it to enable me in future to direct my letters to you? If so, it is a vain expectation. It is quite enough for me that in your signature you adopt my example, and be content to cease from following such vanities.

"If that great theologian was really correct and just who when asked, "What is the root of all theology?" replied *humility*. "What is the tree?" *humility*; and "what the fruits?" *humility*; then I beg you earnestly to consider how easily it may be shewn that you have neither the root nor the tree nor the fruits of theology.

"If what I write seems very harsh to you I will not say forgive me, but urge it upon you to acknowledge your fault and amend your conduct. Or should I by mere flattery confirm you in your error? That be far from me. Christ did not teach us thus to practise mutual love. If you desire to live in our fellowship you must become a theologian of the sufferings of Christ, and not of vain glory.

"Perhaps you may think that from this chiding I have a hatred towards you. Beware that you do not add one error to another. For charity and the fear of God urge me freely to correct my brother, and not to suffer his errors. Read the injunction Lev. xix. 17. If you think of me and my affection towards you the very opposite, you will sin against God whom I call to witness that I seek nothing but your edification, and through you that of the church, and if I knew how to attain this object in any other way than by calling you from the error of your self-esteem, and leading you to the truth, I should adopt that way. This way is however the simplest and the most candid, if not for the present (see Hebrews xii. 11), at least for some future benefit; which may Christ grant, to whose gracious Spirit I most heartily commend you.—Yours in truth, although you appear to be ignorant of it,

"COMENIUS.

"Lissa, Feb. 11, 1649."

While engaged in Hungary, Comenius received the intelligence of the departure out of this life, of Lewis De Geer, Lord of Finspong, whom he describes as a man pious towards God, just towards men, merciful to the distressed, and meritoriously great and illustrious among all men, and who had been among the chief instruments of his eternal Benefactor. It was not enough for Comenius to grieve over this loss alone, or to lament with others, or to chant vain trifles in pompous funeral elegies; but for his own consolation, and that of many others moaning with him, he composed "Animæ sanctæ beatum satellitium, &c." *The blessed guard or army of good deeds of a holy soul entering the eternal kingdom with triumph; being a funeral oration on the death of Lewis de Geer, senior.* This was published at Patak, in 1654, and was included in the volume containing the Didactica, as a grateful monument to the memory of a man of whose munificence the writer had partaken during a period of fourteen years.

CHAPTER VIII.

COMENIUS VISITS THE PRINCESS RAKOCZI—PROCEEDS TO TOKAY—SCHOOL AT SAROS-PATAK—COMPILES THE "ORBIS PICTUS"—DESTRUCTION OF LISSA—ESCAPE AND LOSSES OF COMENIUS—HE SETTLES IN AMSTERDAM—HIS DESPONDENCY—OBTAINS HELP FROM ENGLAND FOR HIMSELF AND HIS BRETHREN—TESTAMENTARY BENEVOLENCES—FRATERNAL SYMPATHY.

THE publication of his writings had secured to Comenius the highest esteem of the widow of the deceased Prince George Rakoczi, one of his greatest admirers. Her name was Susanna Lorantfi, and Sigismund, Prince of Siebenbürgen (Transylvania), was the name of her son. Her esteem was still more confirmed by John Tolnai, to whom the direction of the schools of the country had been entrusted. This gave rise to an invitation from the Princess and her son, that Comenius should visit them at their palace at Saros-Patak, with the view of obtaining his advice in the establishment of their schools; and Comenius, in anticipation of much benefit that might accrue to his Brethren, at least in the Hungarian dominions out of the favour of the family of Rakoczi, accepted the invitation. He, therefore, repaired thither by way of Skalik, where he arrived about Easter, 1650. Here the Brethren, aided by donations from abroad, had been enabled to erect a church, and in this new church Comenius officiated at the Easter solemnities. John Ephronius, assisted by Paul Vetterinus, was minister of the congregation. The latter was son of George Vetter (Streyc), who, with Dr. Pressius, was the principal compiler of the Confession, which, in the year 1575, had been presented to the Emperor Maximilian II. by the States of Bohemia.

North-east from Skalic lies the village of Sednik,* where the Brethren had also built a settlement, in which Dabricius (Dabrick), of whom we shall have to speak hereafter, resided.

From Skalic Comenius addressed an appeal and petition to the Reformed of Dantzic, for contributions in aid of the congregation at Pucho,* to enable it to erect a church of its own, as the people of Skalic had done; and shortly after, under the command of the Seniors, who with himself were unwilling to omit any opportunity of testifying gratitude for the protection afforded to the exiled Moravians by the princes of Transylvania, he proceeded to Patak, where he was welcomed with the greatest joy. From thence, in company of the prince and princess, he went to Tokay, where, after several days conferences, he drew up a report of the manner in which the provincial school at Patak could be best constituted, according to the principles he had adopted. His stay here at this time was short, and soon after his return home Susanna Lorantfi addressed a letter, dated May 18th, 1650, to the Elders of the Brethren at Lissa, urgently soliciting their permission for him to return with his whole family for a few years, in order that he might personally organize the system of the schools throughout Hungary. In a letter to Comenius himself she undertook to raise a liberal salary for him, and to present him with a handsome compensation on the completion of his task; to which was added the liberty to educate, free of expense, ten or twelve of the youths of his country, in the training institution she wished him to establish and superintend. Sigismund Rakoczi, and John Tolnai, whose letter in particular contained expressions of the highest admiration of Comenius, wrote in like manner, inviting his compliance.

* About four miles distant from Puchó, in the Hungarian province of Slovakia. It must not be confounded with a place called Lednice, or Eisgrub, which is in Moravia.

Consent to these reiterated applications was very difficult; for, on the one hand, strictly speaking, Comenius was not free to engage in any new undertaking without the consent of the son of M. De Geer, whose assistance was continued to him; and, on the other, he might not, without the sanction of a general Synod, absent himself from his clerical functions during so long a period as would be required for the purpose: yet the importance attached to these most urgent calls, induced him, without asking the former, or waiting for the latter, to follow the advice of his Con-seniors, who had given their consent; and he left Lissa for Saros-Patak in the autumn of the same year, 1650, although apprehensive of extreme danger to his person and manuscripts from the war threatening Hungary.

Agreeably to the wishes of Sigismund Rakoczi, Comenius, left free to found an institution according to his own didactic and pansophistic ideas, resolved to raise this institution under seven classes, two of which were at once begun in 1650, and a third was organized in the following year. But from the beginning, as was to be expected, Comenius had to encounter the almost insurmountable indolence and prejudices of the scholars.

When Prince Sigismund died, in 1652, Comenius wished to retire, but at the solicitations of Prince George, who succeeded in the government, he was prevailed upon to continue. The school itself was limited to three classes, and he remained at his post until 1654, during which period he compiled his celebrated work, entitled "Orbis Pictus," *Pictured World;* and in the month of June that year he returned with his family to Lissa, where they resided until 1656, and where he published, for the use of his Brethren, a new edition of the History of Persecutions.*

The destruction of Lissa is one of the multitudes of examples on record of the malignity which mankind is

* Plitt's *MS.*

capable of exerting, when steeped in the foul waters of alienation from God, through a priesthood become vicious by its suppression of religious freedom, and which had in the course of ages corrupted the pure fountains of life, of whose waters it had impiously arrogated to itself the sole dispensation.

As early as the year 1628 and 1629, Lissa had become the chief eyesore to the enemies of the Gospel, who, adopting the old method of charging those opposed to their malignity as traitors to the civil government, accused the inhabitants to the king, but through the prudence of Lord Lasinsky, to whom the domain belonged, those accusations were made in vain.

But in 1653, when the Swedes were driven by the Imperial forces out of Silesia, new plots were formed at Glogaw to sack Lissa, and put its inhabitants to the sword, or at least to scatter them by means of one or two regiments of Imperial troops which should seize the town by surprise. The promoters of this scheme being unable to keep the matter secret, the whole affair was brought to light, and thus it came to nothing. Not so, however, the envious devices of the adversaries of Lissa : for after the decease of the prince palatine of Belse, on the division of his estates among his sons and heirs, the domain of Lissa fell to his third son Boguslaus, then newly returned from his travels, who ensnared by the prospect of great wordly distinctions apostatized to Romanism. These distinctions were profusely heaped upon him until he became Lord-treasurer of Great Poland; yet he maintained his integrity to his Protestant subjects, preserving entire the privileges, civil and religious, which his father had promised, and confirmed to the people of Lissa, although incessantly urged to the contrary.

Finding this plan unavailing the enemy attempted another, for Antichrist and Satan are always in unity; the Bishop of Posnania now claimed the old parish church of Lissa, to be

H

withheld from the use of heretics, on the ground of ancient right. Appeal to the Bishop was altogether vain, and in 1652 the Lord-treasurer was cited on the question of his hereditary right, before a tribunal of the realm, which consisting of accusers, witnesses, and judges, must necessarily decide against him. He, however, obtained sanction for the Protestants who had thus been ousted from the old to build a new church for themselves; which in due time they successfully accomplished on a much larger scale, to the chagrin of the Romanists, who now, filled with self-torturing envy at the greater accommodation afforded to the Protestants, complained that it had not been built for themselves.

At length the irruption of the Swedes into Poland, in 1655, when the former invaded the latter as far as Cracow, gave the Romanists the long desired occasion of oppressing the people of Lissa, and of rooting out the profession of the Gospel throughout Poland. For although the Papal party had themselves treated with the Swedes at Uscia, and ceded the town of Lissa and other places expressly by name, yet availing themselves of the position of the King of Sweden, who was now employed in Prussia, they resumed arms in order to liberate their country from the Swedes.

The Jesuits and monks, under cover of this outburst of patriotism, sent in all directions to effect so glorious an undertaking as the recovery of the lost territory, most sedulously urged the thunderbolt of excommunication to the sluggish, and issued forth a profusion of promises of relaxation from the pains of purgatory, and of eternal reward to the alert. Thus excited, a rise was effected against the Swedes, and the promoters of the Gospel, who were charged as having instigated the enemy to the committal of great excesses. In the course of a month, by a furious onslaught, a large number of Protestant families was miserably butchered, which state of things continued until the Swedish General Muller advanced to restrain it.

As for Lissa, its owner the Lord-treasurer, desirous of treating for the safety of his country, went to Prussia in the hope of an interview with the King of Sweden, but failing in this he returned about the 1st of April, 1656. This excited the suspicions of the Poles, who flaming with revenge threatened destruction to the town, now industriously declared to be in league with the enemy,* and from which the Lord-treasurer at once withdrew in order to make his peace with his countrymen. But Lissa was devoted to destruction.

The inhabitants of the town were made aware of it, but depending on their strength they failed to avail themselves of the information, until on Easter day a party of hostile Poles approached the neighbourhood. In the Easter week a report was spread that the Swedish army had been repulsed, and its king slain; upon which, although the town was garrisoned by a party of Swedish horse, the people became alarmed; they therefore, keeping a strong guard night and day, sent scouts to watch the movements of the Poles. But as none were found in the vicinity they began to fancy themselves secure.

On the 27th of April, an army of Polish nobles and peasantry appeared in the neighbourhood, and approaching the town-walls,† were met by the Swedish horse, and repulsed,

---

* Gryphius in his dissertation on the writers of the seventeenth century states : "Comenius composed, I know not for what reason, a panegyric or congratulatory address upon the coming of Charles (Gustavus, King of Sweden) to Poland, which is said afterwards to have been the cause of that terrible destruction by which the city of Leszno perished. A refutation of the said panegyric is extant, in which the author is severely censured." This address was probably afterwards pleaded against Comenius as the cause of that calamity.

† Krasinski, ii. pp. 280-283, in giving an account of this catastrophe, states that the Swedish garrison wished to retire, but that Comenius persuaded the inhabitants as well as the garrison to defend themselves to the

with the loss of about a hundred men, but still continued to devastate the neighbourhood. Next day a proposal to remove the women and children to a place of safety, was negatived, on the principle that their presence would excite a determination in the men to defend the place with the greater resistance.

On the 28th, a letter from the leader of the Poles demanded the surrender of the town, under a threat of fire and sword; at the same time declaring that the Lord-treasurer had ordered the besieged to open their gates. This completely cowed the townsmen, who in a panic suddenly abandoned their arms, and with their families took to a promiscuous flight. The Swedes seeing this quitted the town, which in about an hour was thus left to the besiegers, who took possession; but suspecting an ambushment they retired from it at night. In the morning, however, they returned with many waggons laden with combustibles, and began plundering the place, killing or mutilating all they met. Before noon of the same day they set fire to every street within and without its walls, and thus destroyed the hated town, together with an abundant store of corn, victuals, wares, merchandize, household goods and treasures, which had been

last. Comenius was accused by the Poles, during the investment of the town by the Swedes, of having shewn great friendship to the enemies of their country, and hence their implacable revenge. No doubt the former connection of Comenius with Sweden formed, as it well might, the basis of this accusation; for which, however, there does not appear to have been any sufficient evidence. The statement of two Bohemian ministers seen by Mr. Pell—on the 13-23 of July was, that "the inhabitants of Lesna had promised one another to abide there, and not remove any of their persons or goods, lest they should seem to forsake those who had no means to fly, especially Comenius, whose ecclesiastical relation obliged him, as their ancientest pastor, to stay by his flock in the midst of so many hungry and enraged wolves."—(Vaughan's Protectorate, vol. ii. p. 431.)

brought hither from other places for safety. But the inhabitants, among whom was Comenius and his family, and against whom all this mischief was intended, had fled. And now the perpetrators of the mischief began to upbraid each other with their folly; the nobles, in that they had spoiled their mart and treasury, and the clergy in that instead of destroying the heretics with their nest, the birds had escaped; which was a source of much greater grief and vexation to them.*

Comenius, writing to a friend on the 22nd of May, 1656, states that he escaped from Lissa with nothing but the clothes on his back; and, besides his writings, his loss in money, books, and household stuff, was above three thousand reichs-dalers, above seven hundred pounds sterling, with which he had hoped to leave his children two hundred pounds a-piece.† And in a letter to Harsdörfer, from Amsterdam, of the 1st of September, he relates—" On occasion of the adversities in Poland and at Lissa I lost all my property, and arrived, by way of Cropen to Frankfort-on-the-Oder, in Silesia, I might almost say in a state of nudity.

"Not thinking myself safe there I proceeded to the Marquisate of Brandenburg, from whence I travelled to Stettin, and thence to Hamburg, where I was prostrated by two months illness. After numerous hardships and adventures I at length reached Amsterdam, where, driven hither by the storms of Providence, I am now in the midst of friends and well-wishers, who have received me with great kindness; and my Mecænas, who has aided me in my pansophic studies during the last twelve years, does not cease to manifest great sympathy and liberality towards me; so that I begin to overcome, in some degree, my losses. Indeed, I might even

* Relation of the distressed state of the Church of Christ, in the Great Dukedom of Lithuania. London, 1676. folio. Clarke's General Martyrology, pp. 329 to 338.

† Vaughan, ii. p. 430.

declare it to be good to be here, were it not for the grief I experience at being separated from my family, who are still in Brandenburg, and the loss of my library, and almost all my manuscripts, the fruits of nearly forty years' study."

He minutely describes his literary loss to Hessenthaler, in a letter of the same day, as including the whole of his pansophic works, which were quite prepared for the press; the "Sylvam Pansophicam," *Pansophic Forest*, a rich collection of definitions; a complete Latin-Bohemian and Bohemian-Latin Dictionary, the result of six-and-forty years' study;* and Sermons delivered during the past forty years,

---

* In his letter to Montanus, p. 74, Comenius says: "In order to make myself master of my own language, I began while living at Herborn, to compose a Thesaurus of the Bohemian language; that is, a complete lexicon, an accurate grammar, elegant idioms, sententious expressions and adages. In carefully selecting and arranging these, I have accomplished I hope, what no one else, as far as I know, has in a vernacular language.

"For I have endeavoured to establish a perfect harmony in every respect with the Latin, so as to express words, phrases, idioms, adages, and sententious sayings with similar elegance and force—positive things positively; figurative things figuratively; ancient things anciently; jocose things jocosely; proverbial things proverbially, &c.; to the end that any Latin author whatsoever may be translated into the vernacular language with corresponding elegance, and likewise our own vernacular language into the Latin.

"When this work, the labour of forty years, was nearly ready for the press, it was destroyed, together with my whole library and printing office, when the whole city of Leszno perished by conflagration, so sudden and dreadful that nothing could be saved.

"The loss of this work I shall cease to lament only when I cease to breathe; for it might have been, at least it ought to have been, an example for imitation in respect of other languages. Nothing of it remains except the first rudiments of the work, which were preserved elsewhere—a collection of all the Roots of the Bohemian language, with a large selection of derivatives and compounds." And at p. 75 of the same letter, Comenius says: "Having conceived the hope of raising the language of my native country to celebrity, I formed the plan of a great and important work, in which all things should be so described, that of what thing soever my countrymen

on ordinary and extraordinary occasions in his ministerial character, as a servant of his Church, and which were to have been the consolation of his old age, and a legacy for his son. Only a single fragment of his pansophic work had been saved.* Comenius appealed to his friends for presents of such books as were most indispensable to the pursuit of his studies, in the hope, by their united contributions, to collect together another library.

Thus Comenius, in August, 1656, was driven by the storm of oppression to Amsterdam, there to continue with his family during the remainder of his life. And now, in the sixty-fourth year of his earthly sojourn, he, whose experiences commenced long before the "Thirty Years War," the results of which he had ample time and means of contemplating, was overwhelmed with sad and gloomy feelings, in taking a restrospect of the past; unutterably augmented with the consciousness of his country being consigned to the soul-destroying influence of an anti-Christian priesthood.

Attached, soul and body, to his own particular church, and to the principles of the evangelical faith in general, it was impossible that he should ever cease to denounce the servile and demoralizing nature of the Papal system, and its workings, now impiously triumphing in his nation's tears. His

---

might need information, being thus furnished with an epitome of libraries, they might have this information at home."

"This work, which consisted of twenty-eight books, I entitled, 'Amphitheatrum Universitatis Rerum,' *Amphitheatre of the things of the Universe.* Its last revisal and publication were prevented by my sudden exile; and one of the principal parts, book second, which treated of 'Natural things,' in one hundred and twenty-five chapters, was destroyed in the conflagration at Leszno."

* Mr. Pell, in quoting Comenius's letter of the 22nd May, 1656, relates, "Those papers which have been found in the ashes and rubbish of Lesna are little worth in comparison of those which he counts irrecoverably lost, among which latter were the two libraries of the Unity of the Brethren."
—Vaughan, ii. p. 430.

writings shew him to have possessed a noble mind, imbued with an ardent love of his country and his species; constantly aiming at every thing really good, with the view to counteract the evils of his day, and being himself emancipated from the trammels of the world, while he sought no vain enjoyments therein, perhaps there were few who were capable of so much social enjoyment as himself. It is deserving of admiration, that although he never could entertain for a moment a lenient conception towards Romanism, yet its advocates, who were constantly athirst for his blood, rarely had to charge him with using personal offensive language towards them; which, considering the times he lived in, and the circumstances surrounding him, cannot be sufficiently estimated as a distinguishing feature of his character.

He knew well, too, that although Lutheranism was very far from what he wished it to be, yet that its comparative distance from Rome towards Christianity constituted its real excellence, and, therefore it was not only tolerable to him, but enabled him to give to its professors the right hand of fellowship, which he could not possibly extend to Romanists, led astray and ensnared as they were by dark superstition and foul practice. He never could divest his mind of the knowledge of his earliest years, that the Roman Church in his country had been begun in blood, continued in blood, and now triumphed in blood, and that his nation had, through the intrigues and malignity of the Papacy, been deluged by its oppressive and soul-torturing woes, and systematically made a theatre of blood from the days of John Huss and Jerome of Prague.

And the entire history of the Church of the Bohemian Brethren, as far as it has been handed down to us faithfully, shews that, as a body, while its members could not, in the nature of things, for a moment sanction a single one of the multiplied defections of Romanism from truth, as through the sacred Scriptures they became acquainted with the truth, they at the same time only sought for themselves a peaceful enjoyment of the unalienable right of humanity, the right to worship God according to the direction of his holy word, which utterly discards all self-constituted, despotic, foreign, and priestly rule, and allows the same right to others to do the like.

Romanists of sincere minds ought to know that faithful Christians, while they abhor the Papal system, have hearts streaming with love towards the persons of their fellow-men, and at all times yearning to withdraw them from Antichristian delusions which, if persisted in, must prevent them from enjoying the hopes of Christianity. It is truly surprising that a mind constituted as that of Dr. Gindely—of whose labours we have so largely taken advantage, and who speaks of "The Labyrinth of the World," by Comenius, as a work which to have written would have done honour to a saint—should be utterly unable to see that it strikes at the very root of every human invention for the repose of the soul, which can find no true peace except through faith in Christ alone, the one only Mediator between God and man.

In reflecting on the issue of the struggle between the Romanists and Protestants of the seventeenth century we have reason indeed to exclaim, how wonderful is the way of God beyond the comprehension of poor fallen man! Who can help seeing that the very means used by the great Apostacy in casting forth God's servants and dispersing them throughout Protestant Europe, became instrumental in His hands of furthering His cause among the nations, and of consigning the instruments of His will to the blindness in which, through their determination that He should not reign over them, they still continue to grope, in the comparatively noontide light of the present age?

It is positively true that the hope of the good man never fails; and hence, although the strong confidence of Comenius in the providence of God may seem to have been shaken when he beheld the ruthless destruction and dispersion of his countrymen, yet he, nevertheless, did not abandon his hope for the future, notwithstanding that to outward appearance he was a bishop without a flock—shorn of his national episcopate, he was left to make the world his see.

As soon as circumstances permitted, Comenius prepared and published, "Excidium Lesnense anno 1656 factum fide historicâ narratum," *A faithful historical Narrative of the Destruction of the City Leszno in the year* 1656, of which the foregoing account contains the leading particulars.

After the destruction of Lissa, Comenius cared with renewed zeal for the support of his countrymen, and continued throughout his life to interest himself in their behalf.

In 1657 he sent the brethren Hartmann and Cyrillus to England, there to solicit aid for his people.* They were called before the Privy Council, and their appeal met with a friendly reception. The sum of £50 was at once handed over to them to defray their personal expenses.

According to a manuscript account in the Bohemian Museum, of the English collections for the exiles, they also appealed to the Universities of Cambridge † and Oxford for assistance, and within the years 1658 and 1659, the large amount of £5,900 was forwarded to the petitioners. Of this sum £1000 were devoted to the publication of a Bible in the Polish and Bohemian languages; four parts of the residue were distributed among the Brethren driven out of Lissa and Poland, distinguishing such as were natives from such as were sojourners; and the remaining one-fifth was apportioned to natives of Bohemia living in exile, of whom three hundred and sixty families shared in the dispensation.

* Letter of Baron Sadovius to Comenius, dated, London, 14 February, 1657.

† Collections were general throughout the country, and the sums contributed by the University of Cambridge, in May and June 1658, alone amounted to £56.—Dr. Worthington's Diary, &c., pp. 108, 110.

The whole was distributed before the year 1661, and in the meantime smaller private contributions were also received from England. Comenius' own account of the distribution is given in the note below.*

* THE REVEREND FATHER COMENIUS'S ACCOUNT OF THE ENGLISH COLLECTIONS.

"*An Account of the Contributions sent by the holy Anglican Church, in* 1658 *and* 1659, *for the relief of the dispersed Bohemian and Moravian Churches.*

" In the year 1658 £5,900 were transmitted to Hamburgh and from thence to Poland. This sum was divided into five parts, of which four were given to our Brethren in Poland, whose great loss had very recently been experienced : the fifth was given to the Bohemians in Poland. The Brethren in Poland rendered accounts shewing how prudently they had distributed the portions assigned to them. I myself, together with my Bohemian Brethren, felt it incumbent upon me to render an account of the fifth apportioned to our people in Poland; we, therefore, as in the sight of God, render this account with a pure conscience. For although we are unable to produce the personal signatures of each individual who has enjoyed the blessing of these beneficent gifts, especially as many of the recipients were unable to sign their own names, we will most sincerely, not only as in the sight of man, but also as in presence of the righteous tribunal of the all-seeing God, set forth a statement shewing the greatest faithfulness in the distribution, altogether apart from personal advantage or eye-service, and under the guidance of our conscience and the pressing necessities of the several cases.

"The first apportionment of the money sent in 1648 was made in January of the next year, when our people, driven out of Poland, received the fifth part of the money, viz. . . 1486 imperials (thalers)
At the second division, on the 3rd of May,
    we received . . . . 2663¼ ,,
At the third in August, 1660 . . 376¼ ,.

    Total contributions forwarded to us . 4524¾ ,,
This sum was distributed at five different times as follows :—

        1st   1371¾
        2nd 1467⅙
        3rd   811¼
        4th   525
        5th   314
          ——=4489 4/6

Hartmann visited England again in 1668, on a mission to Prince Rupert, through whose influence he sought assistance

"This is solemnly and conscientiously attested by the signatures of the appointed distributors at Brieg (now the principal seat of the dispersed Brethren), Daniel Vetter, pastor and superintendent of all the surrounding districts, and his assistant ministers John Nigrinus, Wenceslaus Prachenius, and John Pardubius, are the principal recipients of this bounty, the vouchers of which are still extant. And thus that fifth part of the sacred bounty sent into Poland was distributed among the dispersed Bohemians and Moravians.

"Another portion of the collections made for us was sent in 1659 to Mr. Laurentius de Geer and myself, John Amos Comenius, amounting to £3000, which produced in Amsterdam 31,620 florins and 8 stubers, that is 12,642 imperials. The condition attached to this donation was, that one-third of it, £1000, be for the publication of the Holy Scriptures in the Bohemian and Polish languages, and of other wholesome books required specially at the present time. Of these and the other £2000 I have now to render account.

"The expenses connected with the books are:—

1. "The Polish Bible," copies of which are so rare that they can hardly be procured at three or fourfold their value, was published in 8vo. with royal type, new and very neat, 2000 copies.

The paper cost	693 imperials
Printing expenses	819 ,,
Casting of new types and brass title	30 ,,
Corrector 15 months board and lodging	156 ,,
Copies put together for easier transmission	20 ,,
Packing and carriage	15 ,,
Total	1733 imperials.

2. "The Bohemian Bible," of smaller size but a larger edition, namely of 3000 copies . . . 753 ,,
3. "Cancionale ecclesiasticum," *Church Hymn-book* 470 ,,
4. Similar book in the Bohemian, but of a smaller size 418 ,,
5. Bayly's "Practice of Piety," in the Bohemian . 136 ,,
6. "Consolatory Exhortation to the dispersed Bohemians" 5 ,,
7. "History of the Bohemian Brethren," by Lasitius 36 ,,
8. "Of the Benefit of Unity and the Rite of Exhortation," addressed to the Churches . . 142 ,,
9. "An Idea of true Christianity, addressed to the fallen," in German . . . 16 ,,

from the King and Parliament, but with what success does not appear.*

10. Catechetical pamphlets for our Youth in the dispersion	20	imperials.
The necessary incidentals to be added amounted to	487	,,
	4216	imperials.

Account of the other £2000 sent to Amsterdam.

First, Although our Polish Brethren are again settling on their former estates, whilst we are still tossed about in the vessel of misfortune, yet many of them being still in great want, we give them out of brotherly sympathy a fifth of the above sum, *i. e.* 1680 imperials, of which they will doubtless give an account in due time. We who still feel the lot of exile have the rest, which, in the space of three years, has been dispensed as follows:—

In 1659 there were distributed among some Barons and others of the nobility, and such of the commoners as received nothing at the first distribution, out of the sums sent to Poland, and were yet needy—all attesting by signatures their receipts .	373	imperials.
In 1660, divided between the same parties and others in great distress	497	,,
As our printing office had been destroyed in the dreadful warfares in our native land, we set up one for the use of the Church, which cost . .	886	,,
In 1661 the expenses very much increased, for when the former contributions sent to Poland had been consumed new misfortunes befel us in our long continued exile, and by reason of fresh calamities in Hungary and elsewhere, we spent up to the month of July of this year	2,287	,,

The Lord has so ordered that this barrel of meal did not waste, neither did the cruise of oil fail until the day when the Lord sent rain upon the earth, 1 Kings xvii. 14.

N.B. The list of those scattered throughout different countries who partake of your bounty, and pray to God for you I here enclose, viz.: more than 360 families.

---

* Letter of Comenius, 31 January, 1668.

Paul Hartmann, Minister of the distressed Churches of the Bohemian Confession, was in England under the Commis-

Account of the last Collections in England.

I have written to the Commissioners in England respecting the £2000, and they knew that of the sum sent immediately after the distress in Poland, four parts were given to the Polish Brethren, and ours received the other fifth. And now although they are returning from exile we have furnished them a fifth part. This has therefore been ceded to them being one-fifth of £2000 or £400, which make 1600 Imperials.

The following sums have been expended with their consent, according to directions, or as the urgency of the case demanded:—

To John Langner, a student	10 imperials.
To Samuel Gadovecius corrector of the press of the Polish Bible, his journey expense	24 ,,
The same, sent to Groningen (the expenses for one year only)	106 ,,
Journey expenses to Bremen for the same	12 ,,
A debt paid for him at Groningen	20 ,,
To Raphael Pruferus (twice 50)	100 ,,
To Fr. Paul Hartmann, by order of my colleague (twice 50)	100 ,,
To Tertius, at his request	16 ,,
To Nicholas, a theological student	6 ,,
To Paul Onias, per order	50 ,,
To John Langner, journey expenses lately repaid him	45 ,,
To Henry de Schöllen, formerly Lord of Orzechov, a magistrate, now reduced to poverty	20 ,,
Julius Alexander Torquatus	83 ,,
Jacob Blankalski, a proselyte	4 ,,
Henry Kuntz of Elbing, and Fenelius Glacius	3 ,,
John Gauske, of Lissa	4 ,,
	497 imperials.

The signatures or marks are extant to evidence these payments. To most of them a Polish Bible was given,

Moreover the Rev. colleague wrote that 300 thalers were reserved for J. A. Comenius and Paul Figulus, and which they were desired to appropriate to themselves out of any sums that might pass through their hands, to obviate the necessity of remitting this sum to them from Poland. If the 200 imperials be obtained from some other source, and 497 be

sion of a Synodal Convention at Leszno, dated 16th February, 1683, and on the 10th of July following the appeal was commended to the benevolent consideration of the pious by the Archbishop of Canterbury and the Bishop of London, as appears from the printed case of the appellants published at the time, and a letter of Hartmann addressed to his Grace James Duke of Ormond.

Annual assistance is believed to have been continued by Stephen, son of Ludwig de Geer—and Laurentius de Geer also assisted—but to what extent is not known. The Directors of the Navy at Amsterdam, in 1658, made a gratuity to Comenius of 500 Dutch florins, or 200 thalers, on his presentation to them of a few copies of his book, " Commentationes de Juventute Christiana Literis, Artibus, Prudentia Pietateque felicius imbuenda," *Observations how Christian Youth may be better instructed in Sciences, Arts, Morals, and true Godliness.*

substracted from 1600 there will remain of the last collection 1003 imperials.

Besides these there are the collections made in Holland in the autumn of last year, and again recently, which were handed over to J. Rulitius and Wittenwagel in four separate amounts, namely,

From Haarlem	$180\frac{1}{2}$ florins	=	$72\frac{1}{5}$ imperials
" Horn	160	"	=	64	"
" Alkmaar	30	"	=	12	"
" Enkhuyzen	24	"	=	$9\frac{2}{3}$	"

$157\frac{4}{5}$ imperials.

These $157\frac{4}{5}$ imperials being divided into five parts like the other sums, the Polish Brethren would receive four-fifths, *i.e.* 126 imperials, and the Bohemians one-fifth or 32. If to these 126 the balance of the English contributions 703 be added, the amount of balance is 829 imperials, which are now invested with Messrs. Schmettau, and those with the 300 above referred to, making in the whole 1,129, we shall distribute among the necessitous poor, and pray God that he would still further provide for the wants of his saints, &c. &c."

In 1665 the Earl of Pembroke sent him a remittance of £50 for his personal use, and £100 for the poor; and Comenius, in 1667, actually possessed 6000 thalers, a sum total of alms received from sources now unknown.* Of these

---

* Letter from Comenius to Gertichius, 16 Nov. 1666.

"To the Venerable Mr. NICHOLAS GERTICHIUS, Court Chaplain to the Prince of Liegnitz.

"May the love of God preserve our souls unto eternal life.

"Beloved brother and colleague,

"In replying to your two letters, rather gravely, but so much the more truthfully, many things greatly retarded me; first, because for a long time I could not obtain remittances, on account of the intricacy of the house of my patron, who, alas! is now removed from us; then my own health, enfeebled by old age and grief; and lastly, the departure of my beloved friend Rulichius, whom, on the 10th of November, we committed to the grave, as on the 13th of September we did his partner in life.

"What will become of me in the future, whom all friends here upon earth have forsaken, is known to God alone, to whom I commend my ways; that He who has guided me from my youth may direct me until He remove me hence, and finally receive me to Himself, when, at His time, I shall be gathered to my fathers, which cannot be long.

"I congratulate you on your prospects in the situation to which God has called you, in which I pray that you may serve Him. But it grieves me, that your predecessor was driven by envy beyond the limits of his fatherland. Thus all human affairs are subject to mutation, and it is the lot of all the faithful to share in the Cross of Christ, and not to have hope in Him for this life alone.

"I congratulate the halcyon days of the churches throughout Poland, if one dare rely upon it, but the turbulent sea of life everywhere agitated by the blasts from the infernal regions, scarcely permits us to consider anything safe and stable. Meanwhile we must pray and strengthen our minds against every event.

"It is not a good omen to me, that you always desire to be reckoned among the exiled, and even to take precedence of them, by applying to yourselves the alms given for the exiles, though you are not exiles, and by constantly wishing to give us, who are the really exiled, and have been so during thirty-eight years, only the one-fifth part of the contributions. You urge your larger number, but do not add, that you have already returned to your native land, from whence you were never driven for the

3500 were dispensed to the Brethren who had been exiled from Poland and the remainder to the Bohemian outcasts.

sake of religion, and that we have not yet returned. It should also be remembered that you have never obtained what has been obtained, otherwise than through our name as exiles, and with our aid; while you have had no trouble in seeking for aid, unless once or twice you signed your names when sums were paid you. If you are not mindful of this injury inflicted upon us, God will be our judge.

"We would beseech you to act unitedly with us in a brotherly spirit, by giving your counsel, and asking for the sympathy of our friends. And in this matter you see I will make a beginning—I mean of renewed love, by allowing you much more than ourselves. For dividing the whole sum of more than 6000 thalers into twelve equal parts, we will allow you seven and to our people five. There are also 300 imperials, which Mr. Stephanus advised me to keep as my own private share, and of which, according to every principle of right, both human and divine, I might retain for my own use. I send the one-half to my colleague, Mr. C. Bythner, whom I perceive to be in a particularly distressing state of poverty. Thus far, I myself have received nothing; besides which, I have given to you a part of a present given me by my patron. Accept, therefore, through Mr. Schmettau, out of those 6000 thalers 3500, but at present only 2000, the remaining 1500 you will receive in about a year's time, together with interest, which at four per cent will amount to 60, though at this time others allow only three per cent.

"I pray an early reply, that I may know how you are disposed towards me and mine, and be guided as to future contributions.

"Of news here, and especially respecting England, Br. Cornu (Horn) has been instructed to inform you, I having to write to Rev. Mr. Bythner. My fraternal love to him, and renouncing the desire of a happy meeting here below,   "Yours,

"J. COMENIUS.

"16 Nov., 1666.

"I add I have now two University students, John Cornu and David Cassius, with me, besides my own Daniel, who is also dedicated to God and His church. I propose sending for Felix Timothy, who has written from Frankfort, begging me to send him assistance for his studies, or to call him here. Thus, although I am a poor beggar, I have not been allowed to eat my bread alone; and I do not yet know how they are to be fed who are destined to feed the flock of God; but Christ, the common provider and shepherd of us all, will supply.

The distribution of these benefactions was regulated according to the rank in life, and the actual necessities of the recipients. Thus, for example, the Baron de Lukawitz, an exile who resided at Frankfort on the Oder, on one occasion received 80 thalers for himself, while several other exiles living there at the same time received only 20 thalers. The doles frequently apportioned to persons in humble life, were seldom more than from 5 to 10 florins.

It sometimes happened that considerable sums were distributed to the outcasts, in fulfilment of the testamentary instructions of wealthy Bohemians. Thus Mrs. Esther Sadowsky (maiden name Wehnic), in her will of the year 1629, directed 4,000 schock of grosschen* to be distributed among certain members of the congregations of the Brethren; out of this sum which was distributed at her death in the following year, 50 schocks were given to Johann Cyrillus, 60 to Comenius and his daughter Dorothy Crispina her godchild, 600 to poor Brethren and so forth.† Thus again, Mr. Nicholas Kocorovsky, formerly a resident at Kuttenberg, left his whole property in 1638 to the Unity of the Brethren. This, however, was not at that time very likely to reach them.

These testamentary benevolences were in reality only a continuation of practices, which prevailed among the Brethren, throughout Bohemia, during the whole of the

---

"I have not heard from Br. Paul Hartmann for the last four months, though several letters have reached me from Nigrinus, who says he cannot understand how it is that he has received no answer to his repeated communications. Thus things there are as much disturbed as here. There is endless confusion, inasmuch as the end is approaching. Amen."

* A grosschen is equal in value to about 1½d., eight groschen make 1s. Schock is a very common measure in Germany; nuts, cherries, and many other things are sold by the schock. The term means three score or sixty. A schock of grosschen is 60 grosschen or about 7s. 6d.

† List of this distribution in the Bohemian Museum.

sixteenth century. It is moreover quite evident from existing documents, that in every congregation of the Brethren there was a common fund called *korbona*, from which the poor, the sick, and the clergy were assisted. This money was not supplied by any compulsory taxation of the members, but entirely by voluntary contribution. An original document still exists in the Bohemian language, which gives a very explicit account of all such sums as were distributed between 1628 and 1633 among the exiled Brethren who had removed to Upper Hungary.

If the amounts dispensed in other places bore any proportion to those distributed in Hungary, the assistance rendered the Brethren was really large. According to the above document it appears that George Erastus, then superintendent of the Brethren at Eibenschütz, and afterwards Senior of the exiled Brethren, in 1620, sent the steward or treasurer of some congregation near the confines of Hungary, 1000 florins; a portion of which was still on hand when in 1624 the Brethren were exiled, who took up their abode in Skalic and Pucho. Skalic was the depository of this fund, to which Erastus forwarded from Lissa 350 and 150 thalers in coin for the same exiles, to whom in the course of five years the Brethren remitted in the whole 2694 thalers and 1000 florins; and according to another account 834 florins were sent from Lissa to Upper Hungary in 1636. All which fraternal benevolences were applied to meet the necessities of the nobility, clergy, and others.

Thus the Brethren in adversity and exile, cemented by the ties of Christian love and sympathy, exhibited towards each other that union which a true sense of the love of Christ alone can impart.

CHAPTER IX.

COMENIUS AT AMSTERDAM—PUBLISHES HIS DIDACTICA, ETC.
—DEFENDS CHRISTIAN DOCTRINE AGAINST HETERODOX
OPINIONS—ADOPTS MEANS TO CONTINUE THE EPISCO-
PACY AND PRINCIPLES OF THE UNITY OF THE BRETHREN
—THEIR CHURCH DESCRIBED—LETTER TO MONTANUS—
WORKS NOT COMPLETED—SCHOLASTIC PLAYS—ATTEMPTS
FOR THE CONVERSION OF THE TURKS.

At Amsterdam Comenius found himself in the midst of a community, then enjoying the largest amount of religious toleration to be found in any of the nations of Europe, and with it a great diversity of religious opinion. Unitarians, expelled from their own countries, here united themselves to the friends of speculative philosophy among the Remonstrants and Arminians; the philosophy of Cartesius (des Cartes) here found admirers even among the members of the Reformed national church. The truly evangelical Comenius also had become known to many by his writings, which, together with the influence of his patron's son, Laurentius de Geer, who continued his father's benevolence, induced rich merchants freely to entrust him with the education of their sons, so that with the additions accruing from his literary labours, Comenius found a supply of food and raiment, and was therewith content.

His literary activity was wonderful. It exhibited itself in a continuation of his previous labours, and was directed to the two great objects ever kept steadily before his mind —the expiring remnant of the Church of the Brethren, and the well-being of the whole human race; as was exemplified in his transactions with the Brethren in Poland, and his various writings; some of which were now republished in improved editions, and others were composed, or, at any rate, now for the first time published. These interruptions, from which there was no escape, greatly interfered with the completion of his pansophic work.

In 1657, the first year of his residence in Amsterdam, his didactic works were published in a folio volume, containing dissertations on subjects of elementary and scientific education. A list of its contents is given in the note below.*

---

* Comenius, in giving an account to Montanus of his Latin works, which took their rise from certain circumstances during his exile, says : " Having, at the request of the Brethren, who were grieved at the ruin of their native country, and were desirous, in the first place, if God should favour the attempt, to resuscitate the schools, began to compose certain books in our vernacular language, and some in the Latin and vernacular, adapted to the capacities of our youth ; and having at the same time permitted myself to be carried back to scholastic labours, as a means of supporting life, it happened that the works prepared for our own private use, as they were, did not long remain unknown to others. Hence, various inducements being supplied by different persons, I was of necessity, during full thirty years, continually being carried further and further out into that sea. And thus there arose in several places divers occasions of meditating of composing and of publishing various things, as is manifest from the work published in 1657 at the expense of Mr. Laurence de Geer, and printed by Christopher Cunrad and Gabriel à Roy, with the title, " All the Didactical Works of J. A. C."

In tome first are contained :—

1. A brief narration of the circumstances which first led the author to these studies.

2. The Great Didactics, shewing the method of teaching all things : here first published in Latin.

3. The School of the Maternal Bosom, or provident Education of Children during their first six years. First printed in German at Leszno in 1633, and reprinted at Leipsic by G. Gross.

4. Delineation of a Vernacular School. In regard to which Comenius writes : "Six small books were written, adapted to the six classes of the vernacular school ; these, however, were never published, as there were no opportunities of restoring the schools of my native land ; and as matters appertaining to the Latin schools were urgently demanded by others, there was no time to complete them. I therefore give here a translation of the titles only :—

In 1658 the " Orbis Pictus " appeared separately in print, being a revised edition of the " Janua Linguarum," in several

I. The VIOLARIUM (Violet bed), for Christian Youth, containing most fragrant flowers of first scholastic instruction.

II. The ROSARIUM (Rose bed) of Christian Youth, exhibiting bundles of odoriferous flowers of the instruction continued.

III. The VIRIDARIUM (Garden) of learning and wisdom for studious Youth ; in which is placed, agreeably to juvenile ability, whatever beautiful things heaven and earth and human art contain.

IV. The LABYRINTHUS (Labyrinth) of learning and wisdom for studious Youth ; in which are proposed enigmas and their answers, various interesting questions very useful for sharpening the ability and improving the memory: collected from Scripture and elsewhere.

V. The spiritual BALSAMENTUM for Christian Youth ; in which is shewn the salutary use of various human arts and sciences, and therefore of all things which are wont to occur for examination, or to be done in the course of human life: adapted to the capacity of youth in the fifth year of their scholastic instruction.

VI. The PARADISUS ANIMÆ (Paradise of the Soul), for Christian Youth, containing the marrow of the whole sacred Scripture, the principal ecclesiastical Hymns, Prayers, &c., designed to strengthen the minds of youth in Christian principle and practice."

5. Gate of the Latin Language opened : first published at Leszno in 1631, and shortly afterwards reprinted in many different nations, accompanied by a translation into their respective languages.

6. The Vestibule before this Gate.

7. David Vechner's Model of a Temple of Latinity ; with the reasons why this work did not proceed.

8. A Didactic Dissertation on a quadripartite study of the Latin language, addressed to the inhabitants of Breslau, and printed at Leszno, in 12mo. in 1637.

9. Harbinger of a Circle of all Science, printed at Oxford, in 4to. 1636 ; at London, 12mo. and at Paris, &c.

10. Various Censures on this Harbinger, which afforded occasions for further attempts of the same kind.

11. Explanations of these Pansophic Attempts: published at Leszno in 4to.

In tome second are contained :—

1. New Reasons for continuing to devote attention to Didactic Studies, containing the notice of a Description of the " Pansophia," *Circle of all*

languages, and containing a series of sections, and a woodcut to each, with explanatory notes.*

Science: published at Dantzick in 1643, and reprinted by the Elzevirs at Amsterdam in 1645.

2. New Method of Studying Languages, solidly built upon Didactic Foundations, &c.: printed for the censure and decision of the public, first at Leszno, in 8vo. in 1648, and reprinted in folio at the same place.

3. Vestibule of the Latin Language, adapted to the laws of the most recent method of languages, and exhibiting the cardinal points of *things* and of *language*. To this are annexed Rudiments of a Lexicon and Grammar, 1656. Republished at Tubingen in 1687. Balbini, Boh. Docta, p. 318.

4. New Gate of the Latin Language, exhibiting the structure of *things* and of *language* iu their natural order.

5. A Latin and German Introductory Lexicon, or Sylva of the Latin Language, explaining a multitude of derived words: published at Leszno in 1648, reprinted at Frankfort by Matthew Götz.

6. Key of a new Gate to the Latin Language, or Grammar in the Latin and vernacular language, with short commentaries, in which are assigned reasons for all changes and emendations made in the Grammar: published at Leszno in 1648.

7. Treatise on the Latin Language of the "Atrium" *Court*, exhibiting the ornaments of *things* and of *languages*.

8. Certain Opinions of the Learned respecting these and new disquisitions.

In tome third are contained:—

1. Brief account of a call to Hungary.
2. Delineation of a Pansophic School, or Workshop of Universal Wisdom, consisting of seven classes.
3. An Oration on the culture of innate capacity.
4. An Oration on Books, considered as a primary instrument for the cultivation of the innate capacities.
5. On the Obstacles found to the study of the Pansophiæ, with various deliberations as to the means of removing them.

---

* This was translated into English by Charles Hoole, who dated his preface "From my School in Lothbury, London, Jan. 25, 1658," *i.e.* old style. The 11th edition is dated in 1727; the 12th in 1777, and was by Wm. Jones of Pluckley. There was one edition published in 1672, and one in 1689. Chalmers' Biog. Dict. has a short notice of Mr. Hoole, Vol. xviii. p. 144, 145.

Then in 1659 his "Schola Ludus," *Scholastic play;* a living encyclopædia, containing a summary of arts and sciences,

6. A short and pleasant way of learning to read and to understand the Latin authors, in a triple course of instruction—the *Vestibule;* the *Gate;* the *Court:* reprinted at Amsterdam, in 8vo. in 1657.

7. Scholastic Erudition: Part first, the *Vestibule;* laying the foundations of *things* and of *language.* Published in Latin and Hungarian at Patak; in Latin and German at Tubingen, 1687; and in Latin and Belgian, with engravings, at Amsterdam, by John Seidel.

8. Scholastic Erudition: Part second, the *Gate;* exhibiting the structure of *things* and of *language.* Published in Latin and Hungarian at Patak; in Latin only, with engravings, at Schaffhausen, 1659; in Latin and German at Tubingen; and shortly afterward in Latin and Belgian, at Amsterdam, by John Seidel; also at Zullich in 1734. Balbini, Boh. Docta, p. 318.

9. Scholastic Erudition: Part third, the *Court;* exhibiting the ornaments of *things* and of the *Latin language.* Published at Patak, in 8vo. and at Norimberg by the Endters, 1655.

10. Fortius reanimated, or Idleness driven from the Schools.

11. Moral Precepts for the use of youth: published in 8vo. at Patak.

12. Laws of a well regulated School: published at Patak in 8vo.

13. Pictured World of sensible objects; or Illustration of the Vestibule and Gate of the Latin language: published at Norimberg for the third time by Michael Endter.

14. Scholastic Play, or Comic Praxis of the Gate of Languages: published at Patak in 1655, and at Amsterdam in 1656, by Abraham a Burg.

15. Cornice or conclusion of Scholastic Labours discharged in Hungary. A valedictory Oration.

16. The Blessed Guard, or Army of good deeds of a holy Soul, entering the eternal kingdom with triumph; being a funeral Oration on the death of Lewis de Geer, senior. This is noticed before at p. 93.

In tome fourth are contained :—

1. Life a Gyration; or an account of the circumstances by which it happened that the author was carried to Belgium, and then returned to resume his interrupted Didactic studies.

2. A little Boy to little Boys, or all things to all; being a supplement to the Vestibule of the Latin language; in which the primitive words are formed into little sentences: published at Amsterdam in 8vo.

3. Apology for the Latinity of the Gate of Comenius: published at Amsterdam, in 4to.

the various occupations of man at home and in public. This is in the form of a dialogue between Ptolemy Philadelphus, king of Egypt, his librarian, and other learned men.

4. Wisdom's Winnowing Fan; or the art of wisely reviewing one's own opinions. To which is annexed a short review of all the author's Didactic writings, with corrections.

5. Exit from Scholastic Labyrinths into the open plain; or a didactic machine, mechanically constructed, so as steadily to move onward without halting.

6. Latin resuscitated; or Form of a purely Latin College, or of a new little Roman state; where the Latin language may be learned by constant use as formerly, yet better than formerly.

7. The living Printing Press; or Art of impressing wisdom compendiously, yet copiously and elegantly, not on paper, but in the mind.

8. The Paradise of the Church restored, or Best condition of Schools; delineated according to the idea of the first paradisaical school.

9. Tradition of the Lamp; or a devout commendation of the study of Wisdom, and of the Christian youth and of schools, to God and men; thus placing the Cornice, as it were, on the edifice of Didactic study.

As the works comprised in this latter tome were the last of the kind published by Comenius, and contain the marrow of those preceding them, he wished them to be printed separately for the sake of those who valued such subjects. "They would make but a small book, not exceeding eight or ten sheets in 12mo., and yet would be of great utility."

It must be remarked here that the titles to some pieces of Comenius are not always immediately apparent, but when the works themselves are referred to, the suitableness and applicability of those titles are easily discovered. For example, the rather strange title of the tract, numbered 8 above, by which Paradise is represented as a model school, seems suitable enough when in the work itself we find that, although there were neither preceptors, precepts, nor books in Paradise, yet there was a threefold knowledge which comprised all knowledge—the knowledge of *God*, of the *world*, and of *man*; for Adam obtained the knowledge of God from God by listening to the Almighty Himself; the knowledge of the world from the world, by observing God's works—an instance of Adam's acquaintance with one department of this knowledge of the world is recorded by Moses, when he is said to have distinguished all the animals by names—and the knowledge of himself from himself, by attending to the actings of his own mind, of his own will, and of all the faculties appertaining to him.

About the same time some essays composed in former years; for instance, his pamphlet against the Socinian

The following " Model of Instruction," in accordance with the unrevealed things of eternity, presents a summary of Comenius' views on the subject of Scholastic Teaching; as given at fo. 121 of the Didactica, Vol. iv. " The Son can do nothing of himself, unless he see his Father do it; for whatsoever things the Father doeth, the Son also doeth these things in like manner. The Father loveth the Son, and sheweth all things unto him." John v. 19, 20.

" Hence—inasmuch as the invisible things of God are represented by the visible, Romans i. 20—we have the following results:—

1. Schools ought to be an imitation of Heaven.
2. The intercourse between teachers and learners ought to be such as that between fathers and children.
3. Children can neither know nor do anything of themselves.
4. All things, therefore, whatsoever they ought either to know or do—both here and for eternity—must be shewn unto them.
5. Such shewing forth is incumbent upon parents, that is, upon teachers;
6. Such incumbency implying not only teaching by precepts, but shewing forth by examples.
7. By presenting not only examples on the part of others but also by exhibiting examples on their own part, so that, by their doing them, things that ought to be done may be taught.
8. Imitation of all these must be, paternally, exacted from the disciples;
9. And so perfect, that they do all things in precisely the same manner. When this eternal model is disregarded, there, on the contrary, generally prevail—

1. No regard to any model—much less the best—but all things are done in any kind of manner.
2. Intercourse between teachers and learners; no other than that between mercenary shepherds and their sheep, for the sake of the fat and the fleece. Ezekiel xxxiv.
3. Disciples left to themselves, and *that* required of them which they have not yet been taught; as if they of themselves, could know what the preceptor knows.
4. All things necessary for this and for a future life not taught, but only certain small portions.
5. All things not taught by the teacher himself, but intrusted to others, or to a mute teacher—a book—presented to the learners.

Schäfer in 1658; against the Capuchin Magni's "Rule of Faith," in 1658; "Absurditatum Echo," *Echo of Absurdities*, written under the feigned name of Huldric Neufeld ;*

6. Such things as he does teach, not taught by examples, but by certain precepts, and in case that which he commands is not done, by blows.

7. Or, if he exhibit examples, exhibits those of others only, and does not shew how they may be exactly imitated.

8. Or, if he shew how to imitate, does not impress the duty of doing so with much practice.

9. Imitation not taught so perfectly that the *disciple* by doing things similar to those shewn forth, may become a *master*.

This eternal model is a summary of the whole, and I pray that it be attended to by all who undertake to instruct God's children. Here I conclude, and commend you with your schools and the whole of your youth consecrated to Christ, to the grace of God, and myself to your favour. O may the heart of every one of us so turn to the Lord that each of us may be enabled to say as Paul said: "Lord, what willest Thou that I should do?"

Do Thou, Eternal Wisdom, Jesus Christ, whose joy is in the earth and whose delights are with the children of men; to whom it was a pleasure, while dwelling with us in the flesh, to converse with little children, and to deem them worthy of Thine affectionate embraces, deem those likewise worthy of Thy favour who do not disdain to serve Thy little ones; so that through their means Thy blessed kingdom of grace here and of glory hereafter, may receive increases worthy of Thee, the King of Eternity. Amen!"

Note.—Such as possess the means and desire to study the scholastic labours of Comenius, are referred to Herder's *Humanistic Letters*, "Humanitätsbriefe," of the last century, and of our own days Charles de Raumer's *Pädegogic History*, in which works the labours of Comenius are said to be minutely described, and ample justice done to his merits in these scientific matters. Unhappily the writer has not been able to procure these works.

---

* An edition of this was published in 1668. Balbini, Boh. Docta, p. 316. Ex Chr. Aug. Heumann's Spicilegium to Vincent Placcius on anonymous and pseudonymous writings. Jena, 1711, 12mo. p. 147, § xlvii. "Judicium de regula credendi adversus Valerian Magni," *i.e. The Judgment respecting the rule of believing against the opinion of V. Magni.* This work was first published under the name of Ulrick Neufeld, and after-

and against the Socinian Zwicker, and the conduct of similar rationalists. He also wrote "Oculus Fidei," *The Eye of Faith*, against Turks, Jews, and all Infidels, especially the pseudo-rational Socinians; or the *Natural Theology* of Raymund de Sabund,* freed from tautologies and from rusticity of style, &c.: printed at Amsterdam in 8vo.

In this work, entitled "Natural Theology, or the book of Created Things," the author has distributed all created things into four classes: 1. Substances; 2. Living things; 3. Sensitive creatures; 4. Intelligent creatures: all which appertain to the knowledge of God and man; having a reference to the eternal glory of the former, and to the salvation of the latter. These are so clearly elucidated that none can contradict them. The book consists of 330 chapters, and was published at Venice, at Lyons, and at Frankfort. In reference to it Comenius, writing to his friend Hartlib, about the month of December, 1660, says, " I have in hand a very elegant little book written fully two centuries ago against atheists, infidels, and unfruitful Christians, who do not understand the mysteries of their own faith. It is so judiciously composed that I know of nothing equal to it; yet it has a great fault, the style is obscure, and throughout a great portion barbarous (the barbarity of that age), with infinite tautologies. Hence it is known to few, read by still

wards republished in Holland with the real name of the author (John Amos Comenius) prefixed. Hesenthaler, in a letter to Boineburg, which Struvius has inserted in the "Acta Literaria" (Fasciculus VI. p. 29), affirms that he heard this from the lips of Daniel, son of Comenius.

Geo. Matth. Kœnig, in his Bibliotheca Vetus et Nova, p. 572, gives the following notice of this book: " Ulrick Neufeld wrote on the Rule of Belief by Valerian Magni, Anno 1644."

* A learned Spaniard, rector of the Academy of Toulouse. His work was written between A.D. 1434 and 1436, and entitled ."Theologia Naturalis de Homine et Creaturis, seu thesaurus Divinarum Considerationum," often printed, *e.g.* at Venice, 1581, 8vo. Murdock's Mosheim, by Dr. Reid, p. 543, col. 1.

ewer, and understood by very few indeed. Feeling grieved at this, and thinking that nothing more solid could be opposed to the Socinian audacity, I began two years ago, at spare hours, to put it into a better Latin style, and now the correction is not only made, but ready for the press." Comenius, in a subsequent work,* complains that "the merchandize lies without a purchaser, the world not distinguishing between pearls and trash, attending rather to its own labyrinths than to the means supplied on every hand of being extricated therefrom." Hence we find that this improved edition, which is said to have considerable merit, and to be a rare book, "never became popular, and has met with little notice."

Besides these he addressed two letters against the Marcionite delusion, resuscitated by P. Felgenhauer, to Daniel Stoltius, physician; but since Stoltius, who had fallen into this delusion, (by which the true humanity of Christ is excluded from Christian doctrine,) had, by the help of God and this medicine, returned to a sound mind, the letters were not published.

These labours shew the interest which Comenius took in the movements and innovations in the theological world of that age, and how he exerted all his energies to prevent Christian doctrine from being injured.

In relation to these controversial writings he declares: "As God has given me a heart that is gentle and averse to strife, I have always lived mindful of the apostolic saying, 'God has called us to peace' (1 Cor. vii.), and have constantly advocated pacific counsels, provided they involved no snares, as some manifestly did." This disposition of mind led him to write certain "Irenica," *pacific counsels*, not only in his own language, as already stated, but also in Latin.

About this time Comenius employed his various talent in

* Unum Necessarium. Leipsic Edition, 1742, 24mo. at p. 145. Dr. Worthington's Diary, p. 271, 272.

some philosophical works; as, "De natura Caloris et Frigoris," *On the nature of heat and cold*, Amsterdam, 1660; &c. " Gentis Felicitas, speculo exhibita iis qui num felices sint et quomodo fieri possint, cognoscere velint," *The felicity of a nation exhibited as in a mirror to those who wish to know whether they can and how they can be happy*, was addressed to G. R. T. P. in 1654 and printed in 12mo. 1659. In the same year, 1659, he wrote a refutation of the philosophy of Cartesius, under the title, " Cartesius cum sua naturali Philosophia a mechanicis eversus," *Descartes with his Natural Philosophy overthrown by arguments derived from mechanical principles;* which was published anonymously in 1660.

Meanwhile, the affairs of the Unity of the Brethren engaged his most serious attention, and especially the maintenance of church orders through the consecration of bishops. In 1657, of all the bishops of the Unity three only survived, himself and the Polish seniors, Martin Gertichius, junior, and John Büttner (Bythner). The death of Gertichius, which happened on the 10th of December, 1657, in Silesia, was communicated by Bythner to Comenius in a letter of the 15th of January, 1658, commending to him the preservation of the episcopal office, in order that what had continued in the Unity for two centuries without interruption might not now become extinct. Comenius quite coincided with Bythner, to whom, in his letter of the 23rd of August in the same year, he says, " You see, my dearest brother, how far we are reduced, you being the only senior left of your (the Polish) branch, and I of mine (the Bohemian), each with his solitary con-senior. But as long as there remains a possibility of preventing our entire extinction, we ought to embrace it, lest it should seem as though we tempted God, who in most marvellous wise killeth and maketh alive, casts down into, and raises up his people from, the lowest depths. Shall the succession terminate immediately upon our decease?" But the execution of their object was delayed by the disturbed condition of Poland, until after the treaty of Oliva, in 1660, when their negociations were resumed.

Bythner inquired if the consecrating power lay in a single bishop, unaided by the co-operation of any other bishop? Comenius saw no impropriety in the thing itself; but as it was contrary to the usage of the ancient church, he proposed that his con-senior, Daniel Vetter, who had accompanied him from Lissa to Amsterdam, should be sent in his name, and with his credentials be present at the consecration. Bythner objecting to this, requested Comenius to make a written declaration that he approved the choice of the Synod, and of his presence in spirit at the solemnity. Comenius complied with this request, and the synodal choice and consecration of two bishops took place accordingly in 1662; namely, Nicholas Gertichius, aulic pastor to the Duke of Lignitz in Silesia, for the Polish churches; and for the Bohemian churches, Peter Jablonsky, known in his exile by the name Figulus, son-in-law of Comenius, and intended to be his successor, but he died on the 12th of January, 1670.

The declaration of Comenius includes the following sentiments: "How much I wish, beloved brethren, that my bodily presence were in your midst, more particularly on occasion of that procedure by which the ordination received from our fathers, and so highly valued by them, will be preserved to your congregation. Why should not the consecration of the man of your choice, and performed in the presence of you all, by one to whom the church has intrusted this power many years ago, be valid? Notwithstanding, I myself, absent in the body, but present with you in spirit, have resolved that the man whom your assembly, calling upon the name of Christ, has chosen for the episcopal office, shall be consecrated in your midst by the senior, my colleague, who is present, in the name of our Lord Jesus Christ, and in His power, according to apostolic practice, with imposition of hands and prayer for the Divine blessing; and I confirm this act according to the power given me by Christ and the Church. But, above all, do Thou, O Bishop of bishops, Jesus Christ, confirm thy servant, and give him an increasing measure of the gifts of Thy Spirit, that he may grow and bring forth fruit, and that his fruit may remain. Amen! Amen! Amen! Written at Amsterdam, April the 2nd, 1662, in the 71st year of my life, and with mine own aged hand,—J. A. Comenius."

Comenius, in his "Ratio Disciplinæ," lamented his efforts in relation to the succession of the episcopate for Bohemia, which during four years he had made with Bythner without success, to bring about the appointment of Figulus, his son-in-law, and while bequeathing the experiences of his church to a future age he regards the decline of the Unity in his native land as a righteous dispensation of God, certainly not on account of its separation from the Papal sway, as Dr. Gindely would leave his reader to infer, but because of its defection from its first love in Christ into a worldly spirit.

Whilst thus doing all within his power to preserve the outward form of the Unity of the Brethren, Comenius at the same time zealously endeavoured to keep alive among the remnant of his Brethren the spirit of their ancestors; hence, in 1658, he prepared for his Bohemian friends, and in their own language, the work entitled "*A Biblical Manual,*"* or the Cream of the whole Word of God, extracted from the Bible, by way of making up for the Bibles that were taken away and burnt. In 1658 a Confession of Faith; in 1659 a Hymn Book; and in 1661 a "*Catechism,* for the scattered sheep of Christ at Fulneck, Gersdorf, Gedersdorf, Klöten, Klandorf, Stechwalde, Seitendorf, and Zauchenthal;" from all which places Brethren emigrated to Herrnhut in the last century. At the close of the dedication he says: "The God of all grace grant you to be strengthened by his Spirit

* Mentioned at p. 36, 37.

in the inner man with might, that you may continue in prayer, be kept from sin, and endure in the hour of temptation and trial, to the praise of His name and your everlasting comfort in His kingdom."

But a larger and more important work than these appeared at Amsterdam in 1660, containing a "*History of the Brethren*," or as the title literally runs: "A brief History of the Slavonian Church, founded by the apostles themselves, propagated by Jerome, Cyrillus and Methodius, taking root chiefly in the Bohemian nation, and appearing in full vigour in the Unity of the Bohemian Brethren."* This little history is prefixed to a book addressed to the English Church, "which after many storms at length had gained some rest, and was now piously deliberating on the best method of organizing the ecclesiastical constitution, *On the benefit of unity and order; of discipline and obedience;*" and dedicated to the most serene King Charles, who was now restored to his kingdom. It was followed by his "Ratio Disciplinæ," *Rule of Discipline*, first written in 1616, published by the Synod in 1632, and now republished with his own original annotations.†

His object, in the history of the Slavonian church, was "to shew by example, how that the Lord leads his own to perfection by a gradual progress, according to the principle by which He controuls the works of creation, the redemption of the human family, and all acts of Divine Providence. And

* John Franciscus Buddæus, a professor of Jena, caused this book to be translated into German, and printed at Schwaback in 1739. Balbini, Boh. Docta, p. 316.

† This account of the ecclesiastical constitution of the Bohemian Brethren, a book, as important for the study of the history of their ancient Church as it is generally instructive, was published by Buddæus at Halle in 1702, and has recently been translated into German, and published by the Rev. Mr. Köppen. It was translated into English and published before the month of April, 1662; and again, probably from the edition of Buddæus, in 1703.

further by evidences of the grace and power of God; and by reminding the remnant of his people of the godliness of their ancestors, to encourage them in cherishing the faithful hope, that God would yet raise up men who should rebuild the now devastated sanctuary; for which building each and all ought, according to their ability, to collect the materials."

These addresses are worthy of grave attention. In the former, Comenius speaks in the language of one of the ancient prophets: "Persecutions, conflicts, internal discussions on points of doctrine within the church, have at all times produced the spirit of a glorious martyrdom and excellent writings, that is, exhibitions of the truth, both in word and deed. The church has invariably arisen out of its ruins in a nobler and better form, and so it will be until time shall be no more. Therefore, let empires, cities, churches, and schools fall before our eyes; God is able to raise, more than we are able to conceive, something better from their ruins, in the preaching of the Gospel to other nations of the earth. When thus contemplating the wisdom of the Divine procedure my grief at the downfal of the church of my people is assuaged.

"I now close the doors of their remaining churches before your very eyes, the last among the outlasting, for nearly the whole of their ministers, bishops, and patrons have ended their course. As in such cases, it is customary to make a will, we hereby bequeath to our enemies the things of which they can dispossess us, our churches, schools, goods and property, together, if it be the will of the Lord, with the lives too of the remnant of our people. But to you, our friends, we bequeath our mother, the Church of the Brethren. Take her in charge. It may be, God will again awaken her in our country; or raise her up elsewhere if she be dead there. You ought to love the expiring church which has given you, the living, an example of faith and faithfulness, even from the third century of our era. As of old the Lord permitted the foundations of the altar to remain, (see Ezra iii. 3) in order that future generations, in the event of their repentance and return to Him, might build thereon; so, in like manner it becomes our present duty (if the Lord has given us something true, venerable, pure, and noble, and if at any time any praise or any virtue has been found among us; and truly such was the judgment of wise and godly men concerning us) to see to it that all this be not destroyed with us, so that with our fall the foundation be demolished or rendered invisible to our posterity. And this we now do by placing this treasure in your keeping."

Such was the language of the last Bishop of the Bohemian Brethren, full of deep emotion, but still borne up with hope. In his farewell address the veteran father of his church, looking intently around him, speaks as the man who ardently longed for the advancement of Christ's universal kingdom.

The constitution of the Church of the Brethren was apostolic and not schismatic. Animated by the inward spirit which pervaded the whole, it was no merely external form; opposed to no present political frame of government, it adapted itself to all without compromising the liberty of the church, in which something of every existing form was to be found; in her episcopate, the monarchical; in her consistory (directing-board) the aristocratic; in her synods, the democracy. The second form Calvin imitated in his Presbyteries; the first was followed by Bucer in England. Was it really necessary to separate the three?

Moreover the Church of the Brethren possessed the remedy for possible evils, in her discipline; for the furtherance of true godliness; and for the abatement of simony, avarice, pride, contentions, and errors.

"My object," says Comenius, "is to communicate these privileges to the church universal, for the Church of the Brethren is a model of Christian simplicity, avoiding all doctrinal and private contentions; and even when dying we would labour like our forefathers for the universal peace of the church; or like them, in presence of the Emperor Maximilian, for the reformation of the church."

Comenius then inquires what is necessary to a true and perfect reformation of the church, and thus explains his wishes for the church universal: "In order that the church might be the kingdom of Christ upon earth, wherein all should enjoy its blessings, while the teachers lead men to Christ, and the rulers of the world are watchmen of good order in the name of God. Such a congregation of God is known by the four following characteristic marks:

"1. *Unity in the Spirit;* in Europe, Asia, &c.; such as the Unity of the Brethren had for its aim. What *we* have lost I desire may be found by *all;* or that a church may be raised up somewhere as a model for every other church.

"2. *A well regulated church government;* neither a spiritual despotism like the papacy, nor a worldly (political) rule; but a free and mutual co-operation, combined with strict regulation of life and moral conduct; or,

"3. *Good discipline;* and, above all,

"4. *Being filled with the Spirit of Christ.*"

"In the year 1646 a minister of the gospel in one of the German capitals told me he had long desired to know whether the "Ratio Disciplinæ," a book he had once read, was really the description of the constitution of a church that actually existed, or a merely imaginary ideal of such a church?" Why do you doubt it? "Because I cannot conceive the existence of a true church in this world." "Yes, it is an historical fact and no fiction. The constitution was really there; but it was not adhered to, and hence we now experience the chastisement of the Lord." "O happy people!" said the clergyman, "who still have *both* the keys; we have lost the key of binding. I know in my congregation adulterers and others who sit at the Lord's supper, and whom I cannot prevent. I have attempted it, and they called me a Papist and a Calvinist." He said no more, but sighed and wept.

"But what if such a reformation were to take place, more complete than that of Luther and others? For this purpose God, who ever employs instruments in all his works, must send the man or the men. The reformer will act at the bidding of God, by establishing that which is divine and removing what is human, neither according to his own pleasure, nor with tumultuous hurry, but through the aid of united co-operation; so that one universal church may be formed, in which *light* and *right,* i.e. a *Christian knowledge of the truth* and *Christian virtue* (walk and conversation) alike prevail."

The letter of Comenius to Peter Montanus is dated December 10, 1661, and was published by the latter at Amsterdam in 1662. In this he narrates his experiences and writings, for a list of which Montanus had repeatedly applied, until by urgent importunity Comenius was prevailed upon to yield compliance, availing himself, in case any vanity should shew itself in the attempt, of the apostolic apology, "*I have been made a fool; ye have compelled me;*" and protesting that originally he had no intention of writing—much less of publishing any thing in the Latin language. He concludes:

"Thus then, Montanus, in accordance with your desire, or that of those who have importuned you, I have given a full account of my desires, wishes, and attempts, in regard to literature and books, stating what I have done and what remain incomplete."

"If by all these efforts I have done, and am doing nothing, and neither have obtained nor am obtaining my object in some even if it were but small amelioration of the evils that every where prevail among the affairs of men; I must then acknowledge how truly Solomon has observed: '*Incorrigi-*

ble are the perverse ways of the world, and its wants are numberless.' Eccles. i. 15.

"It is truly lamentable that we all, who publicly or in private attempt any thing, exhaust our strength in vain efforts, effecting really nothing. Therefore, after repeating for the thousandth time the complaint of Seneca: '*That the life of man passes away in hoping for good; but in witnessing and enduring evil;*' the pious must seek their ultimate consolation from mortality itself, believing that we shall not be left here for ever in darkness and confusion, but shall pass through the gate of death by the merit of Christ, into everlasting light.

"With such consolation I here conclude this little narration of my Labyrinths also, and the Ariadnean threads, by which means I have endeavoured to escape them; cheered by the hope of the nearly approaching liberation from my imprisonment within this now aged, feeble, and decaying frame, and at the same time from this vast common workhouse (pistrino) of the world. Thanks unto Thee, O Lord Jesus, who hast given us a hope of better things. Farewell, Montanus."

Besides such unpublished works as are already mentioned, Comenius, in his letter to Montanus, p. 92—96, says: "I am now preparing for publication,

"1. '*The Gate of Things*,' the science called the First Wisdom, the light of the mind; and, more commonly, '*Metaphysics;*' so opened as to afford, through it, an entire view into the whole circle of things; into the whole interior order of things, and into all the co-eternal truths appertaining to things.

"2. Practice of the first Wisdom, entitled the '*General Triertium,*' that is, the Triune Key, bearing the impress of the friendly salutation of Grammar, Logic, and Practical Metaphysics, and opening up the Science, Art, and Use of Human Thought, Speech, and Actions.

"The love of peace led me to desiderate and cause to be attempted a great work, 'The whole Philosophy of Christianity;' to shew how Christians, by ceasing to contend about uncertainties, and by acquiescing in such things as are indisputable and sure, would then better know their real benefits, and, possessing these more fully, would more truly rejoice in their peculiar felicity.

"I know that many are surprised, nay, even offended that this work has not been published; but I have reasons for giving still longer time to deliberation.

"Neither is it unknown to me that certain persons suspect and surmise that I myself despair of the work; saying that it ought not to have been promised. I am not aware that it ever was promised to proceed from myself alone; my object being merely to stir up a desire for a more full and more truthful wisdom, by shewing what could be done if we seriously and earnestly made the attempt. Diffidence in one's own capacity, especially when that respects a work which is manifestly above the strength of one man, certainly ought not to be imputed to any one as a fault. Indeed, they tell me—even to my face—that no one can write a Pansophia unless he be *all-wise;* an excellence which appertains to God alone.

"Certainly God alone is wise, as is stated in Romans xvi. 27. But ought we all, therefore—as if otherwise His wisdom could in the least be lessened—to remain foolish? Assuredly we were created in the image of God, and we are commanded 'to be renewed in knowledge, according with the image of Him who created us,' Colossians iii. 10. Undoubtedly man ought to be the image, and not a mere fragment of the image of God. And God will yet grant, I humbly hope, that the necessity of my wishes—whether I myself be alive or dead—will become more and more apparent. For it is of the utmost importance for the schools and for youth, for the learned and for learning, for the Church and for the State, that the light of a fuller wisdom

should arise in the world; and that the condition of human
affairs, now everywhere prostrate and buried in confusion and
darkness, should be thus elevated and improved. So long
as I am able I will embrace every opportunity of speaking
on this subject. Let him hear who will, and let him judge
who hears."

With this letter, Montanus published three scholastic
plays written by Comenius:—

1. Faber Fortunæ, *Man the arbiter of his own fortune.*
2. Diogenes Cynicus redivivus, *Diogenes the Cynic restored
to life,* or a compendious method of philosophising.
3. Abrahamus Patriarcha, *The patriarch Abraham.* Acted
at an examination of the public school in January, 1641.

The author's apology for these, which he gives in his
address to the reader of the first, is as follows in the note
below.*

---

* " Peter Van den Berge, my friend, lately inquired of me if among my
papers, rescued from the fire, there yet remained anything worthy to be
printed, observing that he was disposed to print them. At the same time re-
marking that he had found some persons greatly delighted, even with my
short compositions, such as the " Faber Fortunæ" with the " Regulæ
Vitæ," lately published by him. I therefore searched and found records
of a certain scholastic play, when scenic exercises began to flourish about
twenty years ago in the school of Lesna, at that time under my rule.
On perusing these again, when now aged, I judged that they had been
useful in drawing forth natural abilities, and I infer the same to have
been the opinion of others from this, that within the space of one year the
same " Diogenianus Ludus" was demanded for repetition for the sake of
the illustrious guests visiting our illustrious Count, and desiring to witness
it. But I also find a MS. judgment, I know not how preserved, of a very
learned man and grave theologian, master George Vechner, then living in
exile along with us, afterwards invited to undertake the professorship of theology at Frankfort, but he preferred the invitation of the Princes of Brieg in
Silesia to the rectorate of their celebrated gymnasium, and to the superintendence of the churches in that duchy. I here cite this judgment: " S[alutem]
" P[lurimam] much health (to you) my very friendly (compater) god-
" father, your educational tractate, entitled Diogenes, greatly pleases me,
" and I wish that in the same or a similar manner were successively re-

Comenius afterwards wrote on the way and means by which the Turks might be converted to the Christian faith, so that the Slavonians inhabiting the countries on the banks of the Danube might at length be favoured to enjoy a somewhat less intolerable life. In the year 1667 he very seriously contemplated a translation of the Bible into the Turkish language, and in view of this he actually prepared a preface, the original protocol of which is in the Bohemian Museum, dedicated to the Grand Sultan, in which he commends to him the reading of the Holy Scriptures, saying: " Christians have translated the Korân and studied hard to understand its contents; it would therefore be only justice on the part of the followers of Mohamed to begin the study of the Sacred writings of the Christians, in order to make a proper choice." The objection of the Bible being spurious, he meets with many arguments. This undertaking

" presented Pythagoras, Socrates, Plato, Aristotle, Epicurus, &c. More-
" over also the chief of the great heroes, Alexander the Great, Crassus,
" Cyrus, &c. Truly in this if in any way may be impressed vividly upon
" the minds of youth, not only matters appertaining to history, but also
" the more excellent maxims, and in this way antiquity may be excellently
" learned. I do not speak of the progress which they may at the same
" time make in eloquence and prudence:—and even aged spectators will
" not be without some benefit, the more so as it is conjoined with pleasure
" and delight. Perhaps there might be introduced in the delineation
" some things tending to improve their style of language, and something
" in respect of politeness, but I do not now insist on these—it would be
" sufficient when if at any time they are presented to the public, which
" I hope in process of time may be done, &c." Such was his opinion at the time, and which I follow by now presenting to the public a specimen of a composition judged useful. We do not teach to enact Comedies, (*i.e.* to destroy the time due to the serious affairs of life, which is the practice of the impious who regard life as an amusement (Wisdom xv. 12), when we recommend to schools exercises of this kind, but that we may instil by certain gentle methods, things useful for life. Whoever may please to follow our counsel it is well—if none be so disposed it is also well.—Farewell."

did not, however, proceed beyond a mere attempt at a translation.*

* After the death of Comenius, Gerard De Geer resumed the idea of such a translation, and in 1679, assisted by Christopher Nigrinus, began to seek for persons sufficiently versed in the language. This attempt does not appear to have been successful; at least nothing is known of such a translation.

CHAPTER X.

COMENIUS MISLED BY PROPHETIC DELUSIONS—HIS CONNECTION WITH KOTTER, PONIATOVIA, AND DABRICIUS—HE PUBLISHES THEIR VISIONS—HIS OWN STATEMENT REGARDING THEM—THE ONE THING NECESSARY—HIS LAST WILL—HIS FAMILY—HIS DEATH—UNFINISHED WORK ON THE IMPROVEMENT OF HUMAN AFFAIRS—HIS PERSON AND CHARACTER—CONCLUSION.

WE have now arrived at that period in the life of Comenius which greatly influenced his subsequent history, and the estimation in which he was held by his contemporaries on account of his intercourse with the celebrated Nicholas Dabricius. His connection with this man being almost entirely forgotten in our days, shews that the character of Comenius received no indelible stain by it. It shews, moreover, that even the wisest of men, forced by circumstances surrounding them, may become so involved in chimera as to excite the ridicule and disrespect, and even the contempt of their fellow mortals. " Surely oppression maketh a wise man mad." (Eccles. vii. 7.)

The last two works of Comenius relating to the Christian public at large are in very striking contrast with each other in regard to his own mental training and inward experience of heart. The first of these, "Lux in Tenebris," *Light in Darkness*, printed in 1663,* shews us how Comenius bewildered himself in apocalyptic dreams, and became misled by the visions of others, which he regarded in the light of divine revelations. Like every other great man, he had his weak point, and this was his failing, yet closely connected with his inner life and his ardent aspirations and hopes.

The extremely agitated state of the times naturally excited

* Balbini, Boh. Docta, p. 316, says it was published at Amsterdam in 1655.

the mind of every one to look forward to the future, and a man circumstanced like Comenius would almost necessarily feel an impulsive desire to watch the apparent revelations of those better times which should introduce the restoration of his country and church, or be the commencement of a more perfect development of the kingdom of God upon earth. He had from his infancy been accustomed to witness the oppression of those around him, and driven from his home by the cruelties of anti-Christian power, was ever hoping against hope; for he was thoroughly a child of God, a devoted servant of Christ.

During his residence with Baron Sadowsky at Sprottau, Comenius had heard of the revelations of a certain tanner, named Christopher Kotter. Angels, it was said, had appeared to him, and commissioned him to announce the wrathful judgments of the Lord upon the realm of Bohemia, and the approaching deliverance.

In 1629 Comenius became personally acquainted with Kotter at Hennersdorf, near Görlitz, where the latter, having been expelled by the Papists from Sprottau, then dwelt under the protection of the Elector of Saxony. Comenius heard him relate his revelations, and wrote them down "most faithfully, as before the face of the Lord."

The affair of Christina Poniatowski is more immediately connected with the personal history of Comenius. She was the daughter of a Polish nobleman, Julian Poniatowski,[*]

---

[*] Son of John de Duchnik, grandson of Thomas de Poniaty and Duchnik, of noble descent. Having renounced the errors of the Roman system in which he had been a monk, he professed the truths of the Gospel. He was a gentle, modest, and pious man, and a learned theologian; interesting in conversation on civil matters; a philosopher and an astronomer, and pastor of the Church of Lescin in Little Poland, in the district of Kijovia. His known uprightness, humanity, and other mental and moral excellencies, had such an influence on an *aulic* servant, who, by command of a certain Romanist nobleman, was about to murder him, as to cause him to stay his hand, and to present the sword, with which he was to have perpetrated the act, to Poniatovius, informing him at the same time of his lord's

who having lived as minister and rector at Jungbunzlau, found a refuge on the estates of Charles de Zerotin, to whom he was librarian. In October, 1627, he took his daughter, then sixteen years of age, and to whom he had given a good and religious education, to the castle of the Baroness Zarubia, lady Engelburg de Zolking, of an Austrian noble family, at Brauna, near the source of the Elbe; a lady of exemplary virtue and piety, whose service Christina was to enter as lady's attendant, where, in the very next month, she fell dangerously ill, having fits and visions, during which she imagined she received revelations from Christ and his angels, chiefly referring to the current events of the day, and to the approaching amelioration of the maddening condition of the evangelic body under the malignant oppression of their persecutors.

She was brought to Lissa in Poland, where she had similar visions; and met with many, who, groaning under the same oppression, sympathized in them. Comenius in particular took a deep interest in her, and in return was regarded by her as her most confidential adviser. She told him of her approaching end; and in answer to the inquiry of the aged bishop Cyrillus, stated: "As surely as God is God, so assuredly these revelations are His work."

command. His next employment was that of preacher to Fabian Cema, commander of the district of Sztumeus in Prussia, then rector of the school of the Brethren, and assistant-preacher at Boleslavia in 1617. He was often obliged to hide himself, and often exiled for the name of Christ; was in great favour with Baron Charles Zerotin, and well worthy of the love of all good men. He died 16th February, 1628, a widower, at Namiest in Moravia. He wrote a treatise on the doctrine of the true and real presence of Christ, which was published at Basil in 8vo.; and a theological dissertation on a question recently agitated in Misnia by Dr. Matthias Hoe, against Wenceslaus, Baron of Budova: "Whether the Angels and the Inhabitants of Heaven perfectly know what God is in His own Essence?" This, which was dedicated in 1619 to Raphael Count Leszna, then Castellan of Kalisch, afterwards Palatine of Belzyce, was printed at Hanover in 1620. Regenvolscius, p. 335, 336, 402.

Soon after this, in January, 1629, she ceased to breathe, and towards the evening was laid out for burial. On the following morning she awoke perfectly well, after having before been paralyzed throughout from hand to foot. She assured Comenius that she had been with the Lord, who had commanded her to return again. From this time her visions ceased. In 1632 she was married to the brother Daniel Vetter, on occasion of the Synod of Lissa. Although her convictions respecting her visions remained unaltered, she did not speak of them, lest she should excite unworthy remarks. She became the mother of five children, Daniel, George, Johanna, Sophia, and Dorothy, and died of a catarrhal fever on the 6th of December, 1644. The entry in the church book at Lissa, respecting her birth, life, visions, marriage, and death, concludes with these words: "Thus she was born at Lissa, died at Lissa, began her life in exile, spent it in exile. She also died in exile, and is at length returned to her everlasting home, conveyed to the haven of eternal rest, after a very short earthly pilgrimage."

After this, Comenius was once more drawn into visionary revelations by Nicholas Dabricius (Dabritsky), a native of Strassnik in Moravia; from 1616 a minister of the Unity of the Brethren, and from 1628 an exile at Ledmitz in the Siebenburgen, where he lived in great poverty as the comforter of his fellow outcasts; his visions, no doubt produced in his mind under the workings of the miseries to which his exile had exposed him, began in 1643, and on the 26th of March, 1651, he imagined himself to receive the Almighty's command to communicate these revelations. Comenius, who was acquainted with him, became convinced that the man had received a divine mission to predict the destruction of the Spanish-Austrian power, as well as of that of the Pope and of the Turks, and of the establishment of the glorious kingdom of Christ. These visions and revelations continued to the 4th of January, 1663, when they closed with exhortations to all nations to repent and pray for the coming of Christ's kingdom. The seer was at length imprisoned, and, together with his writings, publicly burnt. Comenius collected all the declarations of these three visionists, and printed them in the above-named book, " Lux in Tenebris." Comenius' own narration of his intercourse with this man is the following :—

"I have known Dabricius from his childhood at Strassneck. He was five years younger than myself, and his father, a very reputable citizen of the town, held some public office as a magistrate. In 1616 he was set apart for the ministry of the word at Draholaus, near where I was, and we knew each other well, and as pastors of churches contracted a very intimate connection. I can bear testimony in the sight of God and of his church that he was very amiable in his manners, pleasant in conversation, and free from anything that might disgrace a minister of Christ. On the contrary, I can attest and declare that myself and many others discovered in him numerous rare virtues peculiar to a good Christian and minister of the church ; such as, uprightness of mind without any disguise ; love and zeal for justice which could not brook anything unjust even at the risk of offending or exciting displeasure in others ; an almost unequalled readiness to succour his neighbour when in distress, so that it might have been truly said of him, as is often said of a very kind person, *He is ready to divide his very heart.*"

Upon Comenius being driven by persecution from Fulneck he lost sight of Dabricius until many years afterwards, when he agreed that Dabricius should come under church discipline on account of his scandalous conduct :—For, driven from his post, and like many others compelled to leave his native country in 1629, and seek shelter in Hungary, he gave up all hope of ever being able to return to his ministerial duties, and entered into the cloth business ; his wife, the daughter of a cloth merchant, understanding something of the trade. But not content with sinning alone by leaving the bounds of his proper calling, he was charged with giving the same advice to others; saying, it was useless, when they had lost their churches, to obey their superiors and bow to their yoke for the sake of a trifling pittance, while they must neglect themselves and look for nothing but abject poverty.

"For," continues Comenius, "our Elders wished that all pastors deprived of their congregations and their brethren in office should not wander about begging, nor, as did some others, travel into foreign countries to solicit stipends; but wherever the Brethren in exile had found places of refuge that there they should stay with them, and although for the sake of regularity *one* should be pastor of the brethren congregated in each place, all the others should in their turn assist in the ministrations of the sanctuary and in instructing the people. And that, for this purpose, none through exile might become unused to his sacred functions, but that each should the rather stir up the others by diligent co-operative exertion; so that if God should pity and allow us to return from exile, each minister should return more strengthened for his duties. As this appeared a wise regulation it was complied with by all, with the single exception of Dabricius, who giving up all hope of returning, preferred caring for his outward temporal comfort."

"But this was not all. It was apparent that in following his earthly calling he became corrupted, and allowed himself to be drawn into the indulgence of sin by the bad example which drunkards set before him, not without detriment to his own morality. His fellow exiles wearied of his offensive behaviour, wrote to their superiors, who being then summoned to a synod in Poland, at which I was also present, proposed this question for our deliberation, 'What is to be done with brethren who create scandal? such as those who refusing to go into exile, expose either their consciences or their lives to great danger,' of whom there were examples; some of which afterwards proved to be apostates: or such as, when in exile forsook their calling, and disgraced it by a dishonourable course of life, among whom Dabricius was named as one? It was resolved, That the former be admonished to come out of the palace of Caiaphas before necessity should compel them like Peter to lament their temerity, and that the latter be suspended from his ministerial office, and that church discipline be exercised upon him, unless in his outward calling he should conduct himself with becoming propriety.

"Alarmed by this strict sentence Dabricius conducted himself more modestly until God himself reproved him, exhorting him to repentance, and awakening in him thereby the almost extinct hope of a revival of his church and of his own restoration to his former function."

The first vision Dabricius had was in the night of February 23, 1638, when he saw armies coming from the north, and heard a voice: "Fear not, nor be impatient, I myself will bring these armies and lead them onward to destroy your oppressors!" He mentioned this on the morning to his brethren, who said it was merely a dream. He himself lost sight of the matter until five years after; the second vision occurred on January 23, 1643, and others appeared to him until May of the same year. Comenius heard of these visions in July, when at Elbing, and that Dabricius had said, "Send all these words to John Amos Comenius, who will confer with others in the sight of God respecting them." This, calling Comenius' recollection to his former connection with Kotter and Poniatovia, excited uneasiness, and appears to have induced him to heed the visions as revelations from above.

In June 1654, Dabricius was readmitted to the ministerial office at the intercession of many noblemen, who regretted that his gifts should be lost to the church. Meanwhile Dabricius had various visions from time to time, and at the period when Lissa was destroyed.*

Comenius, in stating what gave rise to the publication of the above visions in the book entitled "Lux in Tenebris," relates, that "Having come to this place (Amsterdam), it was proposed to me that I should keep quiet and work out my own private literary labours. Accordingly I began to go through the Didactica, a work designed for the young. But when I received new revelations from Dabricius, with renewed exhortations addressed to myself, I communicated them first to one and then to another, and we frequently deliberated upon what should be done, that we might not anew offend either God or man. At last it was resolved that I should compile a work respecting these three different seers and their revelations, and entitle it "Lux in Tenebris;" partly because this Light was offered to the church now

---

* In the "Library" of Thomasius there is the following notice respecting the "Lux in Tenebris." "John Amos Comenius sent this book to Fabricius for his opinion on it. It is well known that those prophecies, and Comenius himself were subjected to a perplexing diversity of opinions. Nicholas Arnold (once a pupil of Comenius) dared (in 16—) to insult this most upright man, who certainly merited very different treatment from him; and Comenius failed not to brand Arnold with ingratitude. Some refer all the prophecies to Satan. Some admit them. Some approve a part of them and condemn a part. Some suggest the propriety of waiting the issue. Some judge one way and some another. Fabricius judged that there was nothing in the visions supernatural or irreconcileable with the workings of a morbid imagination, inasmuch as persons in the constant practice of reading the Scriptures, and also influenced by conferences respecting Divine aid, very easily and sometimes felicitously apply the judgments of God to the present persecutors of the church.".... But the proofs of a prophetic faculty, which some alleged that they discovered in these prophecies, when strictly examined, were not in the opinion of Fabricius entirely satisfactory."

oppressed with darkness, (see Micah vii. 8, 9, and Psalm cxii. 4,) partly because these visions were as yet to be kept in the darkness of silence. But our intention to keep them secret was not complied with, for they soon began to be extensively communicated.

"If we have erred in this matter, the Divine providence did not err, which knows how to render even the errors of man subservient to His own cause, and which so ordered it that this light could not be hidden under a bushel, but appeared before the public proclaiming our *twofold* mistake. *First*, we believed that by the unexpected arrival of the Swedish monarch with his army in Poland, that event was fulfilled which all three seers predicted; namely, that the East would unite with the North, and the fearful work of God have its commencement. But we overlooked what Poniatovia had foretold, that the union of the lions of the East and North would be not for *action*, but only for a conference at which they would not understand each other, but merely arrange matters for future action and then disperse again without *doing* anything. And as in the vision the Northern monarch was forbidden to enter Poland until after he should have arranged his affairs at home, we believed that he had so done when he revealed his plans to the Turks and Tartars (Russians), and undertook his invasion with their consent. In this we were mistaken.

"*Secondly*, The death of Ferdinand the Third about the same time seemed to confirm our hope, and we considered ourselves bound by the mandate in connection with it, regarding the publication of these words of God.

"This, therefore, and many other concurrent causes animated us not to keep the work, which was now complete, too strictly secret, with the view of its coming into the hands of some who might form a correct judgment respecting it, or of some who might themselves be the parties to fulfil some of its predictions.

"Regret for having done so very soon followed, especially with me, because every thing seemed to go contrary to the announcements after the dispersion of the two lions, which, moreover, did not result in a separation of the two parties, but from their being totally defeated.

"I the more particularly regretted three things:—

"1. That I had published such a book without first giving an outline sketch of its sum and substance in a brief memoir.

"2. That I have given the names of so many living persons, whence it is feared that numerous good and innocent men may thereby be seriously injured.

"3. That I expressed myself in the preface and in the notes so confidently, as though the truth of everything were already proved by the events. I could not but see that this might be prejudicial, and the occasion of much inconvenience; yet I greatly comforted myself in reflecting that my reviewers would hence perceive my own candour, and recognize the naked truth by the great simplicity of the style.

"It was not difficult to anticipate that every one into whose hands the book might fall would not read it with equal candour and judgment, but, taking it to pieces, would raise mountains of absurdity from it.

"It is just that man should ascribe righteousness unto God, but to himself confusion of face.—Dan. ix. 5. It is quite certain that the word of David, which came from his very heart, 'I have sinned!' was the beginning of his salvation. May our God be propitious to us all who confess our sins, from which, day after day, none is free. Amen."*

---

* Extract from Freytag's "Adparatus Litterarius," volume III. p. 776.

"Light in Darkness," that is, the gift of prophecy, with which God graciously condescended to supply and comfort the Evangelic Church, in the kingdom and incorporated provinces of Bohemia, during a period of terrible persecution and extreme dispersion for the sake of the Gospel: being revelations truly Divine, commencing in the year 1616 and continuing until the year 1656, respecting the present and future state of the Church

According to his own conviction Comenius acknowledged in after years that in this affair he had been entangled in an inextricable labyrinth. In strong contrast with which we on earth, communicated through Christopher Kotter of Silesia, Christina Poniatovia of Bohemia, and Nicholas Dabricius of Moravia : now faithfully translated from the vernacular languages into the Latin, are, in obedience to the same oracular authority, published to the glory of God, for the consolation of the afflicted and for the salutary information of all. From the year of the beginning of the liberation 1657 years." In 4to. pp. 171, 95, 204, and 136 ; excepting the prefaces 38 pages.

I have mentioned this extremely rare book, which was produced in Belgium, in my " Analecta" on rare books, p. 457, &c. It was edited by John Amos Comenius, who added an ample preface, in which he endeavours to shew, that the gift of predicting future events has not yet been taken from the Christian Church. To the preface he has subjoined a premonition against scruples. In the work itself we have :—

1. " Revelations made to Christopher Kotter, citizen and tanner of Sprottau, from the year 1616, to the year 1624, faithfully translated from the original into the Latin language."

Unquestionably these revelations had previously been translated into the Bohemian language and published; hence in this edition, the preface of the Bohemian translator, written on the 26th of May, 1625, is given in Latin. To the revelations of Kotter, which are completed in forty chapters, are appended three appendices :—1. Certain dreams of Kotter; 2. Supplements to his visions ; 3. Narrative of his incarcerations, exile, and death, &c. A German version of this edition was published with the title, *Göttliche Offenbahrungen, &c.*

2. " Revelations made to Christina Poniatovia in the years 1627-1629, faithfully translated into Latin from the virgin's own Bohemian MS." To the revelations, which are twenty-four in number, are added a historical appendix, and a disquisition on true and false prophecies, determined from sacred Scripture only, together with an application of the same to modern prophecies, namely those of Christina Poniatovia.

3. " Three hundred and forty-four revelations made to Nicholas Dabricius of Moravia, from the year 1638 to the present time, faithfully translated from the original into Latin."

This edition is fully described in " *Nachrichten von einer Hallischen Bibliotheca,*" tome 7, page 336, &c. In James Brucker's " *Critical History of Philosophy,*" tome 3, p. 628, &c. this work is reviewed ; but this first edition is erroneously there stated to have been published in 1651.

observe in his last work, published in 1668, his own heart ; the glow of his enthusiastic love for the true and the good ; his clear reasonings in combination with the ripened judg-

This " Lux in Tenebris" was attacked by Nicholas Arnold, in a work entitled "*A theological Discourse against the 'Light in Darkness,' of John Amos Comenius.*"—Franeker, 1660, 4to. Against which attack Comenius issued, "*A Vindication of the character and conscience of J. A. Comenius, in reply to Nicholas Arnold.*"—Leyden, 1660, 4to.

Freytag next notices the second edition, which has this title :—" History of the Revelations of Christopher Kotter, Christina Poniatovia, and Nicholas Dabricius ; and various incidents connected with these revelations until their publication in 1657 ; in the sight of God and with the faithful testimony borne to the Church by him, who—God so disposing—was eyewitness, collector, conservator, and editor of them all," 1659, 4to. pp. 272 and 28.

This edition, which was also printed in Belgium, is by no means so full as the former; the preface written by Comenius and many other things being omitted. The short new preface by Comenius to this edition scarcely filling four pages. This preface is preceded by a dedication to enlightened men in the Christian world, &c. The following is the order of the subjects herein adopted by Comenius :—

1. Information to the conscientious respecting the publication of the book entitled "*Light in Darkness.*"
2. History of Kotter.
3. History of Poniatovia, in which he principally follows the work of an anonymous author published in 1659 with this title :—"*The Diary of the Revelations of the noble virgin Poniatovia de Duchnick; which she had in the years 1627 and 1628; partly in Bohemia and partly in Poland.*"
4. History of the visions of N. Dabricius.
5. Judgments respecting the "Lux in Tenebris." Here those especially are opposed, who think that the gift of predicting future events has in our days been taken away from the Christian Church and discredit all apparitions and visions. For this purpose he advances many things from the "*Trial of the Spirits*" of Fabricius, by which he labours to confirm his own opinion on these matters.
6. Conclusion of the History of Revelations.
7. Resignation to the Balance—under the decision—of the Church.
8. Aspirations to God.
9. Encouragement to Christians to watch for and meet God in the way.

ment of an aged Christian. It is entitled "Unum Necessarium," *The one thing needful,* in order to become acquainted with what is necessary during life, at death, and

To my copy and likewise some others is added in the way of an appendix [of 28 pages], "*A continuation of the History of the Revelations of N. Dabricius, from the year* 1659 *to the year* 1663." Respecting this 2nd edition, there are some things worthy of notice in the *Bibliotheca* cited, tome 8, p. 69, &c. See Brucker's "*Critical History of Philosophy,*" at the place cited, and my "*Analecta*" on rare books.

Freytag having described as above the 1st and 2nd editions of these Revelations, proceeds to the abridgment of 1663 ;—" An epitome of Divine Revelations, lately made to certain persons for the use of our age, shewing in the first place, what the present terrible commotion of the world is designed to declare ; then, the incumbent duty of living earnestly in the fear of God, and of immediately making due preparation by true repentance, before the final destruction. "*Write the vision distinctly on tablets, so that he may run that readeth it.*" Habakkuk ii. 2. (A History of these matters will shortly follow), 1663, 8vo. pp. 536, and preface, pp. 22.

This third edition or Epitome of the Revelations of Kotter, Poniatovia, and Dabricius, was edited by Comenius himself, and is described in the above named " Nachrichten," &c. tome 8, p. 72, &c. The History promised was published in 1665, under the title " Lux *e* Tenebris," *Light* OUT OF *Darkness,* as will be seen in our next article, viz. *Light* OUT OF *Darkness, increased with new rays; i.e.* Revelations most solemn and divine made for the use of our age; in which are, 1. Grievous complaints respecting the extreme corruption of the Christian community. 2. God's terrible plagues denounced against the impenitent. 3. The manner in which at length God—having first destroyed the Babylon of Pseudo-Christians, Jews, Turks, Pagans, and of all nations—will constitute a new, truly Catholic Church, refulgent with the light of divine gifts. Then a view of its condition from this time henceforth all along until the end of the world. These Revelations being communicated through visions sent, and salutations angelic and divine imparted. 1. To Christopher Kotter of Silesia, from the year 1616 to the year 1624. 2. To Christina Poniatovia of Bohemia, in the year 1627, 1628, 1629. 3. To Nicholas Dabricius of Moravia, from 1638 to 1664. With the privilege of the King of kings and under favour of all the kings of the earth, these are represented for the instruction of the nations, that all may be made known to all the

after death; which Comenius, wearied with the unnecessary things of this world, and returning to the needful One thing, peoples and languages under Heaven, 1665, 4to. pp. 48, 168, 28, 536, 92, and 30, besides 55 pp. of Index.

This edition, which is by far the best, containing much more than the preceding editions, and enriched moreover with very elegant engravings from brass, was printed in Belgium. After the preface to the Christian reader, there are in the first part four dedications:—1. To Jesus Christ, the Son of God; 2. To the kings of the Christian world, and to all constituted in power; 3. To the angels of the Churches, bishops, pastors, and doctors of theology in Academies; 4. To the readers. To these dedications Comenius has subjoined an Appendix containing a portion of the preface to the first edition.

Then the Revelations made to Christopher Kotter, translated and illustrated with their history, chorographical tables, and occasionally, useful notes; followed by a fuller history of those Revelations of Kotter. Then come three appendices:—1. Revelations made by nocturnal visions; 2. Paraphrase of our Lord's prayer, dictated by angels, to Kotter; 3. This contains nothing supernatural, being a kind of general commentary on the prophecies of Kotter by that judicious theologian, John Felinus.

The second book of this first part contains the Revelations of Christina Poniatovia, translated and illustrated with an interspersed historical relation of these events, newly reprinted in sixty-five chapters. The conclusion, or 66th chapter, which treats of true and false prophets, is dedicated by Comenio (for here he has thus written his name) to his consenior, Wenceslaus Lochatius. This edition seems to have been used by the German translator, who published the Revelations of Poniatovia with the following title " *Höchstverwundersame Offenbahrungen, &c.*"

In the second part are the Revelations (614 in number) made to Nicholas Dabricius of Moravia, minister of the word of God, from the year 1638 to the year 1664; faithfully translated from the original into Latin, and preceded by a dedication to Jesus Christ, and a history of the already past portion of the Life of Dabricius. For an account of Nicholas Dabricius, his Revelations and his disastrous fate because of them, at Presburg in July 1671; see David Köler's " *Dissertation on Nicholas Dabricius, a foolish and turbulent new prophet in Hungary.*" Altorf, 1721, 4to.

The appendix to this second part in the copy I use, contains, besides a brief preface, dedicatory epistles to Leopold, Emperor of the Romans; to Alexander VII., or to him, whoever he may be, that shall next succeed

an aged man of seventy and seven years, presents to the world for its consideration.*

This work was addressed to Prince Rupert, on the 1st of March, 1668, and is, as it were, his own last will and testament, the sum of all his experiences during a long, much disturbed, and heavily afflicted life. The aged man, like Solomon of old, lamenting over so much vanity in knowledge, in all human undertakings and enjoyments, commends the character of Mary and of the true Christian, who choose the

him in the Popedom; to the most serene Kings and exalted Princes; and to the most Christian King Lewis, Emperor of France. Then, 1. Solemn dismission, by the command of God, of this prophetic volume, announcing to the world the judgments of the last age, coming forth out of darkness into light, to the most eminent heads of the Christian world, in the month of May, in the year 1667. 2. Apology for this new edition of the book, with supplications to God and men. 3. Continuation of the Dabrician visions, from the year 1664 to the year 1667. The visions now amount in number to 670.

This most splendid, nay, most rare edition, is elaborately described in tome 7, of the above "*Nachrichten, &c.*" p. 339, &c.

See Bayle's Critical and Historical Dictionary, tome 2, p. 911, &c. 1016, &c. and 1624, &c.

There is obviously much discrepancy among bibliographers respecting this book. Barbier in Anonymous and Pseudonymous books ascribes the edition of 1659 to James Fabricius, and assigns no author to the Epitome of 1663. Clericus does not mention the *Lux* IN *Tenebris*, and assigns no editor to the *Lux* E *Tenebris*. Bunemann, on rare books, speaks of this one as extremely rare, from the King of France having bought almost all the copies; and states the price to be 3 thalers.

---

* An edition of this work was published at Leipsic in 1724 by Samuel Benjamin Walther.

Ahasuerus Fritsch, an eminent jurisconsult, and a man of distinguished piety, author of "Pietas Tauleriana," and many other religious works, wrote notes to the "One thing necessary" of Comenius; but whether these were annexed to any edition of the work, or appeared separately, has not been ascertained.

One thing, the needful, the eternal; which we find through Christ in communion with him, and by him with God; and in having like him the One great object in view. This is the true wisdom for youth and age, for the learned, for servants of the state and of the church, yea, for the whole human family, if we really desire a better state of things than now exists. Towards the conclusion he speaks of himself:—

"Shall I mention my aberrations? I would the rather be silent; but since I am aware that my actions were witnessed by others, and God has placed me in a public position, I must speak as a faithful servant of Christ; it may be for the good of others.

"I thank God that throughout my whole life He has made me a man full of longing, and that, after many wanderings on my part, He has directed all my cravings to Himself, the fountain spring of every good. I discern that all my efforts thus far have resembled the activity of Martha, yet I am unconscious of having acted from any other motive than love to Jesus and his disciples, from which these efforts sprung.

"I may here mention my endeavours to promote *the better education of youth*. Many considered them unworthy a theologian's time; but I thank Christ, my everlasting Love, for inspiring me with such affection towards His lambs, and for regulating my exertions in the form set forth in my educational works. I trust that when the winter has passed they will bring forth some fruit to His church.

"I have repeatedly, and with much solicitude, undertaken the task of *promoting peace* among Christians estranged from each other in matters of faith. Very little has been published of all I have written on this subject.

"Some portion of these writings (his Prodromus Pansophiæ) was edited long ago by my friends, by which I intended to benefit the public at large, believing it easier to assist the whole than only a part of Christendom. Let no one call this a presumptuous task; I trust to the Lord that men aiming at the same object will not be wanting in the future.

"I was also with the *revelations of God* in our day, and the Lord in His providence entangled me in an inextricable labyrinth, as may be seen from my work, 'Lux in Tenebris,' which called forth much opposition and reproach. What shall I do? I know of no remedy but that of committing the whole case to God. I ought to be free to put my hand to my mouth, like David, whenever I see God do, or hear Him speak anything I cannot understand. And what shall I now say, after so many *Sisyphus-labours* of my protracted life? 'Thou, O Lord, shalt guide me with thy counsel, and afterward receive me to thy glory.'

"Whatever I may leave behind me of temporal possessions, I distribute among my indigent relations. May I have a humble cottage instead of a palace; bread and water instead of costly fare. If anything more be given me, let me praise the goodness of my God.

"If I be asked respecting my *theology*, I take up my Bible, and declare with my whole heart, 'I believe all that this book contains.' If they desire to know my *creed*, I refer them to that of the Apostles. But what will the admirers of human wisdom say to this? Probably they will laugh at the childish old man. Be it so. Yet for all that, I have found Christ! He is my all! My whole life has been a pilgrimage; I have nowhere found an abiding city; but my heavenly home is open before me, and Christ has led me to its very threshold.

"The One thing needful for myself, therefore, is this, 'Forgetting the things that are behind, and reaching towards those that are before, I press forward,' &c. (Phil. iii. 13, 14.) Thanks to Thee, Lord Jesus, who didst lead me, though often straying from my path, and lingering in my way on a thousand trifles. I bless Thee for assigning this earth only as a place of exile, and for thereby helping me, yea, compelling me onward to my eternal home!

"And as this my confession before the Lord of my return

to *the One thing needful* is at the same time my last will, therefore, my sons and daughters and my grandchildren, hear my words: 'I have no other inheritance to leave you than this,—that ye fear the Lord.' In like manner, I say to my Brethren, the remnant of my scattered church: 'Love the Lord, serve Him with your whole heart, and on no account shun the reproach of His cross.' I call all Christians, yea, all men, my brethren.

"To you, my people of Moravia, together with your neighbours the Bohemians, Silesians, Poles, and Hungarians, among whom I enjoyed many acts of kindness when in exile, I recommend the Christian wisdom of the One thing needful. Be wise! 'Luxury has corrupted the Bohemians!' was the saying of the wise King of the North. The same will soon be to be said of you Poles, unless you speedily return to temperance.

"My last refuge was in Amsterdam, where I learnt better than ever to know how much we can very well do without. But whoever and whatever community entirely loses itself in outward cares, easily forgets God, and runs into its own destruction. Do Thou, O Lord! have mercy upon all. Amen."

In this spirit Comenius reviewed his whole past course and efforts, affectionately regarding all with whom he had been connected. But, above all, his mind, occupied with a few simple, yet grand ideas, was directed heavenward.

In this his last work the vivacity of the mind of Comenius is strikingly manifest, and to this work in particular the commendation bestowed upon all his works by Herder is peculiarly applicable: "Beautiful in clearness of expression, enviable in symmetry and simplicity of thought, he never wearies in repeating, for the sake of the memory of his readers, the same subject in similar language; his object being always one, which is the welfare of his brethren, who comprised the whole human race."

In the case of such a man as Comenius we instinctively

feel interested in learning particulars respecting his family, of which Dr. Gindely furnishes some notices from the correspondence in the Bohemian museum. One could wish they were more comprehensive.

It has already been related (p. 20) that Comenius was bereaved of his first wife and firstborn son in 1622, and that soon after his settlement at Lissa in 1629, he married Elizabeth, daughter of John Cyrillus, the senior of the Brethren. A landed proprietor (probably a nobleman) in the province of Slowackia, and of the house of Lanecius, which was joined in affinity with the Marias' family of Mariasfelda, had offered him the hand of his daughter Johanna, but owing to her youth, and Comenius being in office in the church, this union was declined, when the same nobleman used his influence to secure for him the hand of the daughter of Cyrillus. They lived in happy wedlock with each other until the end of 1648, or the beginning of 1649, when she was taken from his side by death.

This union was blessed with five children, one son, Daniel, and four daughters. The elder of these was Dorothy Krispina. The second, and only one named by Palacky, was Elizabeth. A third, born 5th September, 1643, Susannah. Of the fourth nothing is known, except that she was born after that year. The probably eldest daughter is supposed to have been married to Johan Moliter, of the house of Lanecius, a nephew of the nobleman mentioned above. This Moliter had been sent by his relations to Lissa for education, and when there forming an attachment for a daughter of Comenius, he opened his mind to her mother shortly before her death, and the father not objecting to their union commended it to Marias de Mariasfelda, the young man's guardian; but it is not quite certain that a marriage took place. The second daughter of Comenius married Peter Figulus, surnamed from the place of his birth Jablonski, whom he had brought out of Moravia in 1627, then in his eighth year, and who was many years a coadjutor in his labours, and for whom Comenius had long entertained a particular affection, and was instrumental in making it possible for him to obtain a regular university education. A descendant of this union, which had been contracted prior to 1650, was Daniel Ernest Jablonski, who became court chaplain to the King of Prussia, and was a justly celebrated man. Comenius continued only for a short time a widower, but no mention is made of the name of this third wife, nor of any children by her. In the latter years of her widowhood she lived in the house of the court chaplain of the Elector, Mr. Schmettau, at Berlin, with whose family the Brethren were connected in a variety of ways. Upon his removal to Amsterdam his family consisted of his wife, his son, his second daughter, and her husband Figulus.

A few years more were appointed for the aged pilgrim, the last of which was saddened by the departure of his son-in-law, Peter Figulus Jablonski, on the 12th of January, 1671. He was only fifty years of age, and had been a Bishop of the Brethren during his last eight years. Comenius followed soon after. On November the 15th, in the same year, his faith was suddenly changed to sight, and his body was conveyed to Naerden and there interred.* He was the last Bishop of the Bohemian branch of the Unity of the Brethren. The Episcopal office was however preserved in the Polish branch until 1735, when it was revived again to the renewed Church of the Moravian Brethren.

Comenius, surrounded by many warm admirers and most nobly patronised by Laurentius, a son of Ludwig De Geer, resided at Amsterdam until his happy death, when he was still employed upon his long-deferred publication, the Pansophia. He constantly cherished the hope of completing this work, and with this view had called Christopher Nigrinus to Holland to assist in his labours. On feeling assured of his

* Dr. Gindely, p. 57. Balbini, Boh. Docta, p. 304.

certainly approaching departure he summoned his son and Nigrinus to his bedside, and drew from them, under a strong asseveration, the promise that his manuscript works should be corrected, arranged, and published. The son, in a letter to Nigrinus, refers to this death-bed scene in a very feeling manner.

The Pansophia, begun so many years before and so frequently interrupted, lay very near the heart of the dying Comenius, who believed that he should render a real service to humanity at large by its publication. It is known that Nigrinus was engaged nine years on his manuscripts at the expense of Mr. Gerard De Geer. The son of Comenius who lived alternately at Amsterdam, in England, and at Berlin, does not, however, appear to have shared in this labour. Crantz (Hist. of the Brethren, p. 70) calls this son *David*, and says that he died at Amsterdam, minister of the Bohemian exiles.

We learn respecting this work, in which he proposed to develope his method of educating all mankind and of improving general science and the whole of those occupations that engage the attention of men, that it was never printed in an entire form. The *Introduction*, or "Prodromus Pansophiæ," and the outlines or *table of contents*, "Diatyposis Pansophiæ," were published. It would, however, appear that a portion of the entire manuscripts was preserved and brought to Halle, if we may judge by the introduction of Professor Buddæus to a work published in 1702, and containing a portion of Comenius' "Opus Pansophicum," entitled "Panegersia, seu de rerum humanorum emendatione," *Universal Science, or concerning the Improvement of Human Affairs.*

In this work the writer, after appealing to all learned and godly men, and men of eminence in Europe for their united co-operation in effecting the requisite improvement of human affairs, divides the subject into three classes, *the Sciences* (or literature), *Religion*, and *Political Economy*, and shews that all three classes are corrupted and need improvement, because every individual claims the right *to know, to enjoy,* and *to rule*, yet not in the right spirit; hence the object is never attained. In literature we find the truth of knowledge; in religion, salvation or peace with God in our hearts; in political economy, outward peace: in which three points consists the character of the human family,—true humanity, the end of all our strivings. But who reaches this goal? We discover error, ungodliness, and disharmony everwhere! Hence the necessity of universal improvement in all things, and by all means; and the present confused state of things makes us feel this need most strongly and hope for it even more ardently. But we must co-operate. How? By a return to simple first principles, in order that reason, will, and resolution may be redeemed from error; by *voluntary action*, for even God does not *compel*, neither is it His will that men should *force* things; and lastly, by a *common concurrence of action* to the proper application of all the ability and means the possession and use of which the Lord has given.

On occasion of a journey to Sweden in 1646, Comenius submitted a draft of his work to the inspection of three competent persons, who pronounced it worthy of publication at the expence of the state, when completed. It is difficult to say whether it was ever entirely finished.

The character of the twentieth and last senior Bishop of the Brethren in Bohemian, is important to the whole church, which in its Bohemian episcopate had existed two hundred and four years. In the person of Comenius there was something truly patriarchal; a high moral dignity, an unparalleled simplicity of manner, a constant readiness to serve, and a purified heart full of sympathy with those in misery and destitution, were his characteristic features, and thus he exhibited those qualities which, although in a greatly inferior degree, may be discerned in the aggregate of his people.

Dr. Gindely, concluding his essay, asks whether the Brethren " would not have advanced the welfare of their native country in a much better manner if they had allowed the moral excellency, of which they were unquestionably possessed, to co-operate in conjunction with the ancient (meaning the Papal) church, which has done such glorious things for Bohemia ?"

To which it must be answered, that the entire absence of moral excellence in that apostacy rendered her altogether unable to recognize good in any shape, excepting in her own deformities, and therefore she subjected those faithful men, who would have restored apostolic faith and practice in Bohemia, to persecution, exile, and death : and eventually, by intrigue and bloodshedding, consigned that country's population, once truly Christian and free, to its present debased and abject condition, under the besotting and feline influence of ignorance, superstition, and hypocrisy in religion, and the cringing servility, helplessness, and hopelessness of the slave in the state.

In 1617 Bohemia had seven hundred and thirty-two cities, and thirty-four thousand seven hundred villages ; when Ferdinand II. died, in 1637, there remained one hundred and thirty cities and six thousand villages; and its three millions of inhabitants were reduced to seven hundred and eighty thousand.*

SUCH WERE THE GLORIOUS THINGS DONE FOR BOHEMIA THROUGH THE MACHINATIONS OF PAPAL ROME ! ! !

* Talvi, p. 195.

INDEX.

Abraham, page 136.
Adam, 121.
Albinus, Bp. 14.
Alexander the Great, 137.
Alexander VI. Pope, 11.
———— VII. 152.
Alkmaar, 111.
Alstedius, John Henry, 22.
Altorf, 152.
Amsterdam, 29, 41, 43, 47, 65, 80, 101, 103, 111, 116, 117, 119, 120, 127, 128, 131, 139, 146, 158, 159.
Anchoran, John, 29.
Andreæ, Tobias, 88.
Anhalt, George, prince of, 26.
Aristotle, 137.
Armenia, 5.
Arnold, Nicholas, 146, 150.
Atticus, 78.
Atto, Bp. of Mentz, 79.
Augsburg, 35.
Augustin, Dr. 11, 12.
Austerlitz, 16.
Austria, 9, 10, 11, 79, 141, 142.

Bacon, Lord, 53.
Balbini, 23, 24, 26, 29, 43, 77, 119, 120, 123, 129, 139.
Bangor, 41.
Barbarossa, Frederick, 79.
Barbier, 153.
Barsand, 61.
Basil, 141.
Batty, 40.
Bayle, 153.
Bayly, Bp. 41, 108.
Belgium, 149, 151, 152.
Belse, Prince Palatine of, 97.
Belzice, Palatine, 141.
Berlin, 30, 159.
Bernstein, Peter de, 34.
Blankalski, Jacob, 110.

Bliss, 68.
Bodius, 31.
Bohemia, 1, 7, 9, 148, 160, 161.
Boineburg, 124.
Boleslavia, 141.
Born, Knight of, 22, 46.
Boskovitz, Martha de, 11.
Bothsac (Botzak), John, 69.
Brandenburg, 19, 47, 101, 102.
Brauna, 141.
Bremen, 66.
Breslau, 88, 118.
Brieg, 136.
Brucker, 151.
Brumow, 21.
Brunn, 12.
Bucer, 131.
Buchanan, 30.
Buddæus, John Franciscus, 129, 159.
Budowa, Wenceslaus, Baron, 141.
Bukowiec, p. 47.
Bunemann, 153.
Bunyan, John, 29.
Burg, Abraham A', 120.
Büttner, see Bythner.
Bythner, 56.
———— Bartholomew, 56.
———— C. 113.
———— John, 126, 128.

Caiaphas, 145.
Caladrinus, 75.
Calvin, 131.
Cambridge, 89, 106.
Campen, 29.
Canterbury, Archbishop, 111.
Carpathian Mountains, 24.
Cartesius, see des Cartes.
Cassius, David, 113.
Cato, 30.
Celakowitz, 26.

INDEX.

Cema, Fabian, 141.
Chalmers, Alexander, 38, 56, 57, 119.
Chambers, 23.
Charles IV. Emperor, 2, 8.
Charles IV. of Denmark, 19.
Charles Gustavus, King of Sweden, 89.
Charles, Prince, afterwards King Charles II., 40, 129.
Chelsea, 53.
Chelzichius, Peter, 11.
Chrysostom, 29.
Cicero, 78.
Clarke, Dr. 101.
Clericus, 153.
Colovius, Abraham, 169.
Comenius, Daniel, 113, 124.
Cornu (Horn), 113.
Cracow. 98.
Cranz, David, 27, 46, 159.
Crassus, 137.
Crispina, Dorothy, 114, 157.
Cropen (Cropin), 15, 101.
Culm (Chelm), 69.
Cunrad, Christopher, 117.
Cyrill, 129.
―――― Elizabeth, 37, 157.
―――― John, 36, 37, 42, 114, 141, 157.
―――― Paul, 63, 106.
Cyrus, 137.
Czech, 7.
Czerny, John, 13.
Czerwenka, Matthias, 26.

Dabricius (Dabritsky), Nicholas, 95, 139, 142, 143, 149, 150, 151, 152.
Danet, Jacques, 44.
Dantzick, 38, 62, 64, 69, 70, 73, 90, 95, 119.
Danube, 137.
Daubrawitz, 29.
David, Dr. 41.
De Geer, Gerard, 138, 159.
―――― ―――― Lawrence, 65, 72, 96, 108, 111, 116, 117, 158.
―――― ―――― Ludwig, 53, 54, 55, 59, 60, 61, 63, 64, 65, 66, 67, 68, 69, 70, 72, 73, 74, 75, 77, 88, 93, 111, 120, 158.

De Geer, Stephen, 111.
Des Cartes, 57, 116, 126.
Dietrichstein, Cardinal, 14, 15, 16, 17, 18, 20.
Diogenes the Cynic, 136.
Docem, 38.
Draholaus, 143, 144, 145, 146, 157.
Drazovin, 45.
Dresden, 46.
Dubravius, John, 13.
Duchnik, 140, 150.
Dury, John, 56, 77.

Edmonds, Clement, 40.
Egypt, King of, 121.
Eibenschütz, 115.
Eisgrub (Lednice), 95.
Elbe, 141.
Elbing, in Prussia, 59, 61, 62, 63, 64, 65, 66, 67, 68, 72, 74, 75, 110, 145.
Elzevir, 114.
Emser, Jerome, 14.
Endter, 120.
―――― Michael, 120.
England, 69, 80, 106, 108—110, 129.
Enkhuysen, 111.
Ephronius, John, 94.
Epictetus, 85.
Epicurus, 137.
Erastus, Bp. 36.
―――― George, Bp. 36, 115.
Evinius, Sigismund, 37.

Fabricius, 146, 150.
―――― James, 153.
―――― Paul, 36, 46, 92.
Felgenhauer, P. 125.
Felinus, 152.
Ferdinand, King, 13.
―――― ―――― II. 6, 9, 16, 17, 68.
―――― ―――― III. 20, 147.
Ferdörfer, John, 84.
Figulus, Peter, 63, 64, 66, 91, 110, 127, 128, 157, 158.
Finspong, 93.
Fox, John, 43.
France, 86, 153.
Francker, 150.
Frankfort, 113, 119, 136.
―――― on the Oder, 101, 114.

Frederick, elector of Brandenburg, 19.
―――――― Palatine, 15.
―――――― II. 8.
Freytag, 148.
Fritsch, Ahasuerus, 153.
Fulneck, 16, 23, 24, 25, 27, 31, 32, 143.
Fundanius, 54, 55, 62, 63.

Gauske, John, 110.
Gay, John, 29.
Gedersdorf, 128.
Gersdorf, 128.
Gertichius, Martin, Bp. 36, 126.
―――――― Nicholas, 112, 127.
Giant mountains, 32.
Giessen; 23.
Gindely; Dr. Anton, 22, 41, 55, 56, 63, 69, 72, 89, 105, 128, 157, 161.
Glacius, Fenelius, 110.
Glogaw, 34, 97.
Glottovia, 4.
Görlitz, 30, 140.
Götz, Matthew, 119.
Goez in Zeeland, 41.
Goraj, Zbignxus de, 69.
Grigges, Ambrose, 76.
Gross, G. 117.
Gryphus, 99.
Gustavus-Adolphus, King of Sweden, 42.

Haarlam, 111.
Habrecht, Isaac, 40.
Halle, 129, 149, 159.
Hamburg, 101.
Hanover, 141.
Hartlib, Samuel, 38, 40, 49, 51, 52, 56, 60, 62, 63, 66, 71, 75, 76, 80, 89.
Hartmann, Adam, 90.
―――――― Paul, 106, 110, 111, 114.
Harsdörfer, 101.
Heidelberg, 22.
Hennersdorf, 140.
Henry III., Emperor, 8.
Herborn, 22, 23, 102.
Herder, 123, 156.
Herrnhut, 128.
Hessenthaler, 81, 102, 124.

Heumann, Chr. Aug. 123.
Hexham, vicarage, 68.
Holmes, John, 21.
Holstein, 58.
Homer, 91.
Hoole, Charles, 119.
Hoorne, 111.
Horn (Cornu), 113.
Hortowitz, 29.
Hotton, 54. 55, 62, 67, 72.
Hradisch, 16.
Hungary, 19, 29, 90, 95, 96, 119, 143, 152.
Huss, John, 2, 86, 104.

Ireland, 53.
Italy, 7.

Jablonsky, Daniel Ernest, 158.
―――――― Peter Figulus, 127, 157, 158.
Janssen, John, 38.
Janssens, the, 44.
Jena, 23, 129.
Jerome of Prague, 2, 104.
―――――― St. p. 129.
Jesuits, 14, 15, 17, 18, 79, 98.
Johnstone, 38.
Jones, William, 119.
Joseph, 90.
Jungbunzlau, 141.
Justinus, John, 79.
―――――― Lawrence, 79.

Kalisch, 141.
Kijovia, 140.
Kinner, Dr. Cyprian, 71, 73.
Klandorf, 128.
Klöten, 128.
Knoll, 26.
Köler, David, 152.
König, George Matthew, 124.
Kokorovsky, Nicholas, 114.
Komna, 21.
Koppen, 129.
Kosenbrot, Austin, 12.
Kotter, Christopher, 140, 145, 149, 150, 151, 152.
Kozae, Dr., 66, 67—Kozak, 91.
Kozmin, p. 13.
Kralitz, 14.
Krasinski, Count Valerian, 99.

Kremsier, 15.
Krispina, Dorothy, 157.
Kuenus, 16.
Kuhländel, 24.
Kuntz, Henry, 110.
Kuttenberg, 114.

La Maire, 57.
Lanecius, 157.
Langner, John, 110.
Lansbergius, Philip, 40.
Lasinsky, Boguslaus, 97.
—— — Lord, 97.
Lasitius, 36, 88, 108.
Lech, 7.
Ledmitz, 142.
Lednice, 95.
Lednik, 95.
Leignitz, Prince of, 112, 127.
Leipsic, 117, 125.
Leopold, Emperor, 152.
Lescin, 140.
Lescynsky, Count Raphael, 34, 35, 141.
Leszczynsky, 34.
Leszna, 34, 47, 80, 99, 100, 103, 104, 111, 141.
Lewis, King, 13.
—— King of France, 153.
Lczsyna, 34.
Lipsius, 28.
Lissa, 29, 34, 36, 39, 41, 42, 43, 45, 46, 47, 50, 55, 56, 63, 69, 70, 79, 80, 87, 89, 90, 92, 95, 96, 97, 98, 99, 100, 101, 102, 103, 104, 106, 109, 110, 111, 115, 117, 118, 119, 127, 136, 141, 142, 146, 157.
—— Count Bohuslav, 47.
Lissahora, 24.
Lithuania, 101.
London, 44, 51—57, 118, 119.
—— - Bp. of, 111.
Lorantfi, Susanna, 94, 95.
Lukawitz, Baron, 114.
Luther, 13.

Magdeburg, Abp. of, 2.
Magni, Valerian, 123, 124.
Mahomed, 3.
Malta, 29.
Marcion, 125.
Mariasfelda, 157.

Marienberg, 62.
Martinius, Samuel, 45, 46.
Matthias, 9, 10, 15.
—————— John, 64.
Maximilian II. Emperor, 94, 132.
Mazarine, Cardinal, 63.
Mentz, Bp. of, 79.
Menzel, Abraham, 38.
Mersenne, Marin, 55, 57.
Methodius, 129.
Michael, 11.
Miczislaus, Duke of, 34.
Milicius, of Prague, 2.
Misnia, 45, 141.
Mochinger, Dr. John, 38.
Moguntinus (Mentz), 79.
Moliter, Johan, 157.
Montanus, Peter, 24, 25, 26, 28, 31, 41, 44, 45, 71, 72, 80, 102, 117, 133, 134, 136.
Moser, Martin, 38.
Mosheim, 124.
Müller, General, 99.
Munster, 20.
Murdock, 124.

Naerden, 158.
Namiest, 141.
Netherlands, 22.
Neufeld, Huldric, 123, 124.
Newcastle-on-Tyne, 68.
Nicholas, 110.
Niclassius, Albert, 38.
Nigrinus, 114.
—— an apostate, 64, 67 ? 81.
—— — Christopher, 138, 158, 159.
—— — Daniel, 63, 66, 67 ? 90 ?
—— — John, 90 ? 108.
Nikolbourg, 16.
Noltenius, 40.
Nortcoping in Sweden, 57, 58, 59.
Nudozerin, Laurence Benedict, 30.
Nuremburg, 8, 120.

Optebekius, 75.
Orla, in Lithuania, 66, 67.
Ormond, James, Duke of, 111
Orzechovius, Baron, 110.
Oliva, 126.
Olmütz, Bishop of, 10, 20.
Olyrius, 66, 91.

INDEX. 167

Onias, Paul, 110.
Osnaburg, 83.
Ostrorog, 38.
Ovid, 30.
Oxenstiern, Axel, Lord Chancellor, 23, 58, 59, 64, 81—86.
Oxford, 52, 68, 89, 106, 118.

Palacky, Fr., 22, 26, 29, 41, 81, 157.
Paliurus, Paul, 38.
Pardubius, John, 108.
Paris, 44, 118.
Patak (Saros-Patak), 93, 94, 95, 96, 120.
Pell, Dr. John, 103.
Pembroke, Earl of, 111.
Peschech, Dr., 9, 21, 23.
Pessina, 27.
Peter, 143.
Petreus, Daniel, 63.
Philip, Emperor, 8.
Philo-Judæus, 85.
Picards, 10.
Pilarz, 27, 39.
Pirna, 29, 45.
Pius II., Pope, 9.
Placcius, Vincent, 123.
Plato, 137.
Plitt, John, 21, 26, 32, 42, 45.
Pluckley, 119.
Podiebrad, George, 9, 10.
Poland, 21, 29, 30, 32, 34, 35, 36, 64, 68, 89, 97, 98, 99, 100, 106, 107—112, 116, 126, 127, 140, 141, 147.
Poniatovius (Poniatowski), Christina, 140, 145, 147, 148, 150, 151, 152.
Poniatowski, Julian, 140.
Poniaty, 140.
Posen, 34, 35.
Posnania, Bishop of, 97.
Potter, 21.
Prachenius, Wenceslaus, 108.
Prague, 3, 5, 7, 15.
——— 23, 29, 30, 37, 45.
Prerau, 23, 29, 31.
Presburg, 152.
Pressius, Dr., 94.
Probus, Matthias, 30.
Pruferus, Raphael, 110.
Prussia, 141, 158.

Ptolemy, Philadelphus, 121.
Pucho, 95, 115.
Pythagoras, 137.

Racovia, 47.
Rakoczy, Prince George, 67, 94, 96.
——— Sigismund, 94, 95, 96.
Ratich, Wolfgang, 23, 58.
Ravius, 68.
Raumer, Charles de, 123.
Rees, Abraham, 14, 62.
Regenvolscius, Adrian, 11, 12, 14, 21, 38, 40, 46, 62, 69, 79, 141.
Reid, Dr., 124.
Ritschel, George, 68, 76, 81.
Rossigniolo, 63.
Roy, Gabriel A., 43, 117.
Rudolph, Emperor, 14, 15.
Rulichius, 112.
Rupert, Prince, 108, 153.
Russia, 147.

Sabund, Raymond de, 124.
Sadovius (Sadowsky ?), Baron, 106.
Sadowsky, Esther, 114.
——— Baron, George, 27, 31, 32, 140.
——— John George, 31.
——— Peter, 31.
——— Winceslaus-Ferdinand, 31.
Sakolcenses, 92.
Salamanca, Irish College at, 39, 40.
Saros-Patak, see Patak.
Satumeus, 141.
Savoy Palace, London, 53.
Saxony, 19, 79, 86, 140.
Scalic, 90; Skalec, 92; Skalik, 94, 95, 115.
Schäfer, Melchior, 47, 123.
Schaffhausen, 120.
Schlichting, Jonas, 47.
Schmettau, 111, 113, 158.
Schöllen, Henry, 110.
Schwaback, 129.
Securius, Peter, 90.
Sednik, 95, should be Lednik.
Seidel, John, 120.
Seitendorf, 128.
Seneca, 134.
Siebenbürgen, 94, 142.
Sigismund, Emperor, 9, 34.

INDEX.

Silesia, 30, 32, 34, 71, 97, 101, 126.
Silver, Baron, 31.
Skalitz (Scalica), 79.
Skyte, Dr. John, 58, 59, 64.
Slavke, John, 76.
Slavonians, 137.
Slaupna, 27, 32.
Slovakia, 95, 157.
Smedley, Edward, 5.
Socrates, 137.
Solomon, 51, 133, 153.
Spain, 79, 142.
Sparta, 36.
Sprottau, 33, 140, 148.
Stadius, John, 31.
Stechwalde, 128.
Stephanus, Mr., 113.
Stephen, 11.
Stettin, 101.
Stoltius, Daniel, 125.
Strasbourg, 40, 68.
Strassnick, 22, 142, 143.
Streyc, George, 94.
Struvius, Burcard Gotthelf, 124.
Sweden, 97, 98, 99, 100, 147, 160.

Talvi, 29, 161.
Tartars, 147.
Tauler, 153.
Tertius, 110.
Thomasius, 146.
Thorn, in Prussia, 38, 68, 70, 71, 72, 90.
Thurzo, Stanislaus, 10, 12.
Timothy, Felix, 113.
Timperley, C. H., 38.
Tokai, 95.
Tolnai, John, 94, 95.
Topfer, 21.
Torquatus, Julius Alexander, 110.
Toulouse, 124.
Transylvania, 19, 94, 55.
Trent, 79.
Tressan, 14.
Troppau, 32.
Tubingen, 119, 120.
Turks, 3, 29, 137, 142.

Upsal, in Sweden, 58.
Uscia, 98.

Van den Berge, Peter, 136.
Vaughan, Dr. Robert, 100, 101, 103.
Vechner, David, 118.
———— George, 136.
Vetter, Daniel, 108, 127, 142.
———— Dorothy, 142.
———— George, 94, 142.
———— Johanna, 142.
———— Sophia, 142.
Vetterinus, Paul, 94.
Vienna, 18.
Virgil, 30.
Vladislav, King, 4, 5, 12, 13.
Vladislaus, King of Poland, 71.
Vratislav, Duke, 8.

Waldensians, 10, 24.
Walther, Samuel Benjamin, 153.
Wechner, 41, 49.
Wehnic, Esther, 114.
Weissenberg, 22, 35.
Welde, William, 40.
Westphalia, 20.
———— 81.
Winchester, 53.
Winkler, George, 38.
Wollsog, Wollzog, Wolzog, 64, 65, 70, 88.
Worthington, Dr. John, 89, 106, 125.
Wratislavia, 34.
Wuerben, Count Eugene, 29.

Zamorski, Melchior, 66.
Zarubin, Baroness, 141.
Zauchenthal, 128.
Zelichovia, 47.
Zerawitz, 23.
Zerotin, Charles, 23, 26, 27, 28, 29, 30, 88, 141.
Zolking, Engelburg de, 141.
Zullich, 120.
Zwicker, Daniel, 124.

THE END.

Mothers! remember this,
The infant nestling on the earth
May live, may die, to curse its birth.

THE
SCHOOL OF INFANCY.

The principal guardianship of the human race is in the cradle, as testified by God. Isa. xxviii. 9.

It is easier to prevent than to remove corruption: nay, corruption cannot be altogether removed. Hence the saying, *All things depend on their origin*, and *As is the origin so is the issue*.

Hence also Christ: "Suffer little children to come unto me, and forbid them not, for of such is the kingdom of God." Mark x. 14.

And Solomon: "A young man duly instructed as to his way, even when old will not depart from it."

CONTENTS.

	PAGE.
I. It is demonstrated, that Children, being a most precious gift from God, ought to claim our most watchful care	2
II. Wherefore God gives abundance of Children, and how parents ought to act with respect to them	8
III. That no language can express the necessity of the good education of youth	11
IV. In what things Children ought to be exercised, so that, in their sixth year, they may be found to be proficient in those things	14
V. How a sound and prosperous health of offspring may be obtained	20
VI. How Children should be exercised in the knowledge of things	31
VII. How they ought to be inured to an active life	39
VIII. How they should be instructed in speaking, and the skilful use of language	44
IX. How they should be formed to uprightness in morals	48
X. How they should be imbued with piety	60
XI. How long they should be kept in the maternal school	68
XII. How they ought to be prepared for the public schools	71

TO

PIOUS CHRISTIAN PARENTS, TUTORS, GUARDIANS,

AND ALL

UPON WHOM THE CHARGE OF CHILDREN IS INCUMBENT,

HEALTH!

BELOVED,

Purposing to communicate something to you all respecting your duty, three things seem necessary to be premised:

I. The preciousness of the treasures which God bestows on those to whom He entrusts the pledges of life.

II. To what end or purpose He confers those pledges; and to what objects education ought to be directed.

III. That youth demand good education so greatly that, failing it, they must of necessity be lost.

Having established these three principles, I shall proceed to my purpose, and explain in order the departments of your solicitude respecting this early age—*Under Thy direction, O Father! by whom every generation in heaven and on earth is ordained.*

JOHN AMOS COMENIUS.

I.

That Children, being most precious gifts of God, and an inestimable treasure, should claim our most vigilant attention.

1. THAT children are an inestimable treasure the Spirit of God, by the lips of David, testifies (Ps. cxxvii.), saying: "Lo, children are the heritage of the Lord; the fruit of the womb His reward; as arrows in the hand, so are children. Blessed is the man who has filled his quiver with them; he shall not be confounded." Observe how David declares those to be happy on whom God confers children.

2. The same is also clear from this, that God, purposing to testify His love towards us, calls us children, as if there were no more excellent name by which to allure us.

3. Moreover, He is very greatly incensed against those who deliver their children to Moloch, (Lev. xx. 2; Jer. xxxii. 35.) It is also worthy our most serious consideration that God, in respect of the children of even idolatrous parents, calls them children *born to him;* thus indicating that they are born, not for ourselves, but for God, and, as God's offspring, they claim our most profound respect, (Ezek. xxiii. 37.)

4. Hence in Malachi (ii. 15) children are called the seed of God, whence arises the offspring of God. (Acts xvii. 29.)

5. For this reason the eternal Son of God, when manifested in the flesh, not only willed to become a participator of the nature of children, but likewise deemed children a pleasure and a delight. Taking them in His arms, as little brethren and sisters, He carried them about, and kissed and blessed them. (Mark x. 16.)

6. Not only this, He likewise uttered a severe threatening against any one who should offend them, even in the least degree, commanding them to be respected as Himself, and

condemning, with severe penalties, any who offended even the smallest of them. (Matt. xviii. 5, 6.)

7. Should any one wish to inquire why He is so delighted with little children, and so strictly enjoined upon us such respectful attention to them, many causes will be discovered. And first, if at present the little ones seem unimportant to you, regard them not as they now are, but as, in accordance with the intention of God, they may and ought to be. You will see them, not only as the future inhabitants of the world and possessors of the earth, and God's vicars amongst His creatures when we depart from this life, but also equally participators with us in the heritage of Christ, a royal priesthood, a chosen people, associates of angels, judges of devils, the delight of heaven, the terror of hell—heirs of the more excellent dignities throughout all the ages of eternity. What *can* be imagined more excellent than this?

8. Philip Melancthon, of pious memory, having upon some occasion entered a common school, he looked upon the scholars therein assembled, and began his address to them in these words: "Hail, reverend pastors, doctors, licenciates, superintendents! Hail, most noble, most prudent, most learned lords, consuls, prætors, judges, prefects, chancellors, secretaries, magistrates, professors, &c.!" When some of the standers-by received these words with a smile, he replied: "I am not jesting; my speech is serious; for I look on these little boys, not as they now are, but with a view to the purpose in the Divine mind, on account of which they are delivered to us for instruction. For assuredly some such will come forth from among the number, although there may be an intermixture of chaff among them as there is among wheat." Such was the animated address of this most prudent man. But why should not we with equal confidence declare, in respect of all children of Christian parents, those glorious things which have been mentioned above? since Christ, the promulgator of the eternal secrets

of God has pronounced that "of such is the kingdom of God." (Mark x. 14.)

9. But if we consider even their present state, it will at once be obvious why children are of inestimable value in the sight of God, and ought to be so to their parents; in the first place, on this account they are valuable to God, because being innocent, with the sole exception of original sin, they are not yet the defaced image of God, by having polluted themselves with actual guilt, and are "unable to discern between good and evil, between the right hand and the left." That God has respect to this is abundantly manifest from the above words addressed to Jonah (iv. 11), and from other passages of sacred writ.

10. Secondly, They are the purest and dearly-purchased possession of Christ; since Christ, who came to seek the lost, is said to be the Saviour of all, except those who by incredulity and impenitence shut out themselves from being participators in His merits. For the right of children to the purchased salvation remains, since they are not yet so repelling Christ, and "theirs is the kingdom of heaven." These are the purchased from among men, that they may be first-fruits unto God and the Lamb; having not yet defiled themselves with the allurements of sin; but they follow the Lamb whithersoever He goeth. (Rev. xiv. 4.) And that they may continue so to follow, they ought to be led, as it were, with the hand by a pious education.

11. Finally, God so embraces children with abounding love that they are a peculiar instrument of divine glory, as Scripture testifies, (Ps. viii. 2.) "From the lips of infants and sucklings thou hast perfected praise, because of thine enemies; that thou mayest destroy the enemy and the avenger." How it comes to pass that God's glory should receive increase from children, is certainly not at once obvious to our understanding; but God, the discerner of all things, knows and understands, and declares it to be so.

12. That children ought to be dearer and more precious to parents than gold and silver, than pearls and gems, may be discovered from a comparison between both these gifts of God: for first, gold, silver, and other such things, are inanimate, being only somewhat harder and purer than the clay which we tread beneath our feet; whereas infants are the lively images of the living God.

13. Secondly, Gold and silver are rudimentary objects produced by the command of God; whereas children are creatures in the production of which the all-sacred Trinity instituted special council, and formed them with His own fingers.

14. Thirdly, Gold and silver are fleeting and transitory things; children an immortal inheritance. For although they yield to death, yet they neither return to nothing, nor become extinct; they only pass out of a mortal tabernacle into immortal regions. Hence, when God restored to Job all his riches and possessions, even to the double of what he had previously taken away, he gave him no more children than he had before, namely, seven sons and three daughters. This, however, was the precise double; inasmuch as the former sons and daughters had not perished, but had gone before to God.

15. Fourthly, Gold and silver come forth of the earth; children from our own substance; being a part of ourselves, they consequently deserve to be loved by us, certainly not less than we love ourselves; therefore God has implanted in the nature of all living things so strong an affection towards their young that they occasionally prefer their safety to their own. If any one transfer such affections to gold and silver, he is, in the judgment of God, condemned as guilty of idolatry.

16. Fifthly, Gold and silver pass away from one to another as though they were the property of none, but common to all; whereas children are a peculiar possession, divinely

assigned to their parents; so that there is not a man in the world who can deprive them of this right, or dispossess them of this inheritance; because it is a portion descending from heaven, and not a transferable possession.

17. Sixthly, Although gold and silver are gifts of God, yet they are not such gifts as those to which He has promised an angelic guardianship from heaven; nay, Satan mostly intermingles himself with gold and silver so as to use them as nets and snares to entangle the unwary; drawing them as it were with thongs, to avarice, haughtiness, and prodigality. Whereas the care of little children is always committed to angelic guardianship, as the Lord himself testifies. (Matt. xviii. 10.) Hence he who has infants within his house, may be certain that he has therein the presence of angels; he who takes little children in his arms, may be assured that he takes angels; whosoever, surrounded with midnight darkness, rests beside an infant, may enjoy the certain consolation, that with it he is so protected that the spirit of darkness cannot have access. How great the importance of these things!

18. Seventhly, Gold, silver, and other external things, do not procure for us the love of God, nor as infants do, defend us from His anger, for God so loves infants as for their sakes occasionally to pardon parents; of which Nineveh affords an example, inasmuch as because there were many infants therein God spared the parents from being swallowed up in the threatened judgment. (Jonah iv. 11.)

19. Eighthly, Human life does not consist in abundance of wealth, as says our Lord (Luke xii. 15), since without God's blessing neither food nourishes, nor plaster heals, nor clothing warms (Wisdom xvi. 12, 26); but His blessing is always present with and for the sake of children, in order that they may be sustained. For, if God liberally bestows food on the young ravens calling on him, how much more should he not care for infants, his own Image?

Therefore Luther has wisely said: "We do not nourish our infants but they nourish us; for because of those innocents God supplies necessaries, and we aged sinners partake with them."

20. Finally, Silver, gold, gems, afford us no further instruction than other created things do, namely in the wisdom, power, and beneficence of God; whereas infants are given to us as a mirror in which we may behold modesty, courteousness, benignity, harmony, and other Christian virtues; the Lord himself declaring, "Unless ye be converted, and become as little children, ye shall not enter into the kingdom of heaven." (Matt. xviii. 3.) Since then, God has willed that children should be unto us in place of preceptors, we judge that we owe to them the most diligent attention.

II.

The purposes for which God gives children, and how their education ought to be directed.

1. Should it enter the mind of any one to inquire why it pleased the Divine Majesty to produce these celestial gems not at once in the full number which He purposed to have for eternity, as He did angels, such inquirer will discover no other reason than that, in doing so, he honours human kind by making them as it were his co-adjutors in multiplying creatures. Not however that from that source alone they draw pleasure, but that they may exercise their zeal in rightly educating and training them for eternity.

2. Man accustoms the ox to plowing, the hound for hunting, the horse for riding and driving, because for these uses they were created, and they cannot be applied to other purposes; man, however, being more noble than all those creatures, ought to be educated for the highest objects, so that as far as possible he may correspond in excellences to God, whose image he bears. The body, no doubt, being taken from the earth is earthy, is conversant with the earth, and must again be turned into earth; whereas the soul being inspired by God, is from God and ought to remain in God and elevate itself to God.

3. Parents, therefore, will not fully perform their duty if they merely teach their offspring to eat, to drink, to walk about, to talk and to be adorned with clothing; for these things are merely subservient to the body which is not the man, but his tabernacle only; the guest (the rational soul) dwells within, and rightly claims greater care than its outward tenement. Plutarch, therefore, has rightly derided such parents as desire beauty, riches, and honours, for their

EDUCATION OF CHILDREN.

children, and endeavour to promote them in these respects; regarding very little the adornment of the soul with piety and virtues, saying: "That those persons valued the shoe more than the foot." And Crates the Theban, a Gentile philosopher, vehemently complaining of the *madness* of such parents, declared, as the poet relates:

> "Were I permitted to proclaim aloud everywhere;
> I should denounce all those infatuated and shamefully wicked,
> Whom destructive money agitates with excessive zeal.
> Ye gather riches for your children, and neither nourish them with doctrine,
> Nor cherish within them intellectual capability."

4. The first care, therefore, ought to be of the soul, which is the principal part of the man, so that it may become, in the highest degree possible, beautifully adorned. The next care is for the body, that it may be made a habitation fit and worthy of an immortal soul. Regard the mind as rightly instructed which is truly illuminated from the effulgence of the wisdom of God, so that man contemplating the presence of the Divine Image in himself, may diligently observe and guard that excellence.

5. Now there are two departments of true celestial wisdom which man ought to seek, and into which he ought to be instructed. The one a clear and true knowledge of God and of all his wonderful works; the other prudence, carefully and wisely to regulate self and all external and internal actions appertaining to the present and future life.

6. Primarily, as to the future life; because properly speaking that *is* life, from which both death and mortality pass into exile; since the present is not so much life as the way to life; consequently, whosoever has obtained so much in this life as to prepare himself by faith and piety for a future life must be judged to have fully performed his duty here.

7. Yet, notwithstanding this, inasmuch as God, by bestowing longevity upon many, assigns them certain duties, places

in the course of their life various occurrences, supplying occasions for acting prudently; parents must by all means provide for the training of their children in the duties of faith and piety, so must they also provide for the more polite culture of the moral sciences, in the liberal arts and in other necessary things; to the end that when grown up they may become truly men prudently managing their own affairs, and be admitted to the various functions of life, which, whether ecclesiastical or political, civil or social, God has willed them to fulfil, and thus, having righteously and prudently passed through the present life they may with the greater joy migrate to the heavens.

8. In a word, the purpose for which youth ought to be educated is threefold. 1. Faith and piety. 2. Uprightness in respect of morals. 3. Knowledge of languages, of arts. These, however, in the precise order in which they are here propounded and not inversely. In the first place youth must be exercised in piety, then in morals or virtues, finally in the more advanced literature. The greater the proficiency that youth make in the latter also the better.

9. Whosoever has within his house youth exercising themselves in these three departments, possesses a Garden in which celestial plantlets are sown, watered, bloom, and flourish; a studio as it were of the Holy Spirit, in which He elaborates and polishes those vessels of mercy, those instruments of glory, so that in them, as lively images of God, the rays of His eternal and infinite power, wisdom, and bounty, may shine more and more. How inexpressibly blessed are parents in such a paradise!

III.

That youth imperatively demand education and to be rightly instructed.

1. It must not be supposed that youth can ultroneously and without the application of assiduous labour, be trained up in the manner described. For if a young shoot designed to become a tree, requires to be set or planted, to be watered, to be hedged round for protection, and to be propped up; if a piece of wood designed for a particular form requires to be submitted to the hatchet, to be split, to be planed, to be carved, to be polished, and to be stained with divers colours; if a horse, an ox, an ass, or a mule, must be trained to perform their services to man; nay, if man himself stands in need of instruction as to his bodily actions, so that he may be daily trained as to eating, drinking, running, speaking, seizing with the hand, and labouring: How, I pray, can those duties, higher and more remote from the senses, such as faith, virtue, wisdom, and knowledge, ultroneously come to any one? It is altogether impossible.

2. God therefore has enjoined this duty on parents, that they should wisely convey, and with all due diligence instil into the tender minds of infants, all things appertaining to the knowledge and fear of Himself; and that they should "talk with them respecting these things, whether they sit in the house, or walk along the road, or recline or rise up." (Deut. vi. 7.)

3. To the same purpose Solomon and Jesus son of Sirach, everywhere in their books agree in asserting that youth should be instructed in wisdom, and not too readily withdrawn from the rod. David having seen the necessity of the same

thing was not ashamed, although he was a king, to become a preceptor and director of youth, saying : " Come hither, ye children, hearken unto me ; I will teach you the fear of the Lord." (Psalm xxxiv. 11.) Paul the apostle admonishes parents " to train up their children in the teaching and restraining of the Lord." (Ephes. vi. 4.)

4. Since parents however are often incompetent to instruct their children ; or, by reason of the performance of their duties and family affairs, unable; while others deem such instruction of trifling importance ; it has been instituted, with prudent and salutary counsel from remote antiquity, that in every state youth should be handed over to the instruction, along with the right of chastisement, to righteous, wise, and pious persons.

5. Such persons were called Pædagogues (leaders not drivers of children) masters, preceptors, and doctors. And places destined for such exercises, were called colleges, gymnasia, and schools, (retreats of *ease* or places of literary *amusements*.) It being designed by this name to indicate that the action of teaching and learning is of itself, and in its own nature, pleasing and agreeable; a mere amusement and mental delight.

6. This gladsomeness was however altogether departed from in subsequent times, so that schools were not as their name previously indicated, places of amusements and delights; but grinding houses and places of torture for youth among certain peoples, especially where youth were instructed by incompetent men, altogether uninstructed in piety and the wisdom of God; such who had become imbecile through indolence, despicably vile, and affording the very worst example, though calling themselves masters and preceptors; for these did not imbue the youth with faith, piety, and sound morals, but with superstitions, impiety, and baneful morals, being ignorant of the genuine method, and thinking to inculcate everything by force, they wretchedly tortured the youth ; of

which we are reminded by the singular though trite dialogues. "He appears to have got a very rich vintage of blows upon his shoulder blades," and "He was repeatedly brought to the lash." For other mode of instructions than with severity of rods and atrocity of blows, was unknown.

7. Although our predecessors, together with Ecclesiastical Reformation, somewhat amended this state of things, yet God has reserved for our age some things to be amended by a more easy, compendious, and solid instruction, to His own glory, and our comfort.

8. Now I proceed, depending upon the blessing of God, to the form or idea of the proposed method of education, to be applied, especially in the maternal school, during the first six years of age.

IV.

In what things youth ought to be exercised gradually from their very birth, so that they may be found expert in those things in the sixth year of their age.

1. Every one knows that whatever disposition the branches of an old tree severally obtain they must necessarily have been so formed from its first growth, for they cannot be otherwise. The animal also unless it receive in its very first formation, the foundations of all its members, no one expects that it would ever receive them, for who can amend that which was born lame, blind, defective, or deformed? Man therefore in the very first formation of body and soul should be moulded so as to be such as he ought to be throughout his whole life.

2. For although God can bring an inveterately bad man to be profitable by completely transforming him; yet in the regular course of nature, it scarcely ever happens otherwise, than that as any thing has begun to be formed from its origin, so it becomes completed, and so it remains. Whatever seed any one has sown in his youth, such fruits he reaps in old age, according to the saying, "The pursuits of youth are the delights of age."

3. Let not parents, therefore, devolve the instruction of their children upon preceptors of schools and ministers of the church. Since it is impossible to make the tree straight that has grown crooked, or to produce an orchard from a forest every where surrounded with briars and thorns. But they ought *themselves* to know the modes of managing their own treasures according to their preciousness; to

the end that, under their *own* hands they may receive increases of wisdom and grace before God and men.

4. And inasmuch as every one ought to be competent to serve God and be useful to men, we maintain that he ought to be instructed in Piety, in Morals, and Sound Learning: that parents should therefore lay the foundations of these three in the very earliest age of their children. How far these need to be extended during the first six years must be severally shewn.

5. PIETY, true and salutary, consists in these three things:
 I. *That our hearts, having always and every where respect towards God, should seek Him in all that we do and say and think.*
 II. *Having discovered the steps of Divine Providence, our heart should follow God always and every where with reverence, love, and ready obedience.*
 III. *And thus always and every where mindful of God, conversing with God, our heart joining itself to God, it realizes peace, consolation, and joy.*

6. This is true Piety, bringing to man a paradise of divine pleasure; the foundations of which may be so impressed upon a boy within the space of six years, as that he may know, 1. that there is a God; 2. who, being everywhere present, He beholds us all; 3. that He bestows abundantly, food, drink, clothing, and all things upon such as obey Him; 4. but punishes with death the stubborn and immoral; therefore, 5. that He ought to be feared, always to be invoked and loved as a father; and 6. that all things ought to be done which He commands; 7. that, if we be good and righteous, He will take us to the heavens, &c. I maintain that an infant may be led on in these exercises until the sixth year of his age.

7. Children ought to be instructed in MORALS and VIRTUE, especially in the following: 1. In temperance, that they may learn to eat and drink according to the wants of nature;

not to eat greedily or cram themselves with food and drink beyond what is sufficient. 2. In cleanliness and decorum; so that, as concerns food, dress, and care of the body, they may be accustomed to observe decency. 3. In respect towards superiors, whose actions, conversations and instructions they should learn to revere. 4. In complaisance; so that they may be prompt to execute all things immediately at the nod and voice of their superiors. 5. It is especially necessary that they be accustomed to speak truth, so that all their words may be in accordance with the teaching of Christ; "*that which is, is; that which is not, is not.*" They should on no account be accustomed to utter falsehood, or to speak of any thing otherwise than it really is, either seriously or in mirth. 6. They must likewise be trained to justice; so as not to touch, move stealthily, withdraw or hide any thing belonging to another; or to wrong another in any respect. 7. Benignity ought also to be instilled into them, and a love of pleasing others, so that they may be generous, and neither niggardly nor envious. 8. It is especially profitable for them to be so accustomed to labour, as to acquire an aversion to indolence. 9. They should be taught not only to speak, but also to be silent when needful; for instance, during prayer or while others are speaking. 10. They ought to be exercised in patience, so that they may not expect that all things should be done at their nod; from their earliest age they should gradually be taught to restrain their desires. 11. They should serve their elders with civility and readiness. This being an essential ornament of youth, they should be trained to it from their infancy. 12. From what has been said courteousness will arise, by which they may learn to shew good behaviour to every one, to impart safety, to join hands, to bend the knee, to give thanks for little gifts, &c. 13. To avoid the appearance of levity or rudeness, let them at the same time learn gravity of deportment, so as to do all things modestly and gracefully.

A child initiated in such virtues will easily, as occurred in the case of Christ, obtain for itself the favour of God and man.

8. As to sound learning, it admits of a threefold division, for we learn *to know* some things, *to do* some things, and *to say* some things; or rather, we learn to know, to do, and to say *all* things, except such as are bad.

9. A child in the first six years may begin to know, 1. Natural things, provided it knows the names of the elements, fire, air, water, and earth; and learn to name rain, snow, ice, lead, iron, &c. Likewise trees and some of the better known and more common plants, violets, clove-trees, and roses. Likewise, the difference between animals: what is a bird, what are cattle, what is a horse, &c. Finally, the outward members of its own body; how they ought to be named, for what use designed; as the ears for hearing, the feet for running, &c. Of *optics* it will suffice for children to know what is darkness, what is light, and the difference between the more common colours and their names. 3. In *astronomy*, to discern between the sun, moon, and stars. 4. In *geography*, to know whether the place in which it was born and in which it lives, be a village, a city, a town, or a citadel. What is a field, a mountain, a forest, a meadow, a river. 5. The child's first instruction in *chronology* will be to know what is an hour, a day, a week, a month, a year; what is spring, summer, &c. 6. The beginning of *history* will be to be able to remember what was done yesterday, what recently, what a year ago, what two years or three years ago. This however is puerile, and the remembrance of such things is obscure and as it were through a cloud. 7. *Household affairs*, to distinguish who belongs to the family and who does not. 8. In *politics*, that there is in the state a chief ruler, ministers and legislators; and that there are occasional assemblies of the nation.

10. As to Actions, some have respect to the mind, and the

tongue, as dialectics, arithmetic, geometry, and music; some respect the mind and hand, such as labours and corporeal actions. 1. The principles of *dialectics* may be so far imbibed as that a child may know what is a question, and what an answer; and be able to reply distinctly to a question proposed, not talking about onions when the question is about garlick. 2. *Arithmetic*, the foundation of which will be to know, that something is much or little, to be able to count to twenty, or even all the way to sixty, and to understand what is an even and what an odd number; likewise that three are more than two, and that three and one make four, &c. 3. In *geometry*, to know what is small or large, short or long, narrow or broad, thin or thick; likewise what is an inch, a nail, a foot, a yard, an ell, &c. 4. The child's *music* will be to be able to sing from memory some little verses from the Psalms or Hymns. 5. As to the mind and hand; the beginning of every labour or work of art, is to cut, to split, to carve, to strew, to arrange, to tie, to untie, to roll up, and to unroll, such things being familiar to all children.

11. As to *language*, propriety is obtained by grammar, rhetoric, and poetry. 1. The *grammar* of the first six years in question, will be that the child should be able to express in language so much as it knows of things, though it speak imperfectly, yet let it be to the point, and so articulated as that it may be understood. 2. Their *rhetoric* will be, to use natural actions, and, in case they hear, to understand and repeat a trope or a figure. 3. Their rudiments in *poetry* will be to commit to memory certain verses or rhymes.

12. Care must be taken as to the method adopted with infants in these several things; not apportioning them instruction precisely to certain years or months (as will afterwards be done in the other schools), but generally only; and that for the following reasons:—1. Because all parents cannot observe such order in their homes as obtains in public schools, where no extraordinary matters disturb the regular

course of things. 2. Because in this early infantine age all children are not endowed with equal ability; some beginning to speak in the first year, some in the second, and some in the third.

13. I will therefore shew, in a general way, how infants should be instructed during the first six years. 1. In a knowledge of things. 2. In labours with activity. 3. In speech. 4. In morals and virtues. 5. In piety. 6. Inasmuch as life and sound health constitute the basis of all things in relation to men, it will, above all things, be taught how that, by the diligence and care of parents, infants may be preserved sound and healthy.

V.

How youth ought to be exercised with the view to bodily health and strength.

1. A certain author advises that we ought "*to pray for a sound mind in a sound body.*" But we ought to labour as well as to pray, since God promises the blessing to the laborious, and not to the indolent. Inasmuch, however, as babes cannot yet labour, nor know how to pour out prayers to God, it becomes the parent to discharge this duty, so as zealously to train up what they have procreated to the glory of God.

2. Above all things it should be the parents' first care to preserve the health of their offspring; since they cannot train them up successfully unless they be lively and vigorous; for what proficiency can be made with the sickly and the morbid? Inasmuch as this matter depends mainly upon mothers, it seems requisite to counsel them for their sake.

3. That the mother, bearing in mind that God, the creator of all things, began to form the offspring in her womb, should devote herself on that account even more to piety than formerly, beseeching God daily, with most ardent prayers, that He would bring to light, perfectly formed and sound, what she bears beneath her heart. For this purpose the following prayer may be useful for women so circumstanced.

Form of Prayer for pregnant matrons.

Omnipotent God, Creator of all things visible and invisible, of whom all the whole family in heaven and on earth is named; to Thee, most revered and beloved Father, we, Thy rational creatures, have recourse, inasmuch as Thou, with special counsel and deliberation, didst found our race, forming the body with wonderful wisdom from the dust of the earth, and inspiring the soul from Thyself, that we might be Thine image; and although Thou mightest have produced us all at the same time, even as (Thou didst) the angels, yet it seemed otherwise to Thy wisdom, so that a human race might be multiplied by male and female, in accordance with holy wedlock instituted by Thee; therefore Thou didst deign to bless them that they might increase and multiply, and fill not only the earth, but also the choirs of angels. O eternal God and Father! may praise and glory be to Thy name because of all thy wonderful works in us. I likewise give grateful thanks to Thy clemency that Thou hast willed that I should not only be born of this thy celebrated creature (so that I also should fill up the number of the elect), but likewise hath deigned to bless me by placing me in the matrimonial state, and given unto me the fruit of the womb. The gift is Thine, the paternal grace is Thine, O Lord, Father of spirits and of all flesh! wherefore, with humble heart, seeking counsel and aid, I fly to Thee alone, that what Thou hast formed in my womb may be guarded with Thy strength, and preserved to a happy delivery. For I know, O Lord, that man's steps are not in his own power, and no one is able (of himself) to direct his way; since then we are weak and infirm, we ought to guard against all the snares which, by thy permission, the evil spirit lays for us, and to prevent the calamities into which we are precipitated through our own inconsiderateness. With Thee, however, wisdom is infinite; Thou renderest safe and secure from all evil whomsoever Thou wishest well, through Thine angels. Wherefore I also betaking myself to Thee in this my necessity, O Father, full of mercy, beg that Thou wouldst look upon me with the eye of Thy mercy, and preserve me safe from every dangerous accident. Be Thou a consolation to me and my beloved husband, O God of all consolation! so that we, having seen Thy blessing, may, with joyful heart, adore Thy fatherly love, and with all willingness serve Thee. I complain not of the chastisement which thou hast imposed upon our sex, that our conceptions and birth are accompanied with pain. I humbly beg this only, that Thou wouldst enable me to bear Thy chastisement, and do Thou grant a happy issue. If our prayers in this behalf be heard, and Thou dost grant to us offspring sound and perfect in its members, we promise to consecrate and return it to Thee; so that Thou may continue to be our and our offspring's most clement Lord and Father, as we, with our posterity, purpose to remain Thy faithful children. Hear, O most merciful Father, the prayer of Thy very humble handmaid and the desire of our hearts; for the sake of Jesus Christ, our Saviour, who, for our sakes, being made an infant, deigned to assume flesh in the womb of the blessed Virgin; now lives with Thee, and with the Holy Spirit lives and reigns, God blessed for evermore. Amen. Our Father, &c.

4. Let matrons, therefore, be especially careful of themselves, that they may in no respect injure their offspring. 1. Let them observe temperance and diet, lest by excessive eating and drinking, or unseasonable fasting, by purgations, by blood-letting, by chills, &c., they fall into a condition of depression and liability to injure, or emaciate or debilitate their offspring: they must therefore be particularly cautious against all excess during the period of carriage. 2. Let them not recklessly stagger, stumble, or strike against anything, or even walk incautiously; from any and all these the yet weak and infirm infant may be injured. 3. It is needful for a pregnant woman to hold a tight rein over all her affections, so as to avoid incurring sudden fear, falling into excessive anger, or repining or distressing herself in mind, &c.; for unless she beware of these things she will have an infant timid, passionate, anxious, and melancholy, and, what is worse, from sudden terror and excessive passion it may be brought forth a lifeless abortion, or at

least of very feeble health. 4. In respect of external actions the mother should be careful not to indulge in excessive sleep, indolence, or torpor, but perform with all agility her usual employment, with all the promptitude and celerity of which she is capable; for such as she then is, such will be the nature of her offspring, &c. With respect to other matters, skilful physicians, midwives, honourable matrons will supply advice.

5. Immediately upon the birth of the infant let it be suitably cleansed and washed: let soft and warm fomentations be applied around it; and let the parent at once prepare suitable food for it. And here it ought especially to be observed, that the mother herself ought to be the nurse, and not to repel from her own flesh, nor grudge to the infant the sustenance which she supplied to it prior to its birth. Oh, how grievous, how hurtful and reprehensible is the contrary conduct! that certain mothers (especially of the upper classes), feeling it irksome to cherish their own offspring, should devolve the duty of nourishing it upon other women. This matter imposes the necessity of shewing here the turpitude of such culpability, and of shewing how cautiously they ought to proceed in it; for the deeper this custom has spread its roots and diffused itself, the greater is the necessity of not passing it by in silence, especially here, where we purpose to shew the benefits arising out of good order from the very foundations.

6. I maintain, therefore, that this cruel alienation of mothers from their infants, by handing them over to be suckled with the milk of others (unless in some inevitable case, or when the mother is unable), is opposed, 1st, to God and nature; 2nd, hurtful to the children; 3rd, pernicious to mothers themselves; 4th, dishonourable, and deserving the highest reprobation.

7. That such conduct is strongly opposed to nature is manifest from this: First, that no such thing is found in

nature, not even among wild beasts; the wolf, the bear, the lioness, the panther, and other such ferocious animals, nourish their offspring with their own milk; and shall the mothers of the human race be less affectionate than the dams of all these? Does not God himself indicate this very thing in the Lamentations of Jeremiah (iv. 3), saying, "The dragons make bare the breast and suckle their young: the daughter of my people is cruel as the ostrich in the desert." How, I pray, can it agree with nature that they should thrust from themselves that which is a part of themselves? —that they should at last withdraw the milk from their own offspring, which during so many months they bore and nourished beneath their hearts? God certainly gave not the milk for the use of the mothers, but of the children; for those fountains never spring up unless when offspring come to light: for whose sake then are they, unless they be for the new guests? They, therefore, who can and do not suckle their own offspring, invert the Divine arrangements, and transfer them for any other purpose than that for which they were designed.

8. Secondly, It contributes much to the health of infants that they suck the breast of their real mother, rather than of another; inasmuch as when in the womb they were nourished with the maternal blood, daily experience witnesses that children might approach nearer to the disposition and virtues of their parents than generally happens. Favorinus, not among the least celebrated of philosophers, shews, that as the milk of animals, by some occult virtue, possesses the power of fashioning the body and mind according to the form of its original; and this he demonstrates by citing the case of lambs and kids, saying: "That lambs nourished with the milk of goats have wool much rougher than those sustained by the milk of the mother; on the contrary, kids nourished from the dugs of sheep bear wool much softer than those nourished by the milk of their dams." Who, then, unless he

be blind, does not observe that infants, along with the milk of others imbibe morals other than those of their parents? If married people do not permit their gardens to be sown with foreign seed, why do they allow their plants to be irrigated with foreign water? If the father has communicated his nature to the offspring, why should the mother deny to it her nature? Why admit a third person to perform that? God, moreover, has united only two persons, as sufficient for producing offspring, and why should we not acquiesce in His will? If this custom can be admitted, it can only be in two special cases. First, Should the mother of the infant be labouring under some contagious disease; in order to preserve the sound health of the infant, and to prevent its contracting any taint of the contagion, it may be entrusted to another nurse. Second, If the mother be of such corrupt morals as to occasion obstruction to the virtue of the infant; in case a nurse of upright morals and piety can be found, I should not deny, that in order to secure the graceful endowments of the mind, the infant may be entrusted to her. Inasmuch, however, as in these times even honourable, noble, and pious matrons, deliver their recently born offspring to worthless, disreputable, and impious women, occasionally also in a much more feeble state of health than themselves, such practice can admit of no excuse; for their beloved offspring becomes thus exposed to certain contagion of both body and mind. Assuredly, under such circumstances, parents have no reason to wonder that their children become altogether dissimilar to themselves in morals and in the affairs of life, and that they walk not in their steps,—since, according to a proverb common among the Latins, "Wickedness is imbibed with the milk."

9. Thirdly, As delicate mothers of this kind are afraid, if they should take charge of their children, that they may themselves lose somewhat of their symmetry or elegance of form. It frequently happens, however, that they incur

the loss, not only of their customary rest and beauty, but also of their health; since, when they reject their own sucking infants, they, as it were, reject their physicians, who usually free the mother from superfluous humours and many occult diseases,— as the said philosopher, Favorinus, has shewn at considerable length. Hence also Plutarch deemed it necessary to compose a book for the special purpose of counselling mothers in the duties to which by God and nature they are destined; and Aulus Gellius has left it upon record, "that such women are not worthy the name of mothers, who decline the fulfilment of what God and nature enjoin upon them; and upon such he, moreover, denounces evils of every kind."

10. Fourthly, Finally, it violates maternal honour to refuse the breast to their own children. Didacus Apolephtes calls such not mothers, but stepmothers (novercas), saying that many prefer embracing a whelp rather than to carry their own offspring in their bosom; and many blush more at carrying their own offspring, than a dog or a squirrel in their arms. What animal, I pray, is so savage as to entrust its own young to others? Nay, a race of animals is found in which the male contests with the female about cherishing their offspring. Birds, likewise, although they occasionally produce six and more young ones at a time, and God has not supplied them with milk for their offspring, yet they do not desert them, but feed and cherish them with all possible care.

11. As to what evil may arise if some vile nurse, and not the mother, suckle the infant, I will prove by example from three of the Roman emperors. 1. Titus, from having had a diseased nurse, was throughout life subject to illness, as Lampredius avers. 2. Caligula was a ferocious beast in human form. The cause of this, however, was not attributable to his parents, but to the nurse whose breasts he had sucked; who, besides being grossly immoral and impious,

used to sprinkle her breasts with blood, and then present them to him to suck. From this cause he became of a disposition so ferocious, that he not only delighted in shedding human blood, but also, without the least feeling of aversion, licked it with his tongue when adhering to the sword. He even dared to wish that all mankind had but one neck, in order that they might be cut off at a stroke. 3. Tiberius was exceedingly fond of wine, for his nurse not only was herself a wine-bibbing and drunken woman, but also accustomed him from early life to the juice of the grape.

12. Hence it is evident that no little depends upon what kind of nurse any one has, not only in respect of the body, but also of the mind and morals; for if a nurse be affected with any manifest or secret disease, the infant will also be subject to it. " If she be unchaste, untruthful, or has tarry hands (*i.e.* is a pilferer), or is drunken or passionate, you can expect no other morals from the infant, which, with the milk, imbibes the seeds of all these evils."—*Didacus Apolestes*, part iii. p. 72, &c.

13. Let the above suffice for the present. Pious and prudent parents, anxious for the safety of their offspring, will know how to use these admonitions.

14. When at length infants may be accustomed gradually to other aliment, it must be begun prudently with such nutritious substances as approximate to their natural aliment —namely, soft, sweet, and easy of digestion. It is extremely hurtful (as is the custom with many) to accustom infants to medicine; because by this means obstruction is occasioned to natural digestion in the stomach, and consequently to their growth. For medicine and food are in their nature contrary: the latter supplies the body with blood and vital humours, and increases them; whereas the former opposes, by drying them up and expelling them; besides, medicine taken when not required becomes a habit of nature and loses its power, so as to be useless in time of need, from being

assimilated to nature. Nay, what is still worse, it hence follows that infants used to medicine from their tender years, never attain perfect strength and sound health, being rendered feeble, sickly, infirm, palefaced, imbecile, cancerous; finally, they anticipate fate and die prematurely.

15. Wherefore, O beloved parents, if you would be numbered among the wise, as you would avoid giving them poison, so avoid giving medicine to your children, except in case of necessity. Avoid also drink and food warm and acrid in their nature, such as dishes seasoned largely with pepper or salt, &c. He who feeds his offspring with such food, or refreshes them with such drink, acts in the same manner as an imprudent gardener, who being desirous that his plants should grow and flourish quickly, in order to warm the roots, covers them with lime. No doubt such plants will increase and put forth buds, but they will soon begin to become arid and dwindle away, and, while they seem to be flourishing, perish at the root. If you doubt this, make the experiment, and you will find how insalubrious those nutriments are for children. God has assigned and ordained milk as food for children and other tender creatures; consequently they ought to be nourished on it. As soon, however, as they can be withdrawn from the milk, let them have food of a similar nature, duly tempered,—bread, butter, pottage, potherbs, water, and very light ale; thus they will grow like plants by the running stream, only indulging them in duly regulated sleep, frequent playful amusements, movements of themselves, and, above all, commending their health and safety in pious prayers to God.

16. Hence the Spartans (Lacedemonians), once the wisest of mortals, surpassed all the nations of the earth in paying special attention to the education of their youth. It was strictly provided by the public statutes, that none of their youth should be allowed to taste wine before their twentieth year. Since wine was thus strictly denied to their youth,

what, I pray, should we say respecting that maddening drink, recently discovered to the ruin of the human race—namely, wine eliminated by the force of fire (distillation), brandy, with which now both young and old are equally burnt up. It is time, truly, that we learn to be cautious, lest we corrupt and destroy our children, at least our infants.

17. In other respects also the health of infants should be most carefully watched, since their little bodies are weak, their bones soft, their veins infirm, and none of their members are as yet mature and perfect. Consequently they need prudent circumspection as to the manner in which they should be taken in the hand, lifted up, carried, set down, wrapped up, or laid in the cradle, lest, through any imprudence, they be injured by falling down, or striking against anything, whereby they may lose sight or hearing, or become lame or maimed. An infant is a more precious treasure than gold, but more fragile than glass. It may easily be shaken and injured, and be irreparably damaged.

18. When infants begin to sit, to stand, or run about; to prevent injury from striking against any thing, there is need of little seats, knee-splints, and little carriages, always beginning with the smallest. In some countries the practice prevails of putting upon the heads of infants, a little cap padded on the inside with rolls of cotton, so that in the event of falling, their heads may be preserved from injury; a precaution quite applicable to the other members also. Let suitable clothing and warm covering in winter, defend them from cold and atmospheric changes. To express the matter in few words let their health sustain no damage from bruises, from excess of heat or cold, from too much food or drink, or from hunger or thirst. Observing that all these be attended to with moderation.

19. It is likewise beneficial to observe due order: for example, how often infants should be put to rest in the course of the day; and fed; and refreshed with play; since

this conduces much to health and becomes the basis of subsequent regularity of conduct, Although this may appear frivolous to some minds, yet it is certainly true, that infants may be sufficiently inured to decorous and agreeable order, as is manifested from examples.

20. Inasmuch as our life consists in vital heat, and natural fire unless it have a thorough draft of air and repeated agitation soon goes out, it is in like manner necessary that infants have their daily exercises and excitements. And, for this purpose, before children are able to move themselves and run about, the devices of rocking in the cradle, carrying about, transferring from place to place, and being drawn in vehicles, were adopted. But when the little ones are somewhat advanced and begin to take to their feet, they may be allowed to run and do this or that little matter (at the beck of the mother or nurse). The more a child is thus employed, runs about and plays, the sweeter is its sleep; the more easily does its stomach digest, the more quickly does it grow and flourish, both in body and mind; care being only taken that it in no way injure itself. Therefore a place should be found in which children may run about and exercise themselves with safety. And the proportion of this exercise that may be allowed without injury must be shewn, and guardians of health, nurses, and baby carriers must be procured.

21. Finally, As, according to the proverb, *a joyful mind is half health*, nay, according to Sirachides (ch. xxx. 22). *The joy of the heart is the very life-spring of man;* in this also parents ought to be especially careful never to allow their children to be without delights. For example, in their first year, their spirits should be stirred up by rocking in the cradle, by gentle agitation in the arms, by singing, by rattles, by carrying through some open place or garden, or even by kisses and embraces. Let all these things, however, be done with circumspection. In the second, third, and fourth years, &c. let their spirits be stirred up by means

of agreeable play with them, or their playing among themselves, by running about, by chasing one another; by music, and any agreeable spectacle, as pictures, &c. And to express myself compendiously, whatever is found to be either agreeable or pleasing must on no account be denied to a child. Nay, if some little occupations can be conveniently provided for its eyes, ears, or other senses, they will contribute to its vigour of body and mind. Such things only ought to be denied as are adverse to piety and upright morals. As to the rest, more will be said in its own place.

VI.

How children are to exercised in the knowledge of things.

1. "Being the tender son of my father (says Solomon the wisest of mortals, Prov. iv. 4,) and the beloved of my mother, he taught me, instructing me that wisdom is the beginning of all things, and that prudence must be acquired and secured as a complete possession;" it will therefore be the prudence of parents, not only to provide that their children may have means of living, or possess competent fortunes; but they ought also to labour with all their means, that their minds may be imbued with wisdom. "For wisdom is more precious than gems and pearls, and all things which are desired cannot be compared with it; length of days is in her right hand, and in her left hand are riches and glory; her ways are beautiful, and all her paths are peaceful; the tree of life is to them who have apprehended her, and they who possess her are blessed." These are the words of the Holy Spirit himself. (Proverbs iii. 15.)

2. Do parents consider well when these exercises of wisdom should be begun with children? Solomon says that he was instructed by his father immediately from infancy, and although he was the beloved son of his mother, yet that did not interfere with his education. Our children, therefore, may be instructed in the knowledge of natural things and other matters: but how is that to be done? Even as their tender age permits, *i. e.* according to their capabilities, as is apparent from the following instances:—

3. The *natural* knowledge of recently born infants, is to eat, drink, sleep, digest, and grow; but these things affect

not their intellect. In the second or third year, they begin to apprehend what *papa* is and *mama* is; what food and drink are; and, shortly after this, they begin to understand what it is which we call water, what fire, what wind, what cold, what heat, what a cow is, what a little dog is; and the general varieties of natural things. This their nurse-maids will instil into them, when caressing them in their arms, or while carrying them about, by saying, "Look, there is a horse, there is a bird, there is a cat, &c." In their fourth, fifth, and sixth years, they may begin to make further progress in such knowledge of natural things; so as to be able to tell what a stone is, what sand is, what clay, what a tree, what a branch, what a leaf, what a blossom, &c. Likewise to know certain fruits, such as a pear, an apple, a cherry, a bunch of grapes, &c. Also to call by their proper names, the external members of their bodies, and, in some measure to know their uses. In this matter their father, mother, or bearers may often be occupied, instructing them by shewing them this thing or that, and desiring them to name it by saying, "What is this?" The ear, what do you do with it? I hear. And this, what is it? The eye. For what use is the eye? That I may see. How is this named? The foot. What is the foot for? That I may walk, &c.

4. The beginning of *optics* will be, to look up at the light, a thing natural to children, for the instant it becomes visible their eyes turn to it. They must however be watched, and not permitted to look with fixed eyes on excessive light and brilliance, strongly affecting the power of vision, especially at first, lest that power be weakened, or extinguished by overstraining. Let them have the means of seeing moderate light, especially of a green colour, and gradually any thing that shines. In the second or third year optical exercises will be to present to their contemplation, coloured and pictured objects; to shew them the beauty of the heavens, of trees, of flowers, and of running waters; to bind corals

d

to their hands and neck, and to supply them with beautiful dress, &c.; inasmuch as they delight in gazing at these things; nay, the sight of the eye and acuteness of the mind are stimulated by looking even in a mirror. In the fourth and following years many things ought to be added to optics, when they are occasionally taken into an orchard, a field, or a river, that they may be allowed to look upon the animals, trees, plants, flowers, running waters, the turning of windmills, and other such things; nay, pictures in books, upon the walls, &c. are pleasing to them, and therefore ought not to be denied; for children ought rather to have them designedly presented to them.

5. Children may, in the second or third year at the farthest, learn the elements of *astronomy*, by looking on the heavens, and discerning between the sun, moon, and stars. In the fourth and fifth year, they will be able to understand that the sun and moon rise and set; that the moon sometimes shines full, sometimes a half moon, and sometimes a crescent moon. This may and ought to be shewn to them. In the sixth year they may be incidentally instructed, that the days are shortest in winter, that the night is then longest; whereas in summer that the day is long, and the night short.

6. The elements of *geography* will be, during the course of the first year and thenceforward; when children begin to distinguish their cradles and their maternal bosom. In the second and third year, their geography will be to know the place where they are nursed, &c. in which they ought to learn when to eat, when to go to rest, or when to go abroad; where the light is, and where the heat is to be found. In their third year, they will advance in geography when they remember the distinctions and names not only of the nursery, but also of the hall, of the kitchen, of the bedchamber, of things which are in the area, in the stable, in the orchard, and in and around the house. In the fourth year, they may, by going abroad, learn the way through the

street or market place, by going to their vicinity, to their uncle, to their grandmother, their aunt, or their cousin. In the fifth and sixth years they may fix all such things in their memory; and learn to understand what a city is, what a village, what a field, what a garden, what a forest, what a river, &c.

7. Children ought also to be taught the distinctions of time, namely, that one time is day, and another, night. Likewise what is morning, what is evening, what noon-day, what midnight. Then, how often during the day they should eat, sleep, or pray. Then let them moreover know, that a week consists of seven days, and what days follow each other; that six are common days, but the seventh, the Lord's day; that on that day outward labour should be discontinued, the place of worship attended, and divine service engaged in. That solemn festivals occur thrice in a year; the birth of Christ in winter; Easter in spring; and Pentecost or Whitsuntide in summer; that bread-corn is gathered in autumn, &c. All which things, although children of themselves may understand and remember them, yet nothing hinders from talking to them about such things, according to their several occasions and observances.

8. Children ought to be exercised in *history* and in the remembrance of things, as soon as they begin to talk; at first, by such simple questions as, Who gave this to you? Where did you go to yesterday? When will be Wednesday? Let the child answer, At my grandfather's, at my grandmother's, at my aunt's, &c. What did they give you? What did your godfather promise to give you? &c. Other things will fix themselves in their memories: only there is need of circumspection, in order, as the youthful memory begins to store away treasures for itself, that it may lay up nothing but what is good and useful in obtaining virtue and promotive of the fear of God; all things of a contrary kind ought never to be permitted to meet their eyes or their ears.

9. In the first and following year will be the beginning of *economies* (*i. e.* the due performance of household matters) for children then begin to distinguish their dadas, mamas, and nannas (nursemaids), and afterwards others also in the house. In the third, they will learn that father and mother rule, and that others obey. In the fourth and fifth, let them begin to learn carefulness, what is their clothing for holidays, and what for common days; and let them be careful not to stain nor tear their clothes, nor sweep the floor with them. Then they will easily discover the use of chests, presses, cellars, cupboards, bolts, or bars, and keys, namely that no one may have access to these places. They may comprehend any other necessary domestic furniture by seeing it, or they may learn it by familiar talk with their parents or nurses, or older brothers and sisters. It will greatly contribute to this, that children have for play wooden or leaden horses, tables, little seats, tankards, pots or pans, cows, sheep, little carriages, mattocks, &c. and not for amusement only, but also for promoting their knowledge of things. For this way is to teach the youth according to their own way, and by presenting these little things before their eyes, they will not be ignorant of the greater things which they represent.

10. The *political* knowledge needful for these first years, is indeed but little; for although they hear the names of sovereigns, governors, consuls, prætor, judge, &c. yet inasmuch as they do not visit the places where these functions are performed, they cannot comprehend them and could not if they did; inasmuch as they exceed their capacity. There is no necessity therefore to take them to such places. For it will be sufficient in the place thereof, if they be accustomed to the rudiments of political intercourse. Comprehending by little and little whom they ought to obey, whom to venerate, and whom to respect, (of this matter we afterwards make mention under *morals*) as rational conversation may arise with the father, the mother, or the family. For

example, when any one calls them, to remember that they are bound to stand still, and learn what is desired; also to reply gracefully to questions, although these may be jocular. For we may be agreeably occupied in gently exciting this youthful age, saying this or that playfully with them, for the purpose of sharpening their intellect. They ought therefore to be taught, and that thoroughly, to understand what is said in joke, and what seriously; and at the same time to know when to return a joke with a joke; and again, when the discourse is really serious to be serious accordingly, &c.; which they may easily learn from the expression of the countenance, and from the gesture of the person indicating, or commanding any thing; provided their instructors know how to manage their disposition, and not to joke on every occasion with children, without observing the proper time, especially during serious matters; such as prayer or admonition or exhortation—neither when children are disposed for jesting, should they be frowned at or be angrily used or beaten. For by such means the mind of a child becomes distracted, so as not to know in what way this or that is to be understood. He who wishes a boy to become prudent, must himself act prudently with him; and not make him foolish or stupid before he enables him to understand what he ought to do.

11. It greatly sharpens the innate capacity and intellect of children to be exercised with apologues, stories about animals, and other ingeniously constructed fables, for with such little narratives they are pleased and easily remember them. Moreover, inasmuch as some moral principle is generally included in these ingeniously constructed parables, they become of two-fold use to children, for while they occupy their minds, they instil something into them which may afterwards be profitable.

12. So much respecting the rational instruction of infants in the knowledge of things. I shall add one. Although

their carriers and parents may be of great service to children in all these things; yet children of their own age are of still greater service, when one relates any thing to another, or when they play together, for children of about the same age and of equal progress and manners and habits sharpen each other more effectually, since the one does not surpass the other in depth of invention; there is among them neither assumption of superiority of the one over the other, or force, or dread, or fear, but love, candour, free questionings, and answers, about any thing; all these are defective in us their elders, when we wish intercourse with children, and this defect forms a great obstruction to our free intercourse with them.

13. No one will therefore doubt that one boy sharpens the genius of another boy more than any one else can; consequently, therefore, boys may daily meet together, and play together or run about together in open places, and this ought not merely to be permitted, but even provided for; with this precaution however that they do not mingle with depraved associates, causing more injury than benefit; against liability to this, circumspect parents may easily provide, by carefully observing the kind of society in the neighbourhood, and thus not permitting their offspring to be contaminated, (ea pice inquinari, *to be defiled with pitch.*)

VII.

How children ought to be accustomed to an active life, and perpetual employment.

1. Boys ever delight in being occupied in something, for their youthful blood does not allow them to be at rest. Now as this is very useful, it ought not to be restrained, but provision made that they may always have something to do. Let them be like ants continually occupied in doing something, carrying, drawing, constructing, and transposing, provided always that whatever they do, be done prudently. They ought to be assisted, by shewing them the forms of all things, even of playthings, for they cannot yet be occupied in real works; and by being played with. We read that Themistocles, supreme ruler of the Athenians, was once seen riding with his son on a long reed as a horse, by a young unmarried citizen; and observing that he wondered how so great a man should act so childishly, begged of him not to relate the circumstance to any one until he himself had a son; thus indicating that when he himself became a father, he would be better able to understand the affection of parents towards their children, and cease to be offended at the conduct which he now thought childish.

2. Inasmuch as infants try to imitate what they see others do, they should be permitted to have all things, excepting such as might cause injury to themselves or anything else, such as knives, hatchets, glass, &c. When this is not convenient, in place of real instruments they may have toys procured for their use, namely, leaden knives, wooden swords, ploughs, little carriages, sledges, mills, buildings, &c. With these they may always amuse themselves; thus exercising their bodies to health, their minds to vigour, and their

bodily members to agility. They are delighted to construct little houses, and to erect walls of clay, of chips, of wood, or of stone, thus displaying an architectural genius. In a word, whatever children delight to play with, provided that it be not hurtful, they ought rather to be gratified than restrained from it, for inactivity is more injurious both to mind and body than anything in which they can be occupied.

3. Now advancing according to their years; in the first year it will be sufficient *mechanical* knowledge for children to learn when they open their mouths for food, to hold up their heads, to take anything in their hands, to sit, stand, &c.; all which things will depend rather on nature than nurture.

4. In the second and third years their mechanical knowledge may be extended; for now they begin to learn what it is to run, to jump, to agitate themselves in various ways, to play, to kindle and extinguish, to pour out water, to carry things from place to place, to put down, to lift up, to lay prostrate, to cause to stand, to turn, to roll together, to unrol, to bend, to make straight, to break, to split, &c.; all which things ought to be allowed—nay, when opportunity serves they ought to be shewn to them.

5. The fourth, fifth, and sixth years will and ought to be full of labours and *architectural* efforts; for the too much sitting still or slowly walking about of a child is not a good sign; to be always running or doing something is a sure sign of a sound body and vigorous intellect: wherefore, as it has been said, whatever attracts their attention, they ought not to be denied, but rather to be assisted in; so, however, as that that which is done may be properly done, and with a view to future real labours.

6. Children in this maternal school ought also in their fourth and fifth year to be exercised in *drawing* and *writing*, according as their inclination may be noticed or excited; supplying them with chalk (poorer persons may use a piece

of charcoal), with which they may at their will make dots, lines, hooks, or round O's, of which the method may easily be shewn, either as an exercise or amusement. In this way they will accustom the hand to the use of the chalk hereafter, and to form letters, and will understand what a dot is, and what a little line, which will afterwards greatly abridge the labours of the preceptor.

7. In this stage *dialectics* (reasoning), anything beyond the *natural*, or such as is obtained in practice, cannot be introduced; for in whatever manner those persons conduct themselves, who associate with children, whether rationally or irrationally, such will the children be.

8. The elements of *arithmetic* can scarcely be propounded to children in the third year; as soon as they begin to count up to five and afterwards to ten, or at least to pronounce the numbers correctly, although they may not at first understand what those numbers really are; for then they will of themselves observe the use to which this enumeration is applied. In the fourth, fifth, and sixth years it will be sufficient if they number or count up to twenty in succession, and be able clearly to distinguish that seven is more than five, and fifteen more than thirteen; what is an even and what an odd number, which they may easily learn from the play which we call *par impar*, odds or evens. To proceed further than this in arithmetic would be unprofitable, nay, hurtful; for nothing is so difficult to fix in our minds as numbers.

9. About the second year the principles of *geometry* may be perceived, when we say of anything that it is large or small: they will afterwards easily know what is short or long, wide or narrow. In the fourth year they may learn the differences of forms; for example, what is a circle, what are lines, what a square. At length they may learn the names of the common measures, such as a finger's breadth, a palm, a span, an ell, a foot, a pint, a quart, a gallon, &c.;

and if anything more come spontaneously to their own knowledge, they themselves should be shewn how to try to measure them, to weigh them, thus comparing the one with the other.

10. *Music* is especially natural to us, for as soon as we see the light we immediately sing the song of paradise, thus recalling to our memory our fall, A, a! E, e! I maintain that complaint and wailing are our first music, from which it is impossible to restrain infants; and if it were possible, it would be inexpedient, since it contributes to their health; for as long as other exercises and excitements are wanting, by this very means their chests and other internal parts relieve themselves of their superfluities. External music begins to delight children at two years of age; such as singing, rattling, and striking of musical instruments. They should, therefore, be indulged in this, so that their ears and minds may be soothed by concord and harmony.

11. In the third year the sacred music of daily use may be introduced, namely, that received as a custom to sing before and after dinner, and when prayers are begun or ended. On such occasions they ought to be present, and to be accustomed to attend and conduct themselves composedly. It will also be expedient to take them to public worship, where the whole assembly unites in singing the praises of God. In the fourth year it is possible for some children to sing of themselves; the more slow ones, however, ought not to be forced, but permitted to have a whistle, a drum, or puerile pipes, so that by whistling, drumming, and piping, they may accustom their ears to the perception of various sounds, or even to imitate them. In the fifth year it will be time to open their mouths in hymns and praises to God, and to use their voices for the glory of their Creator. (For this purpose the easier verses of certain cantions have been assigned for morning and evening, before and after food, and

before and after prayer. These verses used by us are such as any nation may imitate in their own language.)

12. These, and such as these, parents and bearers, in singing or playing with children, may easily instil into their minds, since their memory is now more enlarged and apt than previously, and will, with greater ease and pleasure, imbibe a larger number of things in consequence of the rhythm and melody. The more verses they commit to memory the better will they be pleased with themselves, and the glory of God be largely obtained from the mouths of infants. Blessed is the home where voices resound with such Davidic music.

VIII.

How Children ought to be exercised in the skilful use of Language.

1. Two things pre-eminently distinguish men from brutes —*reason* and *speech*. Man needs the former on his own account; the latter for the sake of his neighbour. Both, therefore, equally demand our care, so that man may have his mind and tongue equally trained and exercised as well as possible. We now, therefore, add something respecting instruction in *language*, such as when and how the principles of *grammar, rhetoric,* and *poetry* ought to be propounded. The beginnings of *grammar* appear in certain infants as early as their first half year; generally, however, towards the end of the year, when certain letters in their language begin to to be formed, such as *a, e, i;* or even syllables, such as *ba, ma, ta,* &c. But in the following year more full syllables begin to be formed, when they try to pronounce whole words. When it is usual to propose to them the more easy words to be pronounced, such as *tata, mama, papa,* and *nanna;* and there is need to do this, for nature itself impels them to begin with easier words, since the manner adopted by us adults in pronouncing father, mother, food, drink, &c. is difficult to be pronounced by infants' tongues just becoming loose.

3. As soon however as their tongues begin to be more supple, it is hurtful to indulge them in this practice, which may thus lead them to speaking lispingly; and if this practice be allowed, when children come to learn longer words, and at length to speak, they will be necessitated to unlearn what they had before learned corruptly. Why should not their

mother, sister, or bearer, when amusing infants, now freely opening the mouth, teach them to pronounce letters and syllables properly, distinctly, and articulately, or even entire words, (beginning always with the shorter,) or letters or syllables separately. This will be sufficient grammar for the second year, which exercise may be continued all along to the third year as on account of the slowness of some children is occasionally necessary.

4. In the fourth, fifth, and sixth years, their language will increase with their increase in the knowledge of things, provided exercise is not omitted, so that they may be accustomed to name whatever they see at home, or whatever they are employed in, and therefore they should be often asked, What is this? What are you about? What is this called? always taking care that they pronounce their answers distinctly; in this respect no further instruction is necessary, unless to please them by intermingling some playfulness; for example, who can pronounce better and quicker than the others any rather long word as, *Taratantara, Nabuchodonosor, Constantinopolitan, &c.*

5. The principles of rhetoric arise in the first year, and indeed in a great measure intuitively by gestures, for as long as the intellect and power of speech in this early age remain in their deep roots, we are accustomed to draw them to the knowledge of ourselves and of things by certain gestures and external actions; for example, when we lift them up, put them to rest, shew them any thing, or smile upon them; by all these things we aim at this, that they in their turn should look on us, smile, reach out their hand and take what we give to them. And so we learn mutually to understand first by gesture and then by speech, even as we do with the deaf and dumb. I maintain that an infant immediately in its first and second year, is able to learn so as to understand what a wrinkled and what an unwrinkled forehead mean, what a threat indicated by the

finger means, what a nod means, what a repeated nod means, &c. which in truth is the basis of rhetorical action.

6. About their third year, children begin to understand and imitate *figures*, according to gestures occasionally questioning, sometimes expressing admiration, and sometimes when they relate anything, becoming significantly silent. Of the doctrine of *tropes*, while they are endeavouring to understand the proper meaning of words, they cannot perceive much: yet they may apprehend them if in their fifth and sixth years they hear any such thing from their equals in age or from their bearers. There is however no need of solicitude as to their understanding them, since they will have sufficient time afterwards for those higher or ornamental words. My only aim here is to shew, although this is not generally attended to, that the roots of all sciences, and arts, in every instance arise as early as in this tender age, and that on these foundations it is neither difficult nor impossible for the whole superstructure of rhetoric to be laid; provided always that we act reasonably with a reasonable creature.

7. Almost the same may be said of *poetry*, which binds and, as it were, entwines language in rhythm and measure. The principles of poetry arise with the beginning of speech; for as soon as an infant begins to understand words, it at the same time begins to love melody and rhythm. Therefore bearers, when an infant, from having fallen or somehow, has injured itself, is wailing, are wont to solace it with these or similar rythms:

> My dear baby! O sweet baby!
> What made you go and run away?
> What has it got by running astray?
> If baby had been sitting still
> Baby would never have suffered this ill.

This so much pleases infants that they not only become immediately quiet, but even smile. The bearers also, patting them with their hands soothingly, chant to them these or similar lines:—

> Dearest baby, do not weep,
> Shut its pretty eyes to sleep;
> Go to bye bye, lovely dear!
> And forget all pain and fear.

8. In the third and fourth year such knowledge of rhymes may be beneficially increased; which nurses, when playing with infants, may sing to them, not only to prevent their crying, but also to fix them in their memories for future benefit; for example, in the fourth, fifth, and sixth years they will increase their knowledge of poetry by committing to memory pious little verses; of this, however, I afterwards treat among the exercises of piety in the 10th chapter. Although, therefore, they may not at this time understand what rhythm or verse is, yet by use they learn to notice a certain difference between measured language and prose: nay, when in due time that very thing shall be explained in the schools, it will afford them pleasure to find that they had previously learned something which they now understand better. Puerile poetry, therefore, consists in this, that from their knowing some rhymes and verses, children can understand what is rhythm and poetry, and what is plain speech. So far then should the study of language and its various degrees of progress be exercised in during the first six years.

IX.

How youth ought to be exercised in Morals and Virtue.

1. What those external virtues are, in which youth ought to be exercised in their early years, I have enumerated already in the fourth chapter. Now I will explain how that behoves to be prudently and properly accomplished, or effected. In case it should be asked, how any age so tender, can be accustomed to these serious things? My reply is, even as a young tender tree can be bent so as to grow this way or that much more easily than a full grown tree; so youth can be exercised in the first years of their lives much more readily than afterwards, to good of every kind, provided legitimate means be used; and these are:

    1. A perpetual example of virtuous conduct.
    2. Properly timed and prudent instruction and exercise.
    3. Duly regulated discipline.

2. It is necessary that children should have presented before them a perpetual good *example*, since God has implanted in infants a certain imitative principle; namely, a desire to imitate whatever they see others do. So much so, that although you never desire a boy to do any thing, provided you say or do some such thing in his sight, you will see that he will try to do the same, which perpetual experience confirms. For this reason, there is need of the greatest circumspection in the house where there are children, so that nothing be done contrary to virtue; but let the whole house observe temperance, cleanliness, and neatness, due respect for superiors, mutual complaisance, truthfulness, &c. If this were diligently observed, there certainly would be no neces-

sity for many words to teach, or blows to enforce. But inasmuch, as upgrown persons themselves often fall into excess, it is no wonder that children also should imitate what they see in others, in whom there are sources of error for learners, and our own nature inclines us to evil.

3. *Instruction*, however, and that properly timed and prudent, must accompany example. It will be a suitable time for teaching children by words, when we discover that examples have not sufficiently profited them, or when they really desire to conduct themselves according to the example of others, but yet fail of doing it properly. In such case it will be commendable to admonish them to conduct themselves in this or that way, by saying, " Look, consider how I do—See how father or mother does it—Do not do such things. —Be ashamed of yourself—If you behave so, you will never become an excellent young man—Street beggars, and bad people do so, &c. ;" or the like. It is not yet expedient to have recourse to lengthened admonitions, or discourse on this or that matter, which will be of no use to them afterwards.

4. Occasionally there is need of *chastisement*, in order that children may attend to examples of virtue, and admonitious to it. Now there are two degrees of discipline. The first, that a boy be rebuked if he do any thing unbecoming; prudently, however, not so as to strike him with awe, but to move him to fear, and to a recollection of himself. Occasionally more severe chidings and putting to shame may be added; and, immediately after admonition not to repeat a thing, the admonition may be accompanied with threatening. If, however, you observe amendment, it will be good at once, or a little while after, to praise him; for much benefit results from prudent commendation or blame, not only to children, but to upgrown persons. If this first step of discipline should prove to be ineffectual, the next will be to

e

use the rod, or a slap with the hand, in order that the boy may recollect himself and become more attentive.

5. And here I cannot refrain from severely reprimanding the shallow brained mockery of affection to their offspring in certain parents who, conniving at every thing, permit their children to grow up altogether without discipline and correction. Such parents tolerate their children in committing every kind of evil; to run about in all directions, to bawl, to shout, to howl without a cause, to retort upon their elders, to stick out their tongue at others, and to act in every way without restraint; and then excuse them by saying: " He is a child, he ought not to be irritated, he does not yet understand those things." But *you* the parents yourselves are the children of stupidity, if, discovering this want of knowledge in your child, you do not promote its knowledge; for it was not born to remain a calf, or a young ass, but to become a rational creature. Know you not what the Scripture declares? (Prov. xxii. 15.)—" Folly is bound to the heart of a young man, but it is driven from him by the rod of chastisement." Why do you prefer the child's being detained in its natural foolishness, rather than to rescue it from its folly, by the aid of well-timed, holy, and salutary discipline? Do not persuade yourselves that the infant does not understand; for if it understands how to exercise frowardness, to be angry, to rage, to grin, to puff out his cheeks, to be rude to others; assuredly it will also know what is a rod and its use. Right reason does not fail the infant, but *you* imprudent parents, who neither know nor care to know what will contribute to the safety and comfort of yourselves and your infant. For how comes it that the majority of children afterwards become refractory to their parents and distress them in various ways, unless it be that they have never been disciplined to reverence them.

6. Most truthful is the saying: " He who attains to manhood without discipline, becomes old without virtue." For it

behoves that the Scripture be fulfilled which affirms that "the rod and chastisement confer wisdom, but a froward young man affects his mother with shame," (Prov. xxix. 15.) In the same chapter, ver. 17, the wisdom of God advises, "Chastise thy son, and he will bring rest unto thee, and procure pleasure for thy soul." When parents fail to obey this counsel, they neither get pleasure nor rest from their children, but disgrace, shame, affliction, and inquietude. Hence we often hear complaints of parents: "My children are disobedient and wicked; this one has fallen from the faith, the other is a spendthrift, reckless, and a glutton, &c." And is it strange, my friend, that you reap what you have sown? You have sown in their minds licentiousness, and do you hope to reap the fruits of discipline? This would indeed be marvellous. For a tree that is not engrafted cannot bear the fruit of the grafting. Labour ought to have been bestowed that the tender tree should be planted, duly inclined, and made straight; so as not to have grown up so awry, &c. But as most persons neglect discipline, there is no wonder that youth everywhere grow up froward, impetuous, and impious; provoking God and distressing his servants. A certain wise man has said, that "although an infant seems to be an angel, yet it requires the rod." Did not Eli himself lead a pious life? Did not he give pious instructions to his sons? (1 Sam. ii. 22—25.) But because he spared effectual discipline, it happened ill to him; for by his undue lenity, he brought much sorrow upon himself, the wrath of God upon his house, and the utterly rooting out of his whole race. (1 Sam. ii. 29, &c. iii. 13, 14.) Bearing on our subject; Doctor Geyler, a celebrated pastor of the church of Strasburg, two centuries ago, has represented such parents under the following emblem: "Children tearing their own hair, puncturing themselves with knives, and their father sitting by them with veiled eyes."

7. Hitherto I have spoken generally; now I proceed to

give instructions as to the above-mentioned virtues severally, how they may be exercised in children easily, prudently, and decorously.

8. *Temperance* and *frugality* claim the first place for themselves, inasmuch as they constitute the foundation of health and life, and are the mothers of all other virtues. Children will become accustomed to these, provided you indulge them in only so much food, drink, and sleep as nature demands. For other animals, following the leading of nature alone, are more temperate than we; therefore infants ought to eat, drink, and sleep only at the times when nature disposes them so to do, namely, when they appear to suffer from hunger or thirst, or to be oppressed by sleep. Before this is discovered, to feed them, to give them drink, to put them to sleep, to cram them even beyond their will, to cover them up, or compel them to sleep, is madness. It is sufficient for them that such things be supplied them according to nature. Care must also be taken that their appetites be not provoked by pastry or any innutritious delicacies; for these are oiled vehicles which carry in more than is necessary, and the stomach is enticed to eat more than enough. Such things are really enticements to luxurious living. For although it may not be improper occasionally to give children something savoury, yet to make their food of sweetmeats is as destructive to health (as shewn in the fifth chapter, section 4) as it is also to sound morals.

9. Immediately, in the first year, the foundations of *cleanliness* and *neatness* may be laid, by nursing the infant in as cleanly and neat a way as possible, which the bearers ought to know how to do, provided they are not destitute of sense. In the second, third, and following years it is proper to teach children to take their food decorously, not to soil their fingers with fat, and not, by scattering their food, to stain themselves; not to make a noise while eating (swinishly smacking their lips), not to put out the tongue, &c. To

drink without greediness, without lapping, and without bespattering themselves. Similar cleanliness and neatness may be exacted in their dress: not to sweep the ground with their clothes, and not designedly to stain and soil them; which is usual with children by reason of their want of prudence; and yet parents, through a remarkable supineness, connive at such things.

10. They will easily learn *to respect superiors*, provided their elders take diligent care of them, and attend to themselves; therefore, if you admonish, frequently rebuke and chastise a child, you need not fear that he will not respect you. But if you allow everything to children, a practice followed by many who excessively love them, nothing is more certain than that such children will become froward and obstinate. "To love children is natural, to disguise that love is prudent." Not without prudence has Ben Sirach left it on record, "that an untamed horse will become unmanageable; a son neglected will become headstrong. Cocker a son, and he will cause you fear; play with him, and he will make you sad; do not laugh with him, lest you also grieve with him, and in the end thy teeth gnash." (Ecclus. xxx. 8—10.) It is better, therefore, to restrain children by discipline and fear than to reveal to them the overflowing of your love, and thus open as it were a window to frowardness and disobedience. It is also useful to grant even to others the power of rebuking children, so that not only under the eye of their parents, but wherever they are, they may be accustomed to have due regard to themselves, and by this means to cause modesty and due respect for all men to take root in their hearts. Assuredly they act altogether without circumspection, nay, with extreme imprudence, who allow no one even to look upon their children with an unfavourable eye; but if any one say anything or counsel them, become the advocates of their own children, even in their very presence. In this way their warm blood, even as it spirits up

a horse, gives loose rein to licentiousness and haughtiness. Let there be, therefore, great caution.

11. Youth ought to be instructed with great care as to actual *obedience*, since it will afterwards become the foundation of the greatest virtue, if children learn to restrain their own will and to obey the will of another. We do not permit a tender plant to grow spontaneously, but we bind it to a prop, that, so bound, it may the more easily raise its head and acquire strength. Hence it has been most truthfully said by Terence: " We all are the worse for excessive liberty." As often, therefore, as father or mother, addressing a child, says,—" Touch not that;—Sit still;—Put aside that knife;—Put away this or that"—children ought to be used to do at once what they are commanded; and if any obstinacy appear in them, it may be easily subdued by rebuke or prudent chastisement.

12. We read that the Persians observe with the greatest diligence the training of children in "*temperance* and *truthfulness*," and not without cause, since falsehood and hypocrisy render any person detestable both before God and man. "Lying," says Plutarch, "is a slavish vice, and ought to be vehemently condemned by all men." In respect of God, Scripture testifies that, "false lips are an abomination to Him." (Prov. xii. 22.) Children ought therefore to be compelled, in case they commit any fault, humbly to confess it, and not obstinately to deny it; but on the other hand not to say what really is not. For this reason Plato forbids fables and fictitious stories being recited to children, and he maintains that they should be led directly to truth. I therefore do not know how that can be approved which certain persons do, who habitually instruct children to transfer the blame upon others of some evil committed by themselves, and derive jest and pleasure from accomplishing it. But who, except the boy, becomes really injured? If he become accustomed to interchange lies and jokes, of course he learns to lie.

13. Failure in respect of *justice*. A desire for the property of others, does not greatly attach to this early age, unless the bearers themselves, or those who have the charge of children, introduce this corruption; and this occurs if in the presence of children any one stealthily takes away things belonging to another, and conceals or secures food for themselves clandestinely, or induces another to do the same: whether it be done in jest or in earnest, such infants as see it, are used to imitate it, being in this respect really little apes, for whatever they see, they remember and they do it too. Nurses therefore, and such as are occupied about children, ought in the highest degree to be cautious when present with them.

14. Children will be able gradually to learn and practise *benignity* and *beneficence* towards others in these early years, if they see alms distributed by their parents among the poor, or even if they themselves are ordered to bestow them; likewise if they be occasionally taught to impart something of their own to others; and when they do so, they ought to be praised.

15. The Fathers used to say, and most truly, that "*indolence* is Satan's cushion;" for whoever Satan finds entirely unemployed he will be sure to occupy him, first, with evil thoughts, and afterwards with shameful deeds. It is therefore the office of prudence to allow no man even from his earliest years to be idle, but by all means to exercise him with assiduous labours, that thus a door to the most destructive tempter may be closed. I know labours which the shoulders of children can bear, although they were nothing more (which cannot really be the case) than mere play. "It is better to play than to be idle, for during play the mind is intent upon some object, which often sharpens the abilities." In this way children may be early exercised to an active life, without any difficulty, since nature herself stirs them up to be doing something. But of this I have already spoken in the seventh chapter.

16. As long as infants are learning *to speak*, so long they should be free to talk as they like and prattle freely. When they have acquired the use of speech, it is of the highest importance for them to learn *to keep silence;* not as if I wished to make them statues, but rational little images. "Whosoever thinks silence to be a thing of little importance," says Plutarch, "is scarcely of a sound mind;" because to keep silence prudently is the beginning of sound wisdom: for, assuredly keeping silence hurts no one, whereas talking has injured many; and although no injury were sustained, yet since both those qualities, namely, to speak and to keep silence, constitute the foundation and ornament of all our conversation throughout life, they ought to be so closely united that we may at the same time acquire the habit of both. Parents ought therefore to accustom their children to keep silence. In the first place, during prayer, and divine service, whether at home or in public. Children should sit quietly, and no running about, shouting or making a noise, should at such times be allowed them. Children should also learn to attend silently to the orders of their father and mother in everything. The other benefit of keeping silence, is with a view to well ordered speech, so that before they speak or reply to any question, children may consider what the matter is, and how to speak reasonably, for to utter whatever comes uppermost is folly; neither is it becoming in those whom we would desire to see intelligent beings. However, I incessantly repeat that these things should be done as far as age permits, which circumspect parents should attend to with the greatest care.

17. A child may contract a *habit of patience*, provided excessive softness and immoderate indulgence be carefully avoided. In some children, as early as their first and second year, the vice of an evil inclination begins to creep up, which it is best to root out in the blade as we do thistles; for example, a child of a perverse and obstinate disposition

labours hard by crying and wailing to obtain what it has set its heart upon; another displays anger, malevolence, and desire of vengeance, by biting, kicking, striking, and other such modes. Inasmuch as these affections are preternatural, and only darnel incidentally springing up, parents and bearers ought to use the greater care and choke it in the very germ; this is easier to be done, and is much more beneficial at this very early age than afterwards when the evil has struck deep root. It is vain to say, as some are wont to do, "It is a child, it does not understand:" such persons I have already shewn to be themselves without understanding. No doubt we cannot at once root out unprofitable plants as soon as they appear above ground, inasmuch as we cannot yet distinguish them rightly from the genuine plant, nor grasp it with the hand; nevertheless, it is also true that we ought not to wait until the weeds have become full grown, for then the nettle stings worse, the thistle pricks sharper, and the good fruit or other useful plants will be choked and perish: moreover, when these brambles have once strongly taken root, force becomes needful to pull them up, and often the roots of the standing corn are pulled up too. Therefore, as soon as weeds, nettles, and thistles, are discovered, root them out at once, and the true crop will come forth so much the more abundantly. If you observe a child desirous of eating more than is necessary, or cramming itself with honey, sugar, or any fruit, see that you be wiser than it, by not permitting such things, and having removed the cause of mischief, occupy the child with something; never mind its crying, it will cease when it has cried enough, and will discontinue the habit in time to come with great advantage. In like manner, if a child inclines to be fretful and froward, do not spare it; rebuke it, chastise it, set aside the thing for which it calls; by this means it will at length understand that your will is to be obeyed and not its own pleasure. A child of two years old is sufficiently advanced for this exercise, with this caution, however, that it be in no way hurt or have its anger excited, lest you open up to the child a way to contemn your exhortations and chastisements.

18. There is no need of great labour to accustom infants to *services and officiousness*, since of themselves they generally take hold of every thing, provided they are not prevented and be taught how to do so properly. Let the father or mother therefore enjoin it upon them, to execute immediately some service, which they of themselves or through another may do, saying—" My child, give that to me,—carry this—place it upon the form,—go call Johnny,—tell Annie to come to me,—give this to that little begging child,—run to grandmama, bid her good bye for me, and say that I asked how she does. Come back again as soon as you can;"—and all such things as are suitable to their increasing years. Children ought also to be trained in *alacrity and agility*, so that when any thing is enjoined upon them, they, leaving their play and every thing else, should with the greatest promptitude execute the order. This celerity in obeying superiors may be learned from their earliest years, and will afterwards be a very great ornament to them.

19. Respecting *civility of manners*, parents can instruct their infants as far as they themselves know. There is no need of particular instruction in this respect. The child is amiable which conducts itself courteously and respectfully, both to its parents and towards others. This is as it were born with certain children, whereas others require training, consequently it must not be neglected.

20. That this courteousness and blandness may not be irrational, they ought to be tempered with modesty and gravity. The little story of the ass, may illustrate this: " Once upon a time, an ass seeing a little dog caressing its master with its tail and leaping upon his bosom, the ass attempted to do the same, and for his civility got a cudgelling." This story may be told to children, that they may remember

what is due to every one. Children should be exercised so as to know what is becoming, and what otherwise in external gestures and motions; how to sit straight, to stand upright, to walk decorously, not bending their limbs, or staggering, or lounging. In case they need to ask for anything; how to return thanks when it is given; how to salute any one they may meet; and when they salute, how to bend the knee or stretch forth the hand; how when they speak to superiors to take off their hats, and many other things that appertain to the good and honourable; of which we need not speak more largely. It is sufficient here to to have incidentally noticed these things.

X.

How children ought to be exercised in Piety.

1. "Rejoice not in impious children. If they be multiplied, rejoice not over them; since the fear of God is not in them. For it is better to die childless, than to have impious children." So said the wise son of Sirach. (Ecclus. xvi. 1, 3.) Above all things, therefore, parents ought to be careful to imbue their children with true and not feigned, with inward and not outside piety; apart from which, knowledge and manners, however refined, may be more injurious than beneficial; just as a knife, a sword, or a hatchet in the hand of a maniac; the sharper it is, the more dangerous it becomes.

2. Although in the first and second years, because of their tender age, and from the reasoning faculty not yet being developed in children, little can be effected in this matter towards them, beyond what God through nature and His own internal grace effects; still by all means the beginning of our duty towards them and of theirs towards God must be laid; so that we may in every way cooperate, as far as we can, with God and nature. For although we cannot teach piety to new-born infants, yet we can by exercising piety in respect to them, learn to lay in them also the foundation of piety, through prayer and surrendering them in holy dedication to Christ the Redeemer; imploring likewise for them the internal Teacher, the Holy Spirit.

3. As soon therefore as parents are aware that God wills to grant them the fruit of the womb, they should with ardent prayer solicit from Him blessing and sanctification for their offspring. For Scripture testifies that he who is to

be holy is separated immediately from the mother's womb and sanctified. (Jer. i. 5. Ps. xxii. 10. Isa. xlix. 1.) The pregnant matron, accompanied by her husband, ought daily without intermission to pour out prayer to that effect, and to live through the whole period of her time piously and holily; that their offspring having a place already within their heart, may share with them in the beginnings of the fear of God. (Respect is had to this matter in the prayer given above at chapter V, section 3.)

4. After God has brought His gift from darkness to light, and presented it to their eyes, the parents (as a certain pious theologian advises) ought in honour of the hand of God, as manifested in this recent work, to receive the new stranger into this world with a kiss. For true is the confession of the holy Maccabean mother, who said, "We know not how infants are conceived in the womb; we ourselves give to them neither breath nor life, neither do we knit together the members of their body. But the Creator of the world is the maker of the human race, &c." (2 Macc. vii. 22.)

5. If parents see the fruit of the womb alive, sound and complete in its members, they ought forthwith to return humble thanks to the munificent Donor, and fervently pray that through His holy angels He would protect it from all evil; and make its education felicitous by granting to it a heavenly blessing.

6. The parents will then make provision to return the gift to its almighty Giver through a pious dedication; fervently praying that the most merciful God would deign to save his own creature in Christ, and by granting it the Holy Spirit, as an earnest of salvation, to ratify and confirm His own choice. Likewise piously promising, if God should bestow on their infant life and health, that they will withdraw it from all worldly vanity and carnal corruptions; training it up piously for His glory. So Hannah in fervent prayer devoting her son Samuel to God, before and after

conception, and after his birth, obtained a blessing for him. For it is not in the nature of the Divine mercy, to repel from itself that which is consecrated to it in humility and fervour. On the contrary, if parents, even pious ones, treat this matter with carelessness, God gives them disobedient children, that it may be obvious as it were to the eye, that those blessings are gratuitous and bestowed by Him alone.

7. The efficacious initiation of children into piety may be begun in the second year, when reason, as a little lovely flower, begins to unfold itself and to distinguish things. For then their tongue is loosed, they begin to utter articulate words, their feet acquire strength, and they prepare themselves for running. This is now the most favourable opportunity to begin the exercises of piety also. Yet by little and little, and in what way this may be done step by step I will also shew.

8. First, When the elder children pray or sing before and after food, it should be provided that the infant be familiarized to silence, to sit, or stand quietly, to compose the hands and keep them so. Children may easily be accustomed to this, provided others set before them a good example, and during the requisite time keep their hands composed also.

9. Secondly, That from their lips may now go forth the praise of God, children should be taught to bend the knee, to fold the hands, to look upward, and say little prayers; especially this very little one, " O God my Father, be merciful to me for the sake of thy Son Jesus Christ our Lord, Amen." Within a month or two this prayer may be fixed in their memories. They should next be taught the Lord's prayer; not all at once, but first, the first petition with the commencement within the space of a week; every day, morning and evening, repeating it once or twice; for what else has its attendant to do? It is likewise proper that as the infant advances in reason, it should be accustomed, as often as it requires food, to say its own little prayer. When the child

has mastered the language of and retains in memory the first petition, the second ought to be added and repeated during two weeks. Then the third should be joined to these, and so on to the end. In this way a child will more easily retain in memory the Lord's prayer, than if, according to the usual manner, the whole were recited to it at one and the same time. For thus it is forced to be learning it during two or three years, and even then does not remember it correctly.

10. In the third place, it may be shewn to the child, by pointing with the finger to heaven, that God is there, who made all things, from whom we have food, drink, and clothing. Then, that the child may understand why we, during prayer, look up to heaven, this little prayer may be added: " O my God, grant me a heart fearing Thee, obedient to father and mother, and everywhere in every thing pleasing Thee. Impart to me Thy Holy Spirit to teach and enlighten me, through Jesus Christ Thy beloved Son. Amen."

11. Afterwards the Apostles' Creed should be taught in little portions, so that the child may completely know it before the end of the third year; of the fourth, however, in slower children. This may easily be done by reciting morning and evening, and before and after food, in the first month a first portion only, in the second month a second portion with the first, in the third month a third portion with the second and first, and so on in succession. When a new portion is learned, it may be repeated even without prayer, until the child has completely mastered the words. It may also be permitted to children, when prayer is concluded, to rise from their knees and recite the Confession standing, that thus they may be accustomed to distinguish between what is and what is not prayer.

12. Now also will be the proper time to speak occasionally of God, so that, when He is mentioned, children may be accustomed to reverence, venerate, and love Him. To this, however, they should be instructed according to their capa-

city; for example, pointing up to heaven you may say, "God dwells there;" turning their attention to the sun, "Lo, God made that sun, by which He shineth upon us;" when it thunders, "Lo, He threatens the impious," &c. Likewise promising them, if they willingly pray to God and obey father and mother, that God will give them beautiful attire, but if not, that He will kill them. And when any new clothing is given them, or a repast or any thing that pleases them, it ought to be said that God gives them those things. If they visit where there is a dead body, or accompany the funeral, shew them the dead body as covered with earth in the grave, or any animal that has been killed, and say, "That God destroyed them because of wickedness." All these things should be done in order that a constant memory of God may be impressed upon their mind.

13. If the things here written seem puerile to any one, my answer is, that they are so; for the matter here treated of belongs to children, with whom we cannot proceed otherwise than in a child-like manner. God Himself, in His Word and in this life, speaks to us adults in no other way than as children; for in truth we are children, understanding divine and heavenly things, not as they are in themselves, but according to our capability (1 Cor. xiii. 11); and yet God descends to our infirmity; why then should not we condescend to the weakness of our infants?

14. When they have learned the Confession of Faith, the ten Commandments may be gradually given them, and in the same order which has been advised with respect to the Lord's prayer and the Confession of Faith: so that the ten Commandments may not be proposed to be learned all at the same time (for in this way the natural ability may be blunted and impaired) but by portions. For example, the first precept daily for a whole week, in the morning, after food, and in the evening—afterwards the second precept should be annexed—and as it is somewhat longer it may

occupy two or three weeks—the fourth precept, during the same time; the fifth during two weeks; the sixth to the ninth should be taken together, and learned in the course of two weeks; and when the tenth has been learned, the whole should be repeated distinctly at the several prayers. And now the child itself may recite; yet in the presence of its father or mother, or nurse, or any other person appointed to the duty of seeing that it make no mistake, and of setting it right when hesitating. Attention to gesture, however, ought not to be forgotten, for the child should not be allowed to look this way and that, to swing itself to and fro, or move its hands, but by all means be accustomed to devotional propriety. In this it should be instructed and encouraged, nay compelled by rebuke, or chastisement, if requisite; sometimes by the rod or by a refusal of its repast, until it obey. With the view to this, children should be counselled before or even during prayer. If after all they transgress, punishment should follow, either immediately at the time, or when prayer is ended, so that they may be aware that proper attention must be insisted upon. All must be done prudently, however, lest instead of loving they should begin to dislike sacred things.

15. In the fifth year, an evening prayer ought to be added to the exercises of piety, for example: "I thank Thee, my Father in heaven, through Jesus Christ Thy beloved Son, that Thou hast graciously kept me all this day by Thy free mercy. I pray Thee to pardon all my sins, which I have naughtily done—kindly keep me by Thy grace all through this night—for into Thy hands I give up myself, my body and soul, and my all. May Thy holy angels be with me, so that Satan may not be able to say I am his. Amen." This prayer to be followed by the Lord's prayer: "Our Father, &c."

16. When children have learned this prayer, the following morning prayer may be learned: "I give Thee thanks,

my heavenly Father, through Thy beloved Son Jesus Christ, that Thou hast kept me all through the past night from all evil. I pray Thee, preserve me all through this day from every sin and wickedness; so that all I do and all my life may please Thee. For into Thy hands I give myself up, body and soul, and my all. May Thy holy angels attend me, so that the devil may not get any right in me. Amen." To this also the Lord's prayer is to be added.

17. Children will now readily learn, from daily recitation, to ask a blessing at table and to return thanks.

18. That the piety now taking root in the heart, may not be subject to hindrances, it will be useful, indeed highly necessary at this age, to guard against occasions of evil, by using every possible effort, that nothing vile or impious, tending to contaminate the mind, may be presented to the eyes or reach the ears of children. For as, according to the testimony of Solomon (Prov. xviii. 17)—*He who is first in his own cause seems just;* and according to the saying of jurisconsults: *What appertains to nobody becomes the property of the first occupant,* so likewise it is everlasting truth that *first impressions adhere most firmly to our mind.* Whatever first attaches to the tender age of children, whether good or bad, remains most firmly fixed, so that throughout life it may not be expelled by any after impressions.

19. In a court of justice, no doubt, the accused may justify his own cause; when, the judge having been better informed, the accused overthrows the cause of his accuser, by refuting the allegations, the colouring being dispersed— for whichever of the two parties, whether the former or the latter pleads his cause most satisfactorily, the judge (being mature in age and understanding) pronounces sentence in favour of that one, commanding the other to depart:—but the mind of this early age just unfolding itself, represents wax upon which any impression may be made when it is soft, so that even when it hardens it retains that impression, and

will receive no other unless with difficulty and violence, and not even *that* otherwise than roughly. These, however, differ still wider, since the wax may be softened by fire, so as to lose the former impression; whereas the brain can by no means be forced to lose what it has once received. I maintain, that no art or method can be devised, by which a man can efface an impression which he has once received, even if he himself desire it, and much less at the command of any body else. It was therefore wisely observed by Themistocles that he would rather desire the faculty of forgetfulness than of remembering; because, whatever the force of our natural memory has apprehended, it easily retains and hardly permits to be removed from it.

20. Nothing, therefore, is more requiring the care of parents, who really desire their children's safety, than that, while instructing them as to all good things, they should likewise secure them against the access of all evil things, by conducting themselves piously and holily, and by enjoining the same on their families and all their domestics. Christ declares in the case of such as act otherwise, " Woe to him that offends one of these very little ones," (Matt. xviii. 6) and Juvenal, although a heathen, has left it upon record:

> The greatest reverence is due to a child. Whatever
> Base things you design to do, despise not the years of your child :
> Your yet mute son withstands you, designing to sin.

XI.

How long children may properly be detained in the school of the mother.

1. As little plants after they have grown up from their seed, are transplanted into orchards, in order to their more successful growth, and to their bearing fruit; so it is expedient that infants cherished in the maternal bosom, having now acquired strength of mind and body, should be delivered to the care of preceptors, so that they may grow up more successfully. For young trees when transplanted elsewhere, always grow tall, and garden fruit has always a richer flavour, than forest fruit. But *when* and *how* is this to be done? I do not advise, that children should be removed from the mother and delivered to preceptors before their sixth year, for the following reasons:

2. First, The infantile age requires more watchfulness and care, than a preceptor, having a number of children under him, is able to afford; it is therefore better, that children should continue under the nurture of the mother.

3. Then it is safer that the brain be rightly consolidated before it begin to sustain labours: in an infant the whole *bregma* is scarcely closed, and the brain consolidated within the fifth or sixth year. It is · sufficient, therefore, for this age to comprehend spontaneously, imperceptibly, and as it were in play, so much as is employed in the domestic circle.

4. Besides, no benefit could arise from a different course. The shoot which is taken to be planted out while too tender, grows feebly and slowly; whereas the firmer one grows

strongly and quickly. The young horse prematurely put to the car becomes weakened; but give him full time to grow, and he will draw the more strongly, and more than repay you for the delay.

5. In truth, it is no great delay to wait until the end of the sixth year, or the beginning of the seventh; provided always, that care be taken, as has been advised, that there be no failure at home, during those first years of their age. If it happen that a child completes at home, according to the manner prescribed, its elementary instruction in piety, good morals, especially reverence, obedience, and due respect to superiors; in wisdom, in celerity of action, and distinct pronunciation of words; it will by no means be too late to enter upon scholastic instruction at the termination of the sixth year.

6. On the other hand, I am unwilling to advise, that children should be kept at home beyond the six years; because within that time, whatever ought to be learned at home, according to the manner shewn, may be easily completed. And unless a child after this, be at once delivered over for higher instruction, it will invariably become accustomed to unprofitable idleness, and again become like "a wild ass's colt." Nay, it is to be feared, that from this imprudent idleness some vice may attach to the child, which afterwards, as a noxious darnel, can with difficulty be rooted out. The best way therefore is, to continue without intermission what has once been begun.

7. This advice, however, is not to be so precisely understood as if, without due consideration of circumstances, no transfer ought to be made at the expiration of the six years. The proposed termination may either be delayed or anticipated by a half or even a whole year, according to the child's capacity and progress. Some trees bear fruit in spring, some in summer, some in autumn. Early flowers, however, fade the soonest, while late ones acquire greater

strength and durability; in like manner early fruit is useful for the day, but will not keep; whereas late fruit may be kept all the year.

8. As some natural capacities would fly, as it were, before the sixth, the fifth, or even the fourth year; yet it will be beneficial rather to restrain than permit this; but very much worse to enforce it. By acting otherwise, the parent who would have a *Doctor* before the time, will scarcely have a *Bachelor*, and occasionally may have a *Fool*. Even as the vine at first luxuriating too much and sending forth clusters thickly, will, no doubt, grow to a great height; but its root will be deprived of its vigour, and nothing will be durable. On the contrary, there are also slower natural capacities with which it may scarcely be possible to begin anything useful in the seventh or eighth year. Consequently the counsel here given must be understood as applying to children of ordinary abilities, whose number is always the greater. In case any one have a child of superior or inferior talent, such would do well to consult with the preceptors or inspectors of the school.

9. The signs by which infantine aptitude to attend the public schools may be discovered, are the following:

(1.) If the child has really acquired what it behoved it to learn in the maternal school.

(2.) If there be discovered in the child attention and appreciation of questions, with some power of judgment.

(3.) If a child display some desire for further instruction.

XII.

How parents ought to prepare their children for school.

1. ALL human affairs, if to be properly transacted, require due reflection and preparation. This is noticed by the Son of Sirach (xviii. 23, xxxiii. 4), "Preparation is demanded before prayer, before (passing) judgment, and before uttering a word, even although the question be quite obvious;" and certainly it is proper, that a creature who is a participator of reason, should do nothing without reason and judgment, without prudence and circumspection; so as to reflect before hand, why he does any thing, and what may result from it, or what may follow if done in this or any other way. Parents, therefore, ought not to hand over their children inconsiderately for instruction in the schools, but they themselves seriously reflect what is suitable to be done in this matter, and thus to open the eyes of their children to look forward to the same.

2. Parents act imprudently, who, with no preparation, lead their children to schools as calves to market, or flocks to the herd. Afterwards the schoolmaster becomes harassed with them, and will punish them as he thinks fit. Such parents, however, are surpassed in folly by those who exciting terror from the preceptor and torture from the school, do yet drive their children there. This is done when parents or domestics incautiously declaim in the presence of children respecting scholastic punishments and the severity of preceptors, and that they will no longer be allowed to play, and the like, by saying, "I *will* send you to school," "you *shall* be made gentle," "they will beat you with *rods*," "only wait a little," &c. By this means occasion is supplied them

not for gentleness, but for greater ferocity, despair, and slavish fear towards parents and preceptors.

3. Therefore prudent and pious parents, tutors and guardians, should act in this matter as follows: First, as the time for sending children to school draws near, they should endeavour to inspire them with pleasure, as if fair-days and the vintage were approaching, when they will go to school along with other children, learn with them and play with them. Their father or mother may also promise them a very beautiful dress, an elegant cap, a polished tablet, a book, and the like; or they may occasionally shew those things which they have ready for them. They ought not, however, to give them until the proper time, but only promise that they will give them, so as to increase their desire more and more; saying to them, such words as these: "Come, my dear child, pray diligently that the time may soon come; be pious and obedient, &c."

4. It will also be beneficial to tell them how excellent a thing it is to frequent schools and acquire learning, for such become great men, Provosts, Doctors, Preachers of the Divine word, Senators, &c.; all of them excellent men, celebrated, rich, and wise, whom the rest of mankind are necessarily bound to honour; likewise, that it is better and more becoming to attend school than to drone away in idleness at home, or run about the streets, or learn any grovelling habits, &c.; moreover, that learning is not labour, but that amusement with books and a pen, is sweeter than honey, and that of this amusement children may have a foretaste. It may be useful to put chalk into their hands, with which they may delineate on a slate or on paper, angles, squares, circles, little stars, horses, trees, &c.; and it matters not whether these be correctly drawn or otherwise, provided that they afford delight to the mind. It cannot fail of being beneficial for the child to be accustomed to form letters easily, and to distinguish them. Whatever else can be

desired to excite in them a love of school ought not to be omitted.

5. Parents, moreover, should endeavour to incite in their children confidence and love towards their future preceptor, and this may be done in various ways; for instance, making mention of him as amiable, calling him father's friend, mother's friend, or good neighbour; and generally praising up his learning, wisdom, kindness, and benignity: that he is a distinguished man, knows many things, and yet is kind to children and loves them; and though it be true, that some are punished by him, yet that these are only such as are disobedient and wicked, and deserve to be punished by everybody; but that he never chastises obedient children; besides which that he shews children every thing, how to write, how to say by heart, &c. By conversing in a childlike manner with children in this or some such way, parents may remove all fear and dread from them. Sometimes also they may be questioned thus: "Will you be obedient?" If the child answer *yes;* it should be told, "Assuredly then your schoolmaster will affectionately love you." And in order that the child may contract some acquaintance with its future teacher, and discover that he is an able man, and so be confirmed in the opinion, the father or mother should send occasionally some little present to the schoolmaster by the child, either alone or with a servant, when the preceptor, if he is mindful of his duty, will speak kindly to the child, shewing him something he may not have seen before, a book, a picture, some musical or mathematical instrument, or anything pleasing to a child. Sometimes also he may give a writing tablet, an inkhorn, a penny, a piece of sugar, some fruit, or the like. However, that this may not be at his expense, the parents, whose interest it really is, should remunerate him, or previously send the gift. In this way a child will readily acquire a love for, and joyous anticipation of the school and preceptor, especially where the disposition of the

child is generous; and the work so well begun is now half-done: for when to children the school becomes an amusement, they will make proficiency with delight.

6. Since however, "all wisdom is from the Lord, as it is with Him from eternity, He moreover is the leader and the ruler of wisdom, and in His hands are we, and our words; likewise all providence and knowledge;" (Ecclus. i. 1 & 6. Wisdom vii. 15); the present matter necessarily requires, that parents should in devout prayer again commend their children to God, begging Him to grant His blessing on their scholastic instruction, and to make out of them vessels of grace, nay, if it please His benignity, the instruments of His glory. So Hannah with prayer delivered her Samuel to Eli; so David delivered Solomon to the prophet Nathan; so the mother of John Huss, the Bohemian martyr, as she was taking him to school, occasionally during the journey, falling on her knees with him, poured out her prayers. And how God heard and blessed these prayers, all Christians know. For how can God thrust away from him what is dedicated to him with a full and warm heart, with prayers and tears; first, in the womb, afterwards in faithful dedication, and now a third time? It is impossible for Him not to receive so holy an offering.

7. Therefore, the father or mother may use the following prayer: "Almighty God, Creator of spirits and of all flesh, from whom all paternity in heaven and upon earth is named, supreme governor of angels and of men, who in virtue of Thine eternal right over all creatures, didst ordain by the word of Thy law, that all first-fruits of the produce of the earth, of cattle, and of men, should be presented as offerings to Thee our God and Creator, or be redeemed according to Thy will with other victims; behold, I thy unworthy handmaiden (or unworthy servant), having received by Thy blessing the fruit of the womb, (N.B. If the infant be a first-born, say first-fruit of the womb) present it to Thee our

Creator, Father, and most merciful Lord God, with profound humility, that Thou mayest be my God and the God of my offspring for ever. O the vast benignity and mercy conferred upon us who believe, that we, having been ransomed from mankind, have been made first-fruits to God and the Lamb! Do Thou therefore ratify and confirm this blessing in this the fruit of my womb, O most merciful God, that the child may be in the number of Thine elect, and receive a portion with Thy sanctified ones. And since I now deliver it, to obtain richer knowledge, to the director of youth, I pray Thee, add Thy blessing, that being instructed by the internal Leader, Thy Holy Spirit, it may learn more and more what pleaseth Thee, and walk in Thy commandments. Fear of Thee, O Lord, is the beginning of wisdom, therefore fill its heart with Thy fear, O holy God, and enlighten it with the light of knowledge according to Thy will; so that its advanced age, if Thou shouldst deem fit, may be glorious to Thee, useful to its neighbours, and salutary to itself. Hear me, most beloved Father, and fulfil the prayer of Thy servant, (or thine handmaid) for the sake of the intercession of our mediator Jesus Christ, who received little children when brought to Him, embraced them in His arms, imparting to them a kiss and benediction." This is to be followed by the Lord's prayer. "Our Father, &c."

To God alone be praise and glory!

THE END.

www.ingramcontent.com/pod-product-compliance
Lightning Source LLC
Chambersburg PA
CBHW020226170426
43201CB00007B/330